AS OTHERS READ US

As Others Read Us

International Perspectives on American Literature

EDITED BY
Huck Gutman

The University of Massachusetts Press
AMHERST

LC 90-47299
ISBN 0-87023-629-6
Set in New Baskerville by Keystone Typesetting, Inc.
Printed and bound by Thomson-Shore, Inc.

Library of Congress Cataloging-in-Publication Data
As others read us : international perspectives on American literature
  / edited by Huck Gutman.
        p. cm.
    Includes bibliographical references.
    ISBN 0-87023-629-6 (alk. paper)
      1. American literature—Appreciation—Foreign countries.
    2. American literature—History and criticism.   I. Gutman, Huck,
    1943–   .
    PS157.A8   1991
    810.9—dc20   90-47299
                                      CIP

British Library Cataloguing in Publication data are available.

ॐ

Contents

Acknowledgments

An international undertaking of this magnitude does not come to fruition without the assistance of many people.

The existence of this volume is testimony to the vision and generosity of the Rockefeller Foundation, which supported a conference on American literature in multinational perspectives at its Bellagio Study and Conference Center. Susan Garfield, in the Foundation's New York office, and Roberto Celli, administrator of that lovely site on Lake Como, helped to make the preliminary work for this volume a collegial and pleasurable endeavor.

Professors Thomas Rimer of the University of Maryland, Hisao Kanaseki of Komazawa University/Tokyo, John Brushwood of the University of Kansas, Orm Øverland of the University of Bergen, Sacvan Bercovitch and Harry Xu of Harvard University, Robert Gordon and Anthony Magistrale of the University of Vermont were each instrumental in suggesting contributors to this volume. Thomas Ragle, director of the Salzburg Seminar, played a seminal role in first bringing together a number of the other contributors.

The guidance of Louis Budd of *American Literature,* Bruce Wilcox of the University of Massachusetts Press, and Andrew Brown was instrumental in shaping the concerns of this volume as it progressed toward publication.

My colleague James Holstun was an astute and helpful reader of the introduction. Two other colleagues, Anthony Bradley and Luther Martin, offered counsel and support during the editorial process. Patricia Armstrong offered valuable assistance in the grant application to the Rockefeller Foundation, while Virginia Clark provided much-appreciated administrative support for my efforts. The Graduate College of the University of Vermont generously granted financial support to help this collection of essays move toward publication.

I have learned a great deal from the fifteen contributors to this volume, both about American literature and about the diversity of the world in which we all live. Their wide and deep knowledge shines forth in each essay; still, much of the hard work they have done is hidden beneath the seamless ease of their sentences. I have been happy to work with them, and happier yet to find that each has become a friend. It is my belief that this gathering of international scholars reveals that cooperation and a shared achievement are possible across national boundaries. It is my hope that our collective endeavor may be one small step toward a prolonged era of international understanding and peace.

My wife, Buff Lindau, has sustained me in many ways. Human relationships offer in mystic miniature the vision of what human society can aspire to be. My belief in international understanding is rooted in what she has given me and taught me. This book is for her.

August 1990
Burlington, Vermont

AS OTHERS READ US

Introduction

HUCK GUTMAN

In 1608 Captain John Smith, an explorer and leader of the first British colony in the New World, published the first English description of what would later become the United States. Remarkably, at the moment of its very inception the embryonic new nation was already being transformed into a literary text which was consumed abroad. Thus, the production of American literature, and its ensuing circulation in nations eager to discover what the New World promised or portended, dates from the first European colonization of the North American continent.

The economic impact of colonization was not the only, nor even necessarily the most important, result of the settling of North America. From its very first penetration by European explorers and settlers, the North American continent figured importantly in the consciousness and imagination of nations beyond the oceans which bounded it. To a large extent the literary celebration, the transformation of landscape and nascent social structures into imaginative texts, was a necessary strategy in the continuing process that would lead to the creation of an American commonwealth. Europeans had, after all, to be convinced that they should forsake their homelands for the New World. They had to comprehend the possibilities of the geography, of the climate, of the spaciousness of the largely unsettled continent in order to commit themselves to building a new life for themselves there. They had to envision either a post-Edenic wilderness or potential new social structures as the necessary antecedent to building a new society in America, one which would remedy the deficiencies of the society they would leave behind.

Nor did the American experience, expressed in literary terms, fail to exercise an important influence on Europe from that time forward. Whether Jonathan Edwards's recounting of a revivalist moment in his

3

native Northampton, which contributed to an extensive movement that transformed religion in Britain and America, or Benjamin Franklin's self-portrayal of the New American Man as the conjoining of the principles of Rousseau and the Age of Reason, the colonial period showed that cultural intercourse was more bidirectional than the flow of economic benefits or political power.

Carlyle would read Emerson as carefully as Emerson read Carlyle. Baudelaire would read Poe, and the world of letters, not solely in France, would never be the same. Walt Whitman's democratic chants would find sympathetic listeners and resonances in poetic production in South America, Europe, Asia, and Africa. Both the working classes in British cities and the serfs on Russian estates would see their predicament mirrored in *Uncle Tom's Cabin,* as a succeeding generation would in the fiction of Jack London.

The twentieth century saw no abatement in the dissemination of American writing abroad. Far from it: with the advent of the mass media, American best-sellers, American movies, American television, and American music have had colossal impact on world culture. Although the influence of Faulkner has been widespread, as has that of Hemingway, Eliot, and Steinbeck, American popular culture, in large measure the product of the American mass media, has had an international success and outreach that are unrivalled in our century. Or at least they are rivalled only by the ubiquitous presence of American products which are related to that culture: surely Marlboros are as widely known as American westerns, and Coca-Cola as widely as the American dream.

Yet, although the impact of American literature has been widespread, little attention has been paid to this impact in other than a localized sense: the influence of T. S. Eliot on Eugenio Montale, say, or of Hemingway and Richard Wright on French existentialism. To what extent do American texts circulate abroad, and what is the manner of their circulation? Such questions are at the heart of each essay included in this volume; finding preliminary answers to them and a number of allied questions is the underlying impetus for the book you now hold in your hands. The other questions are closely linked to these first ones: how are American texts received abroad, and what is it the receivers—or, in less theoretical terms, the readers—receive? What books do they read and why do they like them? What are they taught to value, appreciate, and like; and is there a difference between what teachers praise and assign in classes on American literature and what readers buy in bookstores or borrow from libraries?

The genesis of this book may be traced to a moment which occurred at the close of an international meeting on American literature held at the Salzburg Seminar four years ago. One of the contributors to this volume, Theo D'haen, asked with justifiable criticism and complaint why American literary scholars always seem to think that the locus of American literary scholarship lies within the boundaries of the United States. Why was it, he questioned, that the only readings of American literature that are regarded as significant are readings by Americans?

Out of D'haen's questions arose a conference held at the Bellagio Study and Conference Center in northern Italy in December 1987. The purpose of that conference, generously sponsored by the Rockefeller Foundation, was to examine international perspectives on American literature. The goal of the conference was to recognize, and chart, the importance and specific shape of the study of American literature beyond the confines of the borders of the United States. Many of the contributors to this volume attended that conference, where they investigated the ways in which American literature was circulated and received in their respective nations and cultures. The sense of excitement that those participants felt as they discovered continuities and differences, as they recognized that the way in which one culture engages another reveals much that would otherwise be hidden or ignored in each of the two cultures, as they saw revealed time and again how in even seemingly nonideological cultural preferences one could see traces of political choices and implications: that excitement is what this volume is intended to convey. Since that conference, many changes have taken place, both in the relations between the major powers and in the political configurations of many nations. The essays have all been rewritten since then, and in many of them the stimulus of transformation, of a future being shaped in the present's swirling political and cultural currents, augments the excitement of discovery.

The excitement of discovery is available to the reader of this book, too. Part of it will be rooted in brute facts. Prior to more sophisticated interpretive evaluation, these facts are significant because they are repeated again and again and finally emerge, through such repetition, as worthy of note; they are the stuff of which interpretive studies might be composed. Here are several of the many remarkable facts which the reader of this volume will encounter as he or she journeys through these essays from different nations and cultures.

The most widely read author in American literature is Jack London. In socialist nations such as China and Bulgaria one might expect him to be given official sanction, since London was a socialist as well as a Spenserian. But London is widely read in Sweden, Greece, and Germany, too. At the conference, as well as in the essays which follow, his name came up more often, and with more emphasis, than Mark Twain's, a circumstance that I still find surprising. Clearly, London is out of favor only in the United States, not in the rest of the world. The same holds true for Steinbeck, in whom there is great interest, among both general readers and literary critics throughout the world.

One of the contemporary American writers most widely read by those with a passion for American literature is Charles Bukowski. On the whole, this post-Beat, vernacular poet and novelist seems more influential and more widely admired than Nobel laureate Saul Bellow (although the examples of Israel, Japan, and Denmark suggest that Bellow is also widely read). Regarded as marginal in the United States, almost unnoticed in American critical commentary, unavailable in most bookstores, untaught in almost all curricula, Bukowski has an audience overseas that is large and appreciative.

Postmodern American fiction, of both the self-reflexive and minimalist strains, finds an extremely wide readership in many countries. As the reader will learn from a number of the following essays, many such novels, some of which sell poorly in the United States, are available in translation abroad on the same day they are published in the United States. To an extent greater than most American intellectuals realize, John Hawkes, Raymond Federman, Walter Abish, Raymond Carver, Ann Beattie, and Jay McInerney are substantial presences abroad.

Black American writing, considered marginal by most American scholars of American literature, is for many nations one of the defining armatures of American literature, a central and not a centrifugal genre. In Japan, for instance, there was an institutionalized scholarly interest in black writing before any other variety of American writing: the establishment of the Black Studies Group preceded any other specialized literary society by a decade. Although not as yet accorded the centrality of black writing by international scholars, writing by American women is also the subject of great interest abroad. A fact that seems to possess great interpretive power is that Sylvia Plath is more widely read than any other contemporary American poet; her protofeminism may well account for that international attention. The great impact of contemporary feminism is revealed often in these essays, nowhere more powerfully, centrally, and surprisingly than in Keiko Beppu's examination of changes in traditionally male and hierarchical Japan.

Other brute facts: Hemingway is, everywhere, a major literary presence, although the side of Hemingway which attracts readers differs from culture to culture, as Mbulelo Mzamane's essay makes clear. While the existential or gendered Hemingway provides self-definition for a legion of readers in many countries, the political Hemingway is of primary interest to South African blacks. Poe is the most popular, the most widely studied, of nineteenth-century American authors, not only for his tales and poems but also for *The Narrative of Arthur Gordon Pym* and *Eureka.* Regarded in the United States as a historical and even local phenomenon, the Beat writers are of major interest worldwide. So are Jewish novelists of the past three decades. And the widely discussed reexamination and enlargement of the canon of American literature is an international phenomenon, and not merely a domestic one.

Many of the contributors to this volume reveal that in the so-called First World the influence of American publishing houses, of the financial imperatives of buying and selling American literary properties, is profound. Related to this, but certainly not confined to it, is the sense of intrusiveness that the essayists ascribe to American literature. Though all are students and admirers of American literature, their ubiquitous use of a particular metaphor is striking. While time and again the essays refer to the excitement of American "pluralism," the word which recurs most frequently in this volume is one with pronounced sexual implications, "penetration." American literature does not just enter foreign cultures, it "penetrates" them. It is left to the reader to explore the significance of the connotations of this term, which range from the despoiling of cultural purity, through the excitement of orgiastic discovery, to a larger analogy to a possible vision of American economic and military presence as rapacious.

To my mind the most fascinating fact that has emerged from the forays collected here is one that the process of writing and revision has made largely invisible, because it is truly marginal to a discussion of serious American literature. Irwin Shaw's *Rich Man, Poor Man* was made into a television miniseries. That series was broadcast in China, a nation of twelve hundred million inhabitants. Television is far more widespread in China than most westerners might imagine: there is about one television set for every three households. The audience for *Rich Man, Poor Man* in China alone may have been over half a billion viewers. The same series—produced in the United States, based on an American novel, shaped by that critically reviled genre, the miniseries—was a major viewing event in Japan as well. And in Sweden.

And in Greece. And in many other nations. In other words, *Rich Man, Poor Man* has had wider exposure than Charlie Chaplin, Muhammad Ali, or even the World Cup. If there can be said to be a world culture, surely this miniseries must be one of its central texts. The reader will find that the essays collected in this volume often gesture toward the impact of American popular literary culture in the course of their investigations: at moments they glance toward the consumption of television and film, and more frequently examine the role of best-sellers, westerns, and romances.

The constant repetition in these pages of certain facts about the international reception of American literature suggests that American scholars can profit from these views from abroad as they reconsider the established canon and the pedagogy of American academe. If American popular culture is influential worldwide, then perhaps it deserves more serious examination than literary scholars have, for the most part, been willing to accord it. If, as many of the essays in this volume inform us, American postmodernist formalism and experimentation are of widespread interest, then perhaps writers such as John Hawkes and Raymond Federman should be given greater prominence by both teachers and reviewers. If, as seems clear, the continuing tradition of American "socially responsible" writing—the writing of social protest, of solidarity with the experience of the oppressed and working classes—is one of the prominent and influential features of the American literary topography to external observers, perhaps Stowe, London, Dos Passos, Steinbeck, and others should be more widely taught, more thoroughly considered, more fully appreciated. It would appear that an American possessiveness toward the literature produced in the United States has created a glaringly stilted canon; listening to voices which are raised abroad might well remedy this situation, and remind—or teach—American scholars what is most lively, most idiosyncratic, most important, in the culture that they claim as their own.

But such brute facts and their implications, while they make reading the essays which follow an interesting activity, are not all the essays have to recommend them. I asked each contributor to address certain issues, which each essay does, although with widely varying degrees of emphasis. The list of questions with which I asked the essayists to begin their research into the reception and circulation of American literature, and the transmission of literary knowledge about that literature in their country, was:

What distinguishes either the shape of interests in United States literature, or the shape of the study of such literature, in your country?

1. What authors (or literary movements) are most widely studied or read?
2. Is there a divergence between what is studied in universities and what is read by the reading public: is there a significant distinction between what we might call the official canon and the readerly canon?
3. What role does translation play in the accessibility and popularity of United States literature; and, secondarily, how is translation accomplished?
4. In what ways do political considerations—either relations with the United States, or domestic political concerns, or even the political currents in universities—play a role in what is read and what is studied, and how these works are approached?

The reader will discover, with pleasure I hope, that the shape of each of the following essays is different from all its fellows. In part this is owing to the individual voice of the essayists and to the personal stance which they take toward shaping their material. More important, however, is that each essay emerges from the very culture whose reception of American literature it attempts to describe. These essays, however personal and even idiosyncratic, also reflect genuinely multicultural perspectives. The culture often has an impact on style, as when Marc Chénetier exudes a Gallic fondness for the melody of each sentence, or when the cogent Swedish practicality of Rolf Lundén is compared to the exuberance of Savas Patsalidis' Greek passion for intellectual exploration. The culture has an impact on approach, as when Elżbieta Foeller-Pituch of Poland—a nation, as Czeslaw Milosz reminds us, which has for almost all of its history been occupied by, and thus rendered dependent upon, another—makes much of the ability of Polish scholars to hold their own on an international stage. Or when Hana Wirth-Nesher emphasizes the dual interest of Israeli readers in the problematics of Jewish writing and of nation-building.

Each essay, then, has its own cultural perspective. All look at certain specific things—what is taught, how the teaching is structured, what is translated, what is published, what is read—but that looking is given determined shape by the way in which the author structures her or his essay along one or both of two axes. Each essay moves in its own unique fashion along what we might think of as the horizontal axis of history and the vertical axis of sociology. Students of structuralism will recognize these as the two axes of the diachronic and the synchronic. In simpler terms, one axis looks back in time to see how one got to where one is, the other looks around at the present moment to see where one is in relation to other things one sees. Every essay included here of course moves along both axes, but each does so in different proportion. The figure described as each essay proceeds differs from the others, depending on which axis is dominant at the moment as well as which is predominant overall. Theo D'haen, for instance, although he begins and ends with a consideration of a sociology of the Dutch interest in things American, is resolutely interested in the historical development of American literary studies in Holland as it proceeded—all too slowly, as he sees it—from a rather hostile and unaccepting Anglophilia toward its present circumstances. Keiko Beppu, on the other hand, although aware of the shifting nature of Japanese studies of American literature, is primarily interested in the forces which shape that study in peculiarly Japanese directions: study groups, centers of influence, gender distinctions. Robert Lawson-Peebles focuses on one specific historic change, a shift of valence between the United States and Britain as cultural center. Hans-Peter Wagner is far less interested in change than in a remarkable continuity: he traces the enduring presence of Germany's past—sometimes visible, sometimes subterranean, embedded in the continuity of structure—into the present. Xiao-huang Yin sees an opposite phenomenon, the cataclysmic changes brought about first by the Cultural Revolution in China, then by the undoing of that change in the intervening years following the death of Mao, and most recently by the reassertion of new conservative policies. Half a world and several subcontinents away, Savas Patsalidis finds in Greece a confluence between politics and literary study, and a consequent landscape of dramatic changes of attitude that is strongly reminiscent of the confluence Yin explores in China. Natalia Klissourska is far less historical, preferring instead to understand the way in which ideology, value, and social structure shape the Bulgarian response to American literature; nevertheless, the impact of *perestroika* forces her to consider the possibility that historical change may have strong effects on cultural reception. Both Scandinavians, Rolf Lundén and Jan Gretlund, primarily eschew the historical to focus on the specific workings of the processes of translation, review, publication, and academe. Marc Chénetier's essay begins by providing a historical background so that it can better survey the shape of French criticism at the present moment; Federico Patán likewise begins his essay historically to underscore the relevance of extraterritorial literary influence in contemporary Mexico. Mbulelo Mzamane both examines the historic importance of the establishment of apartheid in 1948, and compares the literary culture of a South African society dominated by that social structure to the culture of other countries in southern Africa where apartheid does not hold sway.

These essays provide important lessons and perspectives to those who are interested in American literature. They reveal the diversity of America's literary landscape, not only pointing to overlooked or unexplored peaks and promontories but also providing a whole topography that can be revealed only to those who view American literature with critical distance—looking at it from outside the culture which produced it. Although there are benefits to the native-born critic of any national literature—an easy familiarity with nuances of the culture's language and its idioms, an intuitive sense of which images and symbols have an enduring presence, a deep fund of daily experience against which to measure its representations of the real—it is clear that no American can obtain the distance from American culture that is available to those not totally immersed in it. If there is to be a contemporary Tocqueville who will see American literary culture with an acute and fresh eye, an eye informed by interests different from domestic American concerns, it is rather certain that he or she, like Tocqueville himself, will view the culture from outside.

Another lesson these essays can provide is a sense of just how thoroughly—or partially—American culture has penetrated other cultures, and with what sort of impact. Surely there are surprises here for most readers and scholars: Who would have expected that Hawthorne's *The Scarlet Letter* would be far more widely known in China than in neighboring Mexico, or that one might find more professors of American literature in a small regional college in Japan than in all of Sweden? Who would have guessed that a greater percentage of Bulgarians have read Jack London than the percentage of Americans who have read *any* writer in translation? The power of this cultural penetration, its rootedness in personal desire and experience rather than in academic or bureaucratic imperatives, is made clear by the recognition that in many nations American literature is far more widely read by the reading public than it is by university scholars or students.

The profoundly wide and diffuse circulation of American best-sellers and of contemporary American fiction testifies to the appeal of things American, but also identifies the far-flung reaches of the American empire. Some of these essays illuminate the way in which American publishing houses determine the shape of book sales and the schedule of publication abroad. Others indicate that the United States government's efforts to spread American culture have had an impact on the study of

American literature in many nations. Almost all give witness to the remarkable presence of American culture as an international force, one that at moments rivals the ubiquity and significance of American economic and military influence.

The greater familiarity of readers throughout the world with American fiction than with American poetry or even drama confirms that the novel is the primary "high" literary genre of the twentieth century. At the same time, if one considers the widespread vitality of Hollywood cinema and American rock music, it becomes clear that American drama and poetry too have had enormous impact. Rock music lays claim to being, after all, the dominant poetic practice of our times; similarly, movies and television are the primary forms of dramatic presentation in the second half of the twentieth century. It is possible that the prevalence of the novel as the dominant high literary genre of our century derives from its origins as a popular cultural form in the age of industrialization: the novel apparently has managed to straddle both the "low" (mass-oriented, popular) middle- and working-class audience which demanded and welcomed its appearance and the "high" (literary, intellectual, tasteful) audience which has adopted it as a major art form. On the other hand, poetry and drama have had audiences which are rather strikingly bifurcated between high and low. Nevertheless, whether bifurcated or not, the influence of American culture on the lives of the citizens of the twentieth century, especially through the production and dissemination of imaginative works which depend upon the deployment of the American language, has been and continues to be profound.

But there are lessons here that transcend the literary, lessons that have to do with the specific international venue of this volume. These lessons are, I would suggest, of three sorts. One has to do with history, one with politics, and one with the interaction which takes place on the margins of two cultures as one encounters the other. All three lessons are, as one might expect, intermingled with one another, for history, politics, and cultural interaction are themselves always linked.

Each of the essays which follows can and will reveal these lessons. Let us cast these lessons in bold relief by examining four examples of the complex relations between literature, on the one hand, and history, politics, and national culture on the other.

As I have already mentioned, history is one of the central axes shaping these essays. In the essay by Hans-Peter Wagner the reader will find a profound concern with the history of Germany in the twentieth century. Wagner's study is plainly shaped by the very history he examines: both his continuing concern with the Nazi past and his opposition to the values which created that past are evident on every page. Wagner is not only a historian but also an archaeologist, for he searches out traces of that history which still structure and orient literary study in Germany. He proposes that the politics and ideology of an earlier generation are reproduced in the present generation through the enduring presence of people and structures. People who participate in one historical era will re-create, in a later era, traces of the ideology of their past: Wagner takes issue with the notion that there can be fully reconstructed Nazis. More important, Wagner demonstrates that structure is not value-neutral: it continues to be shaped by the use for which it was created. Even when circumstances change, structure endures and imposes, at least in part, the circumstances which governed its creation. The historical past, sedimented in institutions and patterns of behavior, exerts a major shaping power on cultural activity in the present. Both Germany's authoritarian past, which enabled Hitler's rise to power, and the inhumanity of Nazism continue to shape elements of Germany's academic and intellectual life through structures inherited from the past. Wagner's lesson about the heavy shaping force of past social practice on present activities can also be learned from most of the essays in this collection, especially those by D'haen on the impact of Anglophiles on American studies and by Mzamane on the enduring presence of a Boer past on the blacks of South Africa; and in one form or another in most of the essays in this volume.

That politics and literary study, or literary reception, are inextricably linked is shown most clearly in the explorations of contemporary Greece and China. The trajectory of governmental change in both nations—from the military government of the right to a popularly elected democratic government of the left in Greece, from the imposed radicalism of the Cultural Revolution to the more open and heterogeneous attitudes of the ensuing pragmatic leadership in China, to a cautious wariness following upon the events of Tiananmen Square—has been characterized by a dramatic transformation of literary attitudes and values. In tracing the reception of American literature in each nation, Patsalidis and Yin show that a transformation in official ideology is not only reflected in the cultural realm—what is published, taught, and valued—but also in what we might call the phenomenological realm. For the ideological/cultural shift that is consequent to major political redirection is rather quickly experienced on the personal, perceptual plane as a shift of reading priorities, habits, and interests.

In Greece, a new interest in American literature emerged concurrently with the inception of the Marshall Plan; in this Greece is no anomaly, for essay after essay testifies to the importance of a new American economic, political, and military dominance in the postwar years to the development of American literary study. In many nations, the conscious efforts of the State Department, and the United States Information Service (USIS) in particular, to wage cultural combat in the Cold War led to the establishment of America-Institutes, an effort which coincided fortuitously with nascent or renewed interest in the newly emerged global superpower.

Patsalidis shows how the revival of democracy in Greece consequent to the overthrow of the military government of the colonels was accompanied in the cultural realm by an extreme, even anarchic, receptivity. Throwing off political chains meant, in the sphere of literature and writing, an explosion of personal experimentation. Patsalidis proposes as well, in what may be the most far-ranging implication of his essay on American literary culture in Greece, that this "democratic" profusion of literary approaches may be the harbinger not so much of freedom as of a new, late twentieth-century colonialism. He suggests that such colonialism may masquerade as pure freedom, but have a result other than liberation: cultural anarchy opens the way for a rapacious cultural penetration by the power of the wealthy American mass media and by the advertising of American corporations. What seems to be an end to ideology might prove to be but a form of co-optative capitalist control, he suggests, in which the free circulation of ideas is but a cover for the establishment of an American-style, and American-dominated, marketplace.

Yin reveals that China's former policy of challenging an irresponsible intellectualism—the Cultural Revolution, with its attack on the privileged position of intellectuals—precluded, in great measure, any intellectualism from developing at all. By contrast, the cultural space opened up by the more pragmatic Deng government led to a remarkable interest in things American: with the door to the United States open, as he puts it, millions of Chinese rushed to look through it at the world beyond. In such an atmosphere, translation, literary study, and intellectual exchange proliferate. Whether China's recent openness, which led to a great interest in things American, will eventually lead not only to greater acceptance and understanding of American literature, but also to inroads of foreign cultural or even economic domination of China, is yet undetermined, especially as political transition looms ahead. No one yet knows whether the widespread interest in Faulkner or the phenomenal success of the miniseries *The Winds of War,* which was viewed by hundreds of millions of Chinese, may be the opening wedge in the Coca-Cola-ization of China. What is certain, however, from not only Yin's and Patsalidis' essays but from many others collected here, is that changes in government policy can have a profound effect on the way in which foreign literatures are approached, accepted, and acculturated.

Acculturating a foreign literature is the central concern of Hana Wirth-Nesher's essay on Israel. Carefully exploring Israeli interests in American literature, she notes that only in two regards do they vary from similar interests in the United States. Israeli Jews are engaged in a task of nation-building and nation-securing; a goodly number of the inhabitants of Israel were present at that nation's creation, and even at the present moment the process of nation-building is ongoing. Thus, they look to American literature for analogues to their own situation, hoping to find in the American experience an augury of what is to come and a catalogue of errors to avoid. For instance, Israelis evince greater interest in the writings of Thomas Jefferson and other American colonial founders than the citizens of any other nation surveyed here. Likewise, living in a state which must grapple with the relation between religious and civil society, Israelis are deeply interested in the dialogues and conflicts among the Puritans, who themselves had to reconcile the often opposing demands of religious and secular life.

Second, Israelis see in the situation of American Jewish writers an experience which, paradoxically, as it is doubly marginal, is also central to the identity of contemporary Israelis. The Jewish writer in America is, for the Israeli Jew, marginal to the American culture, and the American culture is itself marginal to Israeli culture: yet in this double marginality, this experience on the border of two cultures, lies the possibility for defining the identity of Jewishness which is so important to Israeli Jews. For where else is identity defined, but at the margins between what is, and what is not? What Wirth-Nesher's essay shows is that margins between cultures are important to national self-identity, and that one should not look at the reception of American literature in other nations as revelatory of the nature of American culture alone. We know that American literature, as an emblem of the diversity, richness, and promise of America, has defined alternatives and future possibilities for multitudes of non-Americans. We know also that satiric portrayals of American success, indictments of American materialism, and revelations of identity crises as indices of societal failure, have served as warnings to non-Americans of the dangers of American practices and values. What we do not always understand, and what each of these essays in different fashion reveals, is that in some ways "America" remains today what the continent was when John Smith first approached it: a Rorschach blot which each reader, or nation, must perceive according to its way of perceiving. Insofar as this is the case, the essays which follow will inform the perceptive reader not only about American literature but also about the cultures which engage it.

The final lesson of all these essays, then, is the manner in which the study and reception of American literature reveals national identity. When one culture abuts another, the way in which one encounters or assimilates the other is defining in special ways. The thematic concerns that speak most strongly to the receiving culture define what are, to extend a term developed by Norman Holland in his theory of reading, the "identity themes" of that culture. The approach to material—the appeal of critical realism in China or Bulgaria, say, or of experimental postmodernism in France—that is favored by the receiving nation, the stylistic approach it finds most congenial, does much to define the predominant values of that nation. The structures of education, the processes of creating or affirming a canon, the economics of publishing, the organization of literary or scholarly elites, all these not only govern the way one culture approaches another, but they also reveal the structure, economic concerns, and group dynamics of the receiving culture. Neglected aspects of the sender culture are, of course, revealed as well.

All this is to say that this collection of essays testifies to more than its putative subject would lead one to expect. Of course, it reveals how widespread the reading and study of American literature is. Of course, it reveals the diversity of responses, many extremely sophisticated, to American literature in countries around the world. It also suggests that American scholars would do well to listen to their colleagues beyond the territorial borders of the United States, and to invite them to participate more fully in the voyages of discovery (books, conferences, lectures, anthologies) that are undertaken in the United States, the more so since these international colleagues promise to make heretofore unexpected discoveries. But it also testifies to the ways in which cultures in general interact with one another, and to the importance of national history, of ideology, of indigenous social structure, in transcultural interaction. That history, politics, and sociology can be constraints to international communication we already know; that they can lead to enriching perspectives, and to greater self-definition for all concerned, is one of the profound lessons of the essays collected herein.

Dean Acheson and the Potato Head Blues

or, British Academic Attitudes to America and Its Literature

ROBERT LAWSON-PEEBLES

I will begin with two dates. The first is 3 August 1958. It has—as far as I know—no significance whatsoever, except to me. It was my sixteenth birthday, and a friend gave me a record of Louis Armstrong's Hot Seven. I can still vividly remember, thirty years later, the shock of first hearing "Potato Head Blues," particularly Satchmo's second trumpet solo, which leaps like a golden gazelle away from the stalking stop chords of the band. The British jazzman Humphrey Lyttelton has said that, after that solo, jazz would never be the same again. Neither would I. Until then, I had looked with a typically British mixture of amusement and amazement at the American consumer products like Coke, bubblegum and westerns that were lightening the rationed gloom of a postwar childhood. After "Potato Head Blues," not just jazz but America generally became exciting and exotic. I determined to find out more about it.

The second date is 6 December 1962. Quite unlike the first, it is an important one for Anglo-American affairs. The London *Times* that day reported a speech made on 5 December at West Point by Dean Acheson, who had been United States secretary of state and was now an advisor to President Kennedy. In that speech Acheson suggested that Britain's function as an independent great power was "about played out." She had "lost an empire and . . . not yet found a role." His remarks caused a great public uproar in Britain and provoked Prime Minister Harold Macmillan into responding that: "Mr. Acheson has fallen into an error which has been made by quite a lot of people in the course of the last 400 years, including Philip of Spain, Louis XIV, Napoleon, the Kaiser and Hitler."

Amongst the many letters which appeared in *The Times* in the following days was one from Roy Jenkins, nowadays chancellor of Oxford University (in succession, ironically, to Harold Macmillan) but at the time a Labour Member of Parliament. He remarked that the public furor and Macmillan's words were "a striking example of the loss of self-confidence to which our poor recent performance and indeterminate position have led." They had, in short, proved Acheson's point. So too did an article published (no doubt coincidentally) in *The Times* of 6 December. Written by the novelist Thomas Hinde, it questioned the future of the serious novelist in a society which refused its support and seemed to want only to be entertained. Within the next few years Hinde found the answer to the problem. His 1968 novel, *High,* concerns the adventures of a novelist who supports himself by teaching college in Flatville, U.S.A.

I have talked of these two dates because they help to simplify a complex network of literary creation and criticism, international politics, and personal and national attitudes and aspirations which inform and direct the study of another nation's culture. The network that links Britain and the United States is of course a long and particularly intricate one. Winston Churchill liked to claim that the two nations had "a special relationship" based on a natural unity of "the English-speaking peoples." Many politicians have followed his cue, when it has suited them. The reality is much more complicated. The United States and Britain have been at war twice and have contemplated it at least twice more, once within the last sixty-odd years. Furthermore, America and (to a lesser extent) Britain are both federal nations comprising a variety of races and languages, each with its own specific viewpoint. The attitude of a Shetlander to the Texan presence in the North Sea oilfields is likely to be different, say, from the attitude of an Oxbridge don to a counterpart at Harvard. British emotions toward America run the gamut from love to hate. Admiration, excitement, and awe are balanced by, indeed often mixed with, disdain, distrust, and condescension. If there is one constant thread running through all these attitudes, it is that every Briton claims to be an expert on America and is willing to express an instant and deeply held opinion. This is not a comfortable or supportive environment for the professional student of American literature and culture.

Having said that, it is possible to trace the outlines of British academic attitudes to American literature. Those outlines are to be seen in my two opening examples and are rooted in a reversal of the old polarity, explored most comprehensively by Henry James, between American innocence and European experience, between the stultifying virtues of a fresh New World and the alluring corruptions of an Old World steeped in sin. As my terminology suggests, the whole subject is beset with paradox and irony. I shall try to keep to a simple path, first by following the reversal of polarity in a small group of British novels; and second by looking at the consequences of that reversal for the study of American literature.

Nineteen sixty-three was, according to Philip Larkin, an "Annus Mirabilis." It was the year when sexual intercourse began for his protagonist—but just too late. The complex of attitudes to be seen in Larkin's poem is also apparent in a number of novels published in that year. Two that I have chosen apply that complex to America and show a movement in the reverse direction, from experience into innocence. Although they are accomplished works they have not, of late, received much critical attention; but they throw my topic into bold relief.

Night and Silence Who Is Here?—An American Comedy was published in May 1963 by Pamela Hansford Johnson. In that year she was fifty years old, was married to C. P. Snow, and the novel was her eleventh of seventeen. It concerns a well-heeled, upper-middle-class Englishman who has been to Eton and Oxford and has done very little since. Matthew Pryar is the world expert—because, as he admits, he is the only expert—on the work of the English poet Dorothy Merlin, and it is to complete his book on her that he has been invited to take up a visiting fellowship at Cobb, a liberal arts college in New Hampshire. The title of the novel, extended by its epigraph, indicates the cultural dichotomy which will be worked out as the novel proceeds. It comes, of course, from Puck as he stumbles on Lysander in *A Midsummer Night's Dream:* "Night and Silence—who is here? / Weeds of Athens he doth wear." Pryar is the modern Athenian, the inheritor of the tradition of imperialism, urbanity, and civilization symbolized by the Greek city state. Like Lysander, Pryar finds himself in a land where nature reigns supreme, but one also that seems to be empty. Cobb is in the middle of nowhere and seems to be inhabited by nobody. There are no manservants to bring Pryar's breakfast—on the first morning he waits and waits, but in vain—and no valet service for his laundry. Everything, it seems, is done by machines. He concludes that Americans live in luxury but not in comfort. Indeed, it appears that they equate comfort with "overheated rooms and admirable water-closets," an ironic allusion to Edmund Wilson's remark that "the admirable American bathroom" is a greater mark of civilization than the cathedrals of Europe.

Like Henry James's heroes, Pryar encounters many situations and usually handles them with finesse. Asked, for instance, to comment on American food, he congratulates the natives on the delicacy of their palates, for "they really can taste food that seems tasteless to me." But occasionally the structural solitude of American life undermines his equanimity, and he is forced to agree that America merits Captain Scott's assessment of the South Pole: "God, this is an awful place." Luckily, Pryar is rescued from his polar existence by a wealthy widow with the significant name of Mrs. Merle. Here is another ironic allusion, this time to James's *Portrait of a Lady*. Pryar, unlike Isobel Archer, is hardly an innocent, and certainly a willing victim of Mrs. Merle. The novel ends in an attitude of pleasant expectation, with Pryar awaiting his future wife and surveying the streets of Manhattan from his lofty hotel room. Here, in the heart of urban America, he knew that "there was a world elsewhere and that it was a real one."

That phrase, "a world elsewhere," anticipates by some three years Richard Poirier's incisive development of the romance hypothesis first fully explored in Richard Chase's *The American Novel and Its Tradition* (1957). Pryar has reached the same conclusion: that the verifiable world of social intercourse is not to be found in America. Indeed, it is Cobb rather than Eton that he regards as the symbol of innocence, and his time spent there is comparable with his youth. Up until 1963, this was not an unusual conclusion for British fiction. Dickens's *Martin Chuzzlewit* (1844), Eric Linklater's *Juan in America* (1931), and Kingsley Amis's *One Fat Englishman* (1963) all look at America with a disdainful, sometimes horrified curiosity. In another context, Graham Greene's *The Quiet American* (1955) regards Pyle's innocence as positively dangerous. American criticism and British fiction therefore agree. Sophistication, wit, social graces—the solidity of a so-called civilized world—are not to be found in the vacuities of America. The place is best avoided, preferably with a cosmopolitan Mrs. Merle.

The attitudes expressed by *As Far As You Can Go* are quite different. It was published in January 1963 by Julian Mitchell. He was then twenty-eight years old, and the novel was his third. Its protagonist is Harold Barlow, a young stockbroker who is bored. He is bored with his life, his job, and his girlfriend. In an attempt to escape this condition he accepts a commission to visit America. Once there the tenor of his life changes. He enjoys the openness and freedom of American space. He follows the westering course of empire and finds that California is as far as he can go, in terms of experience as well as travel. He is adopted by Eddie Jackson, whom he had met in London. The difference there was immediately apparent: while Barlow wore drab suits, Jackson wore skintight black trousers, a black leather jacket over a white sweatshirt, flame-colored socks, and black suede shoes. In California the different dress blossoms into a different mode of behavior. Jackson acts as a kind of free-range James Dean. He is a bisexual who enjoys group sex, despises work, and speeds from party to party by stealing cars. The distance between Barlow's innocence and Jackson's experience could not be greater. Eventually it becomes too great. Jackson is castrated by his girlfriend's brother and commits suicide by driving a stolen car the wrong way down a freeway—thereby demonstrating the inaccuracy of that term and showing that absolute freedom has its costs.

As Far As You Can Go shows that the cultural polarity has been reversed. Pryar was a sophisticate affronted by the American waste land. Barlow has none of his urbanity and none of the confidence that the tenor of English life will provide him with the experience he seeks. The only course is to escape to America. While America is still characterized by space, it is not a space to be avoided. As he travels across America, Barlow tries to read James's *The Ambassadors,* but finds that he is continually drawn away from the novel into the American scene. The enticements of the land reach a climax on the closing page of *As Far As You Can Go.* Barlow muses on the death of Jackson as he drives toward Death Valley, his elbow on the window of the car testing "the rushing air like a bather's toe." He becomes exhilarated as he realizes that the harsh land is "something against which a man could measure himself in all humility." The rite of passage is clear. America is the means of maturation.

In contrast, England is the cruelest place, mixing innocence with despair. This is made apparent in three spheres of Barlow's pre-American life. The first is political. Barlow believes that all the liberal causes are interchangeable and "essentially negative and usually rather pointless." Here is another reversal. Previously, it had been America that had been characterized by negatives. Whatever Europe was, America was not. The best-known list of negatives is the "Epsom, Ascot" passage in Henry James's *Hawthorne,* but there are many similar American complaints. But in *As Far As You Can Go* it is England that provides negations. This is made even more clear in the second, sexual sphere of Barlow's life. When he asks his girlfriend to make love, her response is immediate and unequivocal:

"Certainly not," said Helen. She had very firm ideas about love-making, and one of them was that it was indecent to start till it was dark, and then only with the lights out. The latter indignity Harold had overcome occasionally, the former never.

In England there seems to be nothing to fill the void save unpleasantness, as can be seen in the third sphere of Barlow's life, his home environment. He lives in a bachelor bed-sit that is both dreary and disgusting:

> There was a pair of socks hanging on the towel-rack in the bathroom, and the towel lay where he had left it, sopping wet on the floor. He had never got round to buying a bathmat.
> He found a dry spot to change his socks on: at least they were dry, though looking at them reminded him how much he detested washing anything, how soapy his hands felt for hours afterwards, how his skin wrinkled uncomfortably, and detergents set his nails on edge. Once he had got a disgusting rash that lasted for nearly a fortnight after using too much Froth or Ebb or whatever the stuff was called. It was another reason for marrying, really.

I will leave Harold Barlow for a moment in this heroic posture to try and account for the change in tone and attitudes noticeable between *Night and Silence* and *As Far As You Can Go*. It is too simple, of course, to make a direct link between the uproar caused by Dean Acheson's remarks and the publication, within six months, of two novels which offer quite different accounts of the relationship between Britain and the United States. Yet there are times when the slow shifts of political and cultural power seem to gather pace and become widely apparent. Nineteen sixty-three may have been a historical moment of this kind, adding ironies to "Annus Mirabilis" that Philip Larkin never intended. Certainly, the remarks of Roy Jenkins and Thomas Hinde are not isolated incidents. They register a disorientation which has a number of sources. It may be traced to a number of recent political events such as the emancipation of India in 1947, the Suez debacle of 1956, and the creation of the European Economic Community, at this stage excluding Britain, in 1958. Culturally the disorientation is more deeply rooted, and to explain this I must return to Harold Barlow changing his socks in his bathroom.

Perhaps Barlow's environment sounds familiar. If not, the next page clarifies the matter. After changing his socks Barlow descends the stairs:

> The post had arrived . . . but there was nothing for him. Just as well, he thought, stifling the usual disappointment. It would only have been a bill.

This passage not only adds to the litany of negations, but points to the source of the novel. The hero of *As Far As You Can Go* is in the same predicament as the hero of *Keep the Aspidistra Flying:*

> Gordon took out his key and fished about in the keyhole—in that kind of house the key never quite fits the lock. The darkish little hallway—in reality it was only a passage—smelt of dishwater, cabbage, rag mats, and bedroom slops. Gordon glanced at the japanned tray on the hall-stand. No letters, of course.

In Mitchell's novel the dampness and decay, the unsatisfactory, furtive, and also Larkinesque sexual relationship, and the despair of lost causes are all reminiscent of George Orwell. Indeed, *As Far As You Can Go* brings Orwell up to date, for it displays an awareness of the events since 1936, including the publication of *1984*. It also ameliorates the gloomy tone by presenting an alternative. One might traduce the novel for a moment by retitling it *Gordon Comstock Meets the Big Bopper,* simply to point out that the clash of cultures could not be sharper or more to Britain's disadvantage. The only solution is to leave.

As Far As You Can Go, therefore, signals the reversal of the Jamesian polarity. Naturally enough, many Britons did not welcome the transfer of cultural power to America. More senior novelists like Pamela Hansford Johnson and Kingsley Amis continued to maintain that it had not happened. Others adopted a different tactic by reintroducing the old fear of Americanization. Ever since Columbus was accused of introducing syphilis to Europe, the New World has been regarded as a source of moral danger. Democracy, mass production, the cinema, hamburgers, and (I am glad to say) jazz are just a few of the things denounced as evidence of Americanization and hence the decline of British life. In 1962, for instance, the journalist Francis Williams published *The American Invasion,* predicting that within the next couple of decades there would be nothing left of our culture which was specifically British.

One of the most influential Jeremiahs was the literary critic F. R. Leavis. He was one of a number of writers (another was the popular philosopher C. E. M. Joad) who linked Americanism with a machine culture. In his 1930 pamphlet, *Mass Civilisation and Minority Culture,* Leavis noted:

> It is a commonplace that we are being Americanised, but a . . . commonplace that seems, as a rule, to carry little understanding with it. For those who are most defiant of America do not propose to reverse the processes consequent upon the machine.

Those processes had been explored in the fiction of Leavis's guru, D. H. Lawrence. Leavis's own antidote was a great tradition of fiction which stretched back from Lawrence to Jane Austen. Unfortunately, it appeared that the tradition had ended, for Lawrence had died in the year that Leavis published *Mass Civilisation and Minority Culture*. This and (amongst other things) the greater prominence of American material culture in Britain in the postwar years made Leavis's criticism of America increasingly sharp and his tone increasingly shrill. One of his later books, the appropriately named *Nor Shall My Sword*, contains a number of hostile remarks attacking "the energy, the triumphant technology, the productivity, the high standard of living and life-impoverishment" of America. Leavis's attack was supported by another influential acolyte of Lawrence, Richard Hoggart. Hoggart's widely read 1957 book, *The Uses of Literacy*, expands Leavis's great tradition to include elements of the working-class culture in which he, Hoggart, grew up. His writing, too, is elegiac. He believes that British culture is being swamped by what he calls "shiny barbarism . . . the ceaseless exploitation of a hollow brightness . . . a Candy Floss world." Of course, as its name implies, candy floss is American, rotting the teeth and the spirit of British youth.

I would like to argue that the literary and critical tradition associated with Orwell, Leavis, and Hoggart could not accept the ways in which Britain was changing, despaired of its role in the postwar world, and demanded a conservatism from its novelists. The result was a dissociation between the British literary imagination and its natural environment. It first became apparent in *As Far As You Can Go* and is developed in the novels of Malcolm Bradbury and David Lodge. Bradbury's *Stepping Westward* (1965) takes the cultural nervousness of *As Far As You Can Go* a few steps further. Indeed, one of its characters, a German emigré named Dr. Jochum, makes precisely the point I have just made, that the Jamesian polarity has now been reversed and it is European innocence which seeks American experience. The innocent in question is James Walker, a Nottingham novelist who was once an angry young man and is now just a confused liberal. He is invited to teach creative writing at Benedict Arnold University. The university is in a town called Party, somewhere in the Midwest and once part of the frontier, in an area which has been "reclaimed from nothing." This, it becomes clear, is an earlier version of Flatville, and like Flatville it is not a void but rather an arena in which Americans can introduce Europeans to the twentieth century.

Unfortunately, the twentieth century is too much for Walker, and at the end of the first term he escapes westward with a modish college girl called Julie Snowflake. Snowflake melts into his arms and the relationship is consummated, suitably, in the Rockies. But this rite of passage through the Continental Divide is of no help. Walker retreats eastward to England, as innocent as when he set out. Significantly, the retreat will provide no spiritual sustenance. Although some of the inhabitants of Party regard England in Leavisite terms as the "fulcrum of moral sanity," this is a view tenable only from the west side of the Atlantic. Dr. Jochum knows better. London has become "Nowhere," and the provinces are no better. Formerly the vibrant theatre of the great tradition, they have now become as "resourceless and minute" as Walker's imagination. His soul is not enlivened but simply dampened by the fog and rain of Lawrence's Nottingham.

The bad weather is also the most notable aspect of the provinces in David Lodge's *Changing Places: A Tale of Two Campuses* (1975). As the novel's title suggests, the plot mechanism is a faculty exchange. The English university is set in the town of Rummidge, a lightly fictionalized version of Birmingham, perpetually overcast by a black cloud and with damp penetrating the buildings and the bodies of the inhabitants. The innocent is Philip Swallow, who visits the State University of Euphoria, often called Euphoric State and located somewhere between northern and southern California. The date is 1969, and Euphoric State seethes with student radicalism and police brutality. The streets are alive with beautiful bodies and the smell of tear gas. As a witness—and at one point as a participant, for he gets busted by the police—Philip feels that he "is part of the historical process." Like Harold Barlow and James Walker before him, he reverses the Jamesian polarity, but now with greater firmness:

> Now it was not Europe but the West Coast of America that was the furthest rim of experience in life and art, to which one made one's pilgrimage in search of liberation and enlightenment; and so it was to American Literature that the European now looked for a mirror-image of his quest. He thought of James's *The Ambassadors* and Strether's injunction to Little Bilham, in the Paris Garden, to "Live . . . all you can; it's a mistake not to," feeling himself to partake of both characters, the speaker who had discovered this insight too late, and the young man who might still profit by it.

There is perhaps an echo of Larkin's "Annus Mirabilis" here, but far away from Larkin-land. Euphoria, it is clear, is in a state of being, and Philip partakes of that state of being while he lives there. Rummidge, in contrast, seems to be in a state of becoming. Indeed, at one point the academic who has exchanged with Philip, the wonderfully named Morris Zapp, feels that he has stumbled upon a new American frontier. But, unlike Party, Rummidge is a puny frontier and presents an illusory state of becoming. There is some radical unrest, but it is easily tamed by the university's vice-chancellor with the aid of Morris Zapp, and is dismissed with a typically British phrase, "a spot of bother with the students." Rummidge easily reverts to its state of soggy innocence.

As Far As You Can Go, Stepping Westward, and *Changing Places* are united in the mobility of their titles and in their themes. That unity is supported by a web of allusion and provides a comprehensive riposte to the Eurocentrism of Henry James. There are several other novels which reflect on the same topic. In addition to Thomas Hinde's *High,* the subject is handled perceptively and often with great humor in Andrew Sinclair's *The Hallelujah Bum* (1963), David Caute's *The Occupation* (1971), and Tom Sharpe's *The Great Pursuit* (1976), as well as in other novels by Bradbury and Lodge. The reversal of polarity seems to be firmly and substantially effected. It has, moreover, important implications for the study of American literature, not least because Bradbury and Lodge are distinguished critics as well as novelists. It is to literary criticism that I shall now turn.

The distaste for things American apparent in *Night and Silence* and in the criticism of Leavis and Hoggart has a long history in British academic circles. For instance, when Cambridge University was offered in 1866 funds for a lectureship in the "History, Literature, and Institutions of the United States," the proposal was regarded as an attack upon Britain's royalist and Christian principles and was turned down. Such attitudes have lasted a long while. When the English poet Charles Tomlinson went to Cambridge in 1945 he noticed that his tutors seemed to be unaware of the existence of American literature. When Marcus Cunliffe began teaching the subject at Manchester University in the 1950s his request for books was refused by the university librarian on the grounds that "we don't want book-of-the-month club stuff here." American history has been treated in a similar fashion, and such attitudes are still far from dead.

Yet it was impossible to deny the existence of America forever. Things had to change, and if there was one person responsible for the change it was, ironically, F. R. Leavis. A distinction must be drawn between Leavis's attitudes to Americanization and his attitudes to some American literature. In a way, Leavis had been cornered by the intensity of his beliefs. He venerated Lawrence, and Lawrence had shown in his *Studies in Classic American Literature* (1924) that he had a clear eye not only for the horrors of Americanization but also for the virtues of American literature. Indeed, Leavis admitted in *D. H. Lawrence, Novelist* that Lawrence was a good literary and cultural critic and that *Studies* was a fine book. It followed therefore that American literature existed after all, and even had some value.

This did not mean that American writers were allowed to remain American. They were, instead, accorded honorary status in the English pantheon. Leavis makes this clear in a 1952 essay, "The Americanness of American Literature," now reprinted in *Anna Karenina and Other Essays*. The essay is an attack on Van Wyck Brooks's *The Confident Years*, also published in 1952. According to Leavis, Brooks is too preoccupied with the idea of Americanness. In consequence, he spends too much time on the novelist William Dean Howells. Leavis has no time at all for Howells; he "just doesn't exist as a creative writer." Brooks should instead have devoted his energies to Hawthorne, Melville, and James. It is these writers, Leavis concludes, who take their places with Austen, Dickens, Conrad, and Eliot as the heirs of Shakespeare.

This tactic has been adopted before. As Robert Clark has pointed out, when Henry James published his little book on Hawthorne (with its marvellous negative catalogue) it was in a series entitled "English Men of Letters." Amongst the many things that Hawthorne was not, it seems that he also was not American. With this and the imprimatur of Leavis in mind, university English departments began to pay selective attention to American literature. They tended to focus on the writers of the so-called American Renaissance, Emerson and Whitman as well as Hawthorne and Melville. A number of others were admitted because they had taken British nationality or had been cleansed by their British contacts. Examples are James, Pound, Eliot, and Frost. Yet others were admitted because they wrote on "international" themes (Hemingway), or could be fitted within international literary movements (Stevens and the symbolists, Faulkner and stream of consciousness), or seemed to be warning us of the perils of Americanization (Fitzgerald). In each case the social and historical context was ignored or simply sketched in as a series of stereotypes. The new work was therefore safely contained within the present teaching abilities of the average English department. A visit to America was regarded as unnecessary or even as injurious. Writers whose work depended upon some knowledge of context, such as the polemical Stowe or the realists Howells, Dreiser, and Lewis were—as Mrs. Thatcher would put it—out.

Leavis's influence was perhaps more fertile in its influence on British writing about American literature. Some critics, perhaps, follow him too closely. The echo of Leavis's 1936 *Revaluation* in Martin Green's *Reappraisals* (1963) is confirmed by its decided subtitle, *Some Commonsense Readings in American Literature*. It is to be found, too, in the book's trenchant tone and in a series of opinions which are crankily but insightfully unorthodox. Thus, "Salinger is a hundred times more intelligent and interesting than Faulkner." Green, furthermore, anticipates remarks that Leavis would make in *Nor Shall My Sword* when he attacks American critics for their "great bustling bazaar of symbols and theories and readings and discussions which have lost their relation to the books they allegedly discuss." Any non-American visitor to the annual Modern Language Association convention must have felt some sympathy for the common sense of this viewpoint.

This criticism can, however, be turned against two of the most distinguished British critics, if only to indicate the strength of their work. Tony Tanner and Peter Conrad both move easily between English and American literature, and they can do so, I think, because they use America as an idea rather than as an entity. American literature, therefore, becomes an end in itself. Tanner and Conrad tend not to see it in terms of society, politics, and culture. They need no training outside their literary training. This is not to say that they refrain from making interesting and cogent points about the nonliterary, but rather that they do so from a standpoint firmly within the literary. This has allowed them, paradoxically, to move away from the narrow moralism of Leavis's attitudes.

Tony Tanner's first book, *The Reign of Wonder: Naivety and Reality in American Literature* (1965), introduces its theme of the innocent eye—the new angle of vision in such writers as the transcendentalists, Twain, James, and Hemingway—by situating it in a tradition coming from Rousseau, Wordsworth, and Carlyle. *City of Words: American Fiction 1950–1970* (1971) discusses the simultaneous need to place a pattern upon unconstructed reality and to escape the restrictions of that pattern. Tanner concludes that modern American novelists are oppressed by a sense of futility. These are telling observations and, in some instances, they are certainly accurate. Tanner makes them, however, not in relation to American society but rather to an intellectual and philosophical tradition which is common to Western culture. He begins his discussion by reference to the Spanish philosopher José Ortega y Gasset and ends it by reference to the Austrian philosopher Ludwig Wittgenstein. Tanner's most recent book, *Scenes of Nature, Signs of Men* (1987), continues the enterprise. The book's one illustration, Erastus Salisbury Field's *The Historical Monument of the American Republic* is, he says, typical of much of the literature he examines, in which "images of the real past are dislodged and reassembled at the whim of the poet as he spins out his web." The same point could be made about Tanner's criticism itself, which here spins out a brilliant web entrapping writers from Fenimore Cooper to William Gass, and cocooning them from the taint of their environment. There are signs aplenty, but not many scenes.

Peter Conrad adopts the same strategy, but in a more controversial way. His 1980 book, *Imagining America,* examines British literary visitors to America over the last century and a half, and shows that each found a different place. The Trollopes, Dickens, Wilde, Brooke, Kipling, Stevenson, Wells, Lawrence, Auden, Huxley, and Isherwood found institutional, aesthetic, epic, futuristic, primitive, theological, psychedelic, and mystical Americas. This voraciously pluralistic approach to America has caused a fair amount of disquiet. Anthony Burgess, for instance, thought that there had to be "a unity, a self-subsistent entity called America, full of Americans and Americana and Americanisms." The frightening conclusion to be drawn from the book was that if the writers' Americas had nothing in common, "they never went there." Similar remarks have been made about Conrad's 1984 book, *The Art of the City: Views and Versions of New York.* Alan Trachtenberg begins his review by quoting Sartre: "I was looking for New York, but couldn't find it." In general he admires the book, but for its insights into Conrad's mind and into itself, and not for its analysis of the city and its artistic life. In both books, then, Conrad tends to recompose his subjects so that they create a brilliant if wayward supertext which, at times, seems only tangentially to deal with America.

Tanner and Conrad exemplify a British tradition of analysis of American literature and culture which is distinguished for its breadth and vigor but which achieves those qualities at the expense of context. Earlier I tried to trace a dissociation between the British literary imagination and its natural environment. The books of Tanner and Conrad counterbalance this trend. They reveal not despair but, in the best sense of the term, playfulness. They display a dissociation between the critical imagination and the American environment. To this extent, they can be regarded as the inheritors of Leavis's critical attitudes to Americanization, although they reject his disdainful piety. They are the inheritors, too, of the Eurocentrism of Henry James, particularly the hovering, barely tethered consciousness of the late James. It is appropriate that both have written sensitively about James.

There is another form of British criticism which draws its strength not from Leavis but from the American studies movement. It is often inter-disciplinary in nature; or, if it confines itself to imaginative literature, attempts to set that literature in context. This tradition is younger than the Leavisite one. It was only after the Second World War that American studies began in Britain. It has three related sources. The first was the growing body of fellowships which allowed the holder to spend a year or more at an American university. Possibly the oldest and certainly the most lucrative was the Commonwealth Fund (later known as the Hark-ness) Fellowship. Alistair Cooke, the well-known commentator on Amer-ican life, held one in the 1930s. After the Second World War, Fulbright, Henry, Procter, and English-Speaking Union Fellowships added greatly to the number of young scholars who stepped westwards, Malcolm Bradbury and David Lodge among them.

The second source funded traffic in the opposite direction. The United States government paid for visiting lectureships by Americans and for conferences of interested scholars. It was these conferences which led in 1955 to the foundation of the British Association for American Studies (BAAS). But money alone was not enough. The third source of American studies was the growing awareness that the United States had become the most powerful of Western nations, and was therefore worthy of study. When in 1980 the *Journal of American Studies* (the official organ of BAAS) published a series of autobiographical pieces by several of the most senior Americanists (as they are called), the authors showed that their work was indebted to this impetus. Moreover, because the formal means for studying America barely existed, their interest was often sparked in unorthodox but productive ways. Movies, the New Deal, the kindness of visiting GIs, the imagery of a land of plenty, Paul Robeson: all were cited as the initial impulse for an aca-demic career. My experience with "Potato Head Blues" may have been idiosyncratic but it was by no means unusual.

Fortunately, the growth of American studies in Britain was followed, in the early 1960s, by the growth of British higher education. It meant that American studies was grafted onto the system with relative ease. It gained a particularly strong foothold in new universities such as East Anglia, Keele, and Sussex. In established institutions more vig-orous battles had to be fought, but they tended to be over the question of autonomy, which is less contentious than the question of finance. In an expanding system there seemed to be money, and therefore room, for all.

At its best, American studies has produced literary criticism which is sophisticated and contextually rich. I have in mind here Marcus Cunliffe's *Literature of the United States,* first published in 1955 and still, in its fourth edition (1986), the best introduction to its subject. Unfortunately, the book is not only exceptional but also unusual. American studies scholars tend to lack the breadth and vigor to be found in the work of Tanner and Conrad. While they playfully ignore questions of context, the Americanists are intimidated by them. As Marcus Cunliffe himself remarked, "in practically every branch of American Studies the organizing ideas, the bold interpretations, the controversy have been introduced by Americans." That was in 1971. In the succeeding years we have done little to change that sad state. We still have produced nothing to equal the frontier theory, the romance hypothesis, or Leslie Fiedler's love and death.

For instance, in 1983 a four-volume series was published entitled *American Literature in Context.* The volumes cover the period 1620 to 1930, and each has the same format. Each chapter begins with a quotation from a primary text, which is then analyzed and placed in context. The effect is of a series of finely detailed and argued fragments which have only a limited overall interpretative power. Similar remarks can be made about a 1985 collection called *The Nineteenth-Century American Short Story.* Individually the essays are excellent, but they do little to disturb the established canon, are limited to the individual insight, and lack an authoritative, synoptic overview. The essays, furthermore, deal without exception with themes of pessimism, cultural sterility, and authorial uncertainty. To be sure, these themes are to be found in American literature, but there are others. Perhaps they reflect the attitudes of the critics.

It is fair to say that this timidity is not confined to literary Americanists. Michael Heale noticed a similar failing when in 1985 he reviewed British writing on American history. Nor is it confined to American studies. When the Oxford structuralist David Robey reviewed Jonathan Arac's *Critical Genealogies: Historical Situations for Postmodern Literary Studies* he noted that "it is striking and embarrassing how few contemporary British critics are referred to in Arac's discussion." Apart from Frank Kermode and Raymond Williams, only two or three others received passing mention.

Why has American studies been so afflicted? There are a number of

possible answers. One obvious one is access to sources. While Americanists often spend extended periods in the United States, such visits do not
allow the familiarity with materials that is achieved through regular
access. There may, though, be deeper reasons, and here again the notion
of the Jamesian polarity may be helpful. I suggested earlier that the
disdain apparent in *Night and Silence* was matched by British critical
ignorance of America. Perhaps the breathless fascination to be seen in *As
Far As You Can Go* is matched by a lack of interpretative confidence. The
unhappy marginality of Britain seems to be accompanied by a search for
imprimatur. Senior Americanists have often said that the way forward
for the discipline lay in comparative studies, as if the British study
of America could only be warranted if it had a non-American component. This view has led to a disproportionate number of studies of
colonial America and of Anglo-American relations. It has also infected
our teaching. While writers like Stowe and Howells certainly appear in
American studies courses, Crèvecoeur's *Letters from an American Farmer*
and Tocqueville's *Democracy in America* exert a particular fascination, to
the extent that these Gallic views of America now make up the "authorized version."

Our own lack of authority may also be caused by the continued decline
of Britain. At times it has seemed as if the only worthwhile British
contributions to Western culture were comedy shows such as Monty
Python. Perhaps, after all, our island would sink giggling into the sea.
There is, however, some evidence that the giggling has stopped. In 1986
the social historian Arthur Marwick suggested that Britain's drift and
decline may have ended with the Falklands War of 1982. He wondered if
the imperialist resolve exemplified by that unfortunate South Atlantic
adventure was being followed by an economic revival. Perhaps a general
recovery of self-confidence would ensue. Certainly, there is the odd evidence that British Americanists are becoming more forthright. Robert
Clark's *History, Ideology and Myth in American Fiction 1823–52* (1984), for
instance, boldly analyzes the work of Cooper, Hawthorne, and Melville
as an articulation of Jacksonian political beliefs. It sees their work not as
an expression of American myth but as a development of the (sometimes
ruthless) politics of individualism and open access to land. The irony is
that the book draws its values not from Thatcherite revivals of Victorian
self-reliance but rather from Raymond Williams and the one group
which has produced a confident and coherent body of writing, the
British Marxist historians.

Furthermore, the so-called British miracle of the last few years has bypassed higher education. Malcolm Bradbury's recent *Cuts* (1987) reflects a depressing retrenchment and uses the term which has become the saddening watchword for the decade. Perhaps it will be some time before the Jamesian polarity reverses itself again. Significantly, a recent issue of *The Times Higher Education Supplement* continued to talk of Britain's "vacuum of identity." The title of the article, "Answering Acheson," showed that the West Point speech still rankles and still has not received a convincing response. On the other hand, as we have seen from *Virgin Land* or *The American Adam*, it only takes a few scholars to make a summer: perhaps somewhere there is someone waiting to be inspired by "Potato Head Blues."

ஜ

One More Window to the World
American Literature in Bulgaria

NATALIA KLISSOURSKA

It would not perhaps be too much to say that over the past thirty or so years American literature has gained a distinguished place in the cultural life of the Bulgarian people. It would not be an overstatement to maintain that Harriet Beecher Stowe, Jack London, Mark Twain, Ernest Hemingway, and John Steinbeck are almost as well established in the national culture as are the nineteenth-century Russian, French, English, and German classical writers whose weighty presence predates that of American authors by more than half a century. The interest in American literature has grown steadily, fostered by its massive translation into Bulgarian and by its study at the university level and in the English-language high schools. Teaching and translation, the latter preceding the former by nearly a century, have provided the two avenues for the reception of American literature in Bulgaria. Literary scholarship has thus depended on the requirements and needs of these two large educational and cultural areas.

Teaching and translation have both been instrumental in shaping the canon of American literature in Bulgaria, each endeavor exhibiting to a greater or lesser degree the workings of some principles of canon formation. Why is it that the above-mentioned American authors should have been so well received? What are the reasons for our preference of them to other writers? What are the criteria governing their translation? What are the factors responsible for their selection? The answers to these questions, and to the many more related to them, will of necessity lead into the field of reception theory as well as into the theory and practice of literary influence. What further complicates matters is that reception theory itself shares many of the concerns of general literary theory,

34

the sociology of literature, and hermeneutics. Different theories of reception depend on different philosophical premises, emphasizing the importance of one or another of the components of the triad, author–literary work–reader. While this essay cannot resolve the issues involved, it makes a modest attempt to discern some of the principles of canon formation as they have functioned in the reception of American literature in Bulgaria.

As translation precedes the study of American literature, some of those principles are to be found on its terrain. When teaching caught up with translation in the late 1940s, the two areas jointly contributed to canon formation. In recent years considerable insight has been provided by the practical criticism in comparative studies on the reception of foreign literatures in Bulgarian culture. Though comparative Bulgarian-American literature studies are in their initial stage of development and thus very few in number, the analyses they offer are particularly valuable and dependable since they are based on a balanced view of the dialectic unity and interaction of the triad's components.

Without claiming to be comprehensive, I would venture to suggest five principles of canon formation which interact and mutually complement one another. My inferences have been drawn from three sources: a comparative Bulgarian-American literature study, the translation of American authors since the 1830s, and the study of these authors at university and high school levels.

The first is the ontological principle which pertains to the recognition of the objective existence of the literary work as an artifact of specific sociohistorical conditions and its movement in time and space. A literary text is transplanted and adopted from a host culture by a recipient culture when both of them undergo analogous historical and socioeconomic developments. These developments may be contemporaneous, but more often than not they do not coincide in time. The second is the epistemological principle manifested in the dichotomy known–unknown (familiar–unfamiliar). The known, reinforced by the experience of the recipient culture itself, makes it possible for the latter to assimilate the unknown, to transform and modify it in a way that will best satisfy its own needs. The third is the literary aesthetic principle which is related to the phases in the development of the interacting nations in terms of literary trends and genres with their corresponding artistic systems of expression. Both the ontological and the epistemological inhere in the aesthetic in that at first, trends and genres may appear concurrently. This makes it easier for the recipient literature either to absorb an aesthetic system intact or, and this is more frequently the case, to transform it in the process of assimilation to suit its national specificities. When the literary processes do not overlap in time, and the unknown for the recipient literature dominates over the known, it adopts the unfamiliar by integrating it into its then extant aesthetic system. The fourth principle may well be termed moral–psychological, related as it is to common human responses to universal verities, and to the satisfaction of spiritual needs conditioned by specific sociohistorical experience. The fifth factor is as much objective as it is subjective. It is represented by the literary institution in the country which includes literary critics and editors, publishers and reviewers, as well as academics. It is subjective in that the reception of foreign literary texts depends on the views, beliefs, and biases of the individual cultural policymakers whose critical methods, with their categories, conventions, and strategies, are those of the literary critical approaches they have adopted. It is objective in that their adoption of one or another critical approach is as much an aesthetic choice as it is a projection of the kind of social and historical individuals they are. It is this factor that can be said to be most susceptible to changes in the larger political sphere. An awareness of at least some major events in Bulgarian history is necessary in order to make meaningful the illustrations of these principles of canon formation.

At the dawn of the modern bourgeois-capitalist world, the economic, sociopolitical, and cultural development of Bulgaria was set back in the fourteenth century owing to its conquest by the Turks. For five centuries it was part of the Turkish Ottoman Empire. Its liberation as a result of the Russo-Turkish War (1877–1878) paved the way for its development along capitalist lines. Until the Socialist Revolution of 1944 Bulgaria went through a series of dramatic events. The monarchy involved it in two wars in the Balkans, and then in World War I. The rise of labor and socialist movements began before World War I, and in the wake of that war there occurred the Soldier's Uprising and the setting up of communes. Then in 1923 there was the fascist coup d'état and the subsequent antifascist September Uprising of that same year, which was bloodily suppressed. In 1925 the fascist dictatorship wiped away the cream of the Bulgarian intelligentsia. The 1930s witnessed fierce battles between labor and capital, while the early 1940s saw the beginning of that organized struggle against fascism, the partisan movement, which culminated in the Revolution of 1944.

The first illustration of the above principles—which have been operative for the reception of American literature and by which canon formation can be gauged—is from the field of comparativist Bulgarian-American studies. Nikolai Aretov's "The Reception of Benjamin Franklin in Bulgaria during the Revival Movement" provides a concrete analysis of the reception of Franklin's writing from which important generalizations may be derived.

The last century of the Turkish rule saw the emergence of the Bulgarian Revival Movement, which was as much sociopolitical in its character as it was cultural; in its first phase it corresponded intellectually if not chronologically to the Enlightenment period in Europe and North America. One of the first writings, perhaps the first one, translated into Bulgarian from French (in 1831 and 1866, and translated from German in 1868 and 1872), was Benjamin Franklin's *Poor Richard's Almanack*. The ontological and epistemological principles manifest themselves in the analogous characteristics of the American Enlightenment and the Bulgarian Revival. Both coincided with a national liberation movement and both were concerned with the establishment of nationhood and independent statehood. Both periods, different in historical time as they are, were characterized by nascent bourgeois-capitalist relations of production established after wars of liberation, relations characterized culturally by the philosophy and morality of the bourgeoisie in its initial democratic stage of development. The moral-psychological principle is evinced in the early translations where Franklin, as disguised in his fictional creation, is perceived as a moral example. He is the bearer of the cardinal virtues of the democratic bourgeois: industry, thrift, temperance, sincerity, justice, order, humility, and charity. The possession of these virtues is seen as the prerequisite for material prosperity. In the later translations Franklin's other facet, that of a fighter for national independence, emerges into stronger relief. The social, moral-psychological and political aspects become welded into a whole: the virtuous become wealthy, but becoming wealthy is possible only when the people are free from foreign domination. The literary aesthetic principle shows forth first and foremost in the similarities between Franklin's prose and that of the Bulgarian Revival. Neither is literary, in the sense that plot and character portrayal appear only in their most rudimentary form. Then, the didactic, sermonizing nature of Franklin's narrative accorded with a strong sermonizing tradition in Bulgarian medieval literature that was carried over into Revival writings as a catalyst for the emergence of the untraditional, that is, plot, composition, world outlook. Furthermore, the Bulgarian mind was attuned to aphorisms, proverbs, and sayings. In addition, both types of prose contain a strong autobiographical element; this was of particular epistemological relevance, since the autobiography itself was one of the sources for the emergence of the new Bulgarian prose. The subjective character of the fifth principle and its proneness to fluctuations in the political sphere can be demonstrated, for example, by those Bulgarian intellectuals who were moderate in their political views, a moderation grounded in their faith in reason. They were attracted by the early Franklin who appealed to the reason of the English king and Parliament, as they themselves did to the sultan and the High Porte, to be considerate of their subjects' grievances and thus avoid military confrontation.

A similar pattern in the interaction of the five principles of canon formation takes shape in the topography of American literature translated into Bulgarian. The following brief survey is confined to the mere mention of American authors and/or their works, in which the belief that an awareness of some of the processes in Bulgarian history will make writers' names and titles speak for themselves.

Uncle Tom's Cabin first reached Bulgaria in 1853 in a Russian translation, which was reissued in 1857; the novel was finally translated into Bulgarian in 1898. Since then it has had numerous translations, countless printings, and today its total circulation is over half a million copies. A more recent title which has been equally successful is *The Catcher in the Rye,* which in only four printings has been issued in 360,460 copies. A short story by Mark Twain was first translated in 1897, while in 1911 his complete works in sixteen volumes (in Russian translation) became available in Bulgaria, as did almost all of James Fenimore Cooper's novels between 1873 and 1898. Edward Bellamy's *Looking Backward: 2000–1887* was first translated from Russian in 1892 and once again in 1921. Jack London's essay "Strike" appeared in 1918, and *The Iron Heel* in 1921, while the thirties launched him as the most widely published of all American writers in Bulgaria to this day. During that decade twenty-seven individual titles—novels, short stories, and essays, including "People of the Abyss"—were translated into Bulgarian. They were simultaneously published with his selected writings in five volumes, along with still another series called *The Library of Jack London.* Since then each decade down to the eighties has added its own share of new or reissued titles in new or old translations, and it would hardly be an exaggeration to say that his entire body of work exists in the Bulgarian language. Up to 1977 the number of copies of his writings amounted to one million, while within the last ten years it rose by another million and a half. The thirties and forties witnessed two directions in the choice of American writers for translation. One centered on the representatives of what Henry Mencken and Robert Spiller have called the literary movement of social criticism of the 1890s and their successors, the other on books in which the socially eventful decades registered a faint echo or none at all. Thus Jack London, Mark Twain, Theodore Dreiser, Willa Cather, Sinclair Lewis (seven titles), Upton Sinclair (fifteen titles), Michael Gold, Thornton Wilder, and John Steinbeck were in the company of Louis Bromfield (fifteen titles) and Pearl Buck (eighteen titles).

The years after the Socialist Revolution of 1944 may be divided into two periods with two peaks in the number of translated titles, one at the beginning of the first period (1945–1976), the other in the middle of the second period (1976–1986). A year after the end of World War II, when the country was in ruins and the wounds that war inflicted on its economic and social spheres had just started to heal, forty-four titles of American authorship were translated into Bulgarian; thirty-eight were translated the following year. Though no title was issued in an edition larger than five thousand copies, the pace in translation indicated a new policy in cultural life. With the onset of the Cold War, however, the number of new titles began to decrease rapidly and dwindled to nought in 1952 and 1953. This dramatic decline was a direct corollary of the radical change in the image of the United States from that of an ally of the Soviet Union against German fascism in World War II (which Bulgaria joined during its second liberation phase), to that of an imperialist power set upon curbing the spread of the "red menace" at home and abroad.

The number of titles began to pick up in the successive years of detente until 1962 with an average of about ten titles a year, after which the average rose to fifteen per year. For six years (1971–1976) the number went down again to the average of ten titles annually, and since then it has held to a steady average of twenty-five titles, with the second peak of thirty-three in 1981. Shortage of paper was an important factor in these vacillations, but much more important was the impact of the fluctuations on the international political scene as two significant realities alternately held sway. The first was the coalescing of image and reality: the United States not only was seen to be, but also actually was, the greatest capitalist country, the nation whose enormous economic and political power dominated much of the globe. The second was the recognition that the political realities of our nuclear age have made all the more imperative the Leninist principle of peaceful coexistence of countries with different socioeconomic systems. The cultural correlative of this guiding principle in international relations for the socialist countries rests upon the idea that the deeper and greater the cultural contacts among nations, the deeper the mutual understanding among them, the greater the chances of securing our collective survival. Thus, in spite of these oscillations, during the first thirty-year period the number of copies of American literary works was over 4,720,000. During the second ten-year period, coincident with a more consistent adherence to the Leninist principle of disassociating a government's policies from a nation's democratic culture, the number more than quadrupled and reached the figure of 17,700,000. Bearing in mind that the population of Bulgaria is a little less than nine million, this means that there are two and a half books of American authorship per capita.

The statistics may look impressive, but what are of greater significance and relevance to our subject are the richness and topography of American literature in Bulgarian culture. It is represented in all of its trends and genres, with all of its ethnic and regional characteristics. One can find in translation all the romantic writers: Irving, Cooper, Emerson, Thoreau, Hawthorne, Melville, and Whitman. Almost all of the realists, critical realists, and new realists from the beginning of this century to the present have been translated: Henry James, Mark Twain, Francis Bret Harte, Sinclair Lewis, Theodore Dreiser, Sherwood Anderson, Ernest Hemingway, F. Scott Fitzgerald, William Faulkner, Robert Penn Warren, John Dos Passos, John Steinbeck, Langston Hughes, Albert Maltz, Richard Wright, Ralph Ellison, James Baldwin, Erskine Caldwell, William Saroyan, Carson McCullers, William Styron, Salinger, Updike, Bernard Malamud, Saul Bellow, Truman Capote, Gore Vidal, John Cheever, Kurt Vonnegut, Philip Bronosky, Joseph Heller, Katherine Ann Porter, Joyce Carol Oates, Doctorow, Anne Tyler, Toni Morrison, Tillie Olsen, and Scott Momaday. The majority of these writers have had more than one of their books translated; some of the texts exist in more than one or two translations.

A recent project involves the publication of selected works of individual writers in a series of several volumes. In addition to editions of the poetry of Whitman, Poe, Longfellow, Emily Dickinson, Carl Sandburg, and Robert Frost, there are two volumes of American and Afro-American poetry which include poets of different generations, including the present one. The plays of Eugene O'Neill, Lillian Hellman, Arthur Miller, Tennessee Williams, Edward Albee, Lorraine Hansberry, Sam Shepard, Marsha Norman, and Beth Henley are watched on stage and on the television screen. There are seasons when three or four plays by American dramatists play at the same time in the Sofia theaters. The translation policy of the last fifteen or so years has been to continue the tradition of translating the works of nineteenth- and early twentieth-century writers and to keep up with the most recent works of contemporary authors. The past ten years have also seen the translation of science and detective fiction, while the experimental, postmodern novel (usually represented in excerpted form) is relegated to literary journals and magazines, as are literary critical essays. Best-sellers, particularly those whose film or television versions have been shown in Bulgaria—*Gone with the Wind* and *Rich Man, Poor Man* are examples—also find a home in publishing houses to meet a demand for that kind of fiction.

The writers who have enjoyed the greatest popularity in Bulgaria are Jack London (2,500,000 copies), Mark Twain (over a million copies), Hemingway (941,253), Steinbeck (674,614), and Salinger (450,797). That these authors should constitute the backbone of the reading canon of American literature in Bulgarian culture can be explained by the turbulent history of the Bulgarian people throughout the centuries. It has made them acutely responsive to literary works which deal with problems relevant to their sociopolitical experience, moral concerns, and spiritual aspirations.

From another perspective, the five principles of canon formation may also be viewed as general criteria for the selection of American literary works for translation. Common sociohistorical and general human experience, common moral-psychological issues and spiritual strivings, curiosity about the unfamiliar and different, are both prerequisites for the reception of American literature on the part of readers and the bases for selection on the part of publishing institutions. The fundamental principle that subsumes them and serves as a leading criterion is the Marxist-Leninist approach to the heritage of world literature generally. Predicated on the conception of literature as a major component of culture, it holds that the literary heritage of the world is the making and crystallization of many centuries of human experience, thought, and feeling and that this heritage should be shared by all. The criterion is to select the best in the humanistic and democratic tradition of world literature and to bring it to all the people for their cultural uplift and aesthetic education. By and large, Bulgarian intellectuals have avoided the two extreme attitudes to literary heritage: the one a complete rejection based on the assumption that if a literature was produced under exploitative social systems it cannot but be reactionary, the other an unquestioning acceptance of all and everything.

The selection of American or other foreign texts for publication is made by publishing houses' editorial boards and by artistic councils composed of professional literary critics, creative writers, translators, and academics, who proceed on the basis of written recommendations or book reviews submitted by specialists in the field. The selected works are then commissioned to professional translators, the majority of whom are organized in the Bulgarian Translators' Union. Solid professionalism is the criterion for membership, and the Union's annual conferences, which assess the yearly production of translated works, help maintain the high standards of quality translation. It has been a long road since American literature was first translated from French, German, and Russian versions in the late nineteenth and early twentieth centuries. The road made its way through translations by a handful of people who used the original English texts in the period before the Socialist Revolution to reach the broad highway of today: there is at present a massive presence of American literature in Bulgarian culture, a presence effected by a small army of professional translators whose ranks constantly increase with the infusion of young talent.

So far it can be correctly inferred that translation is the main conduit of American literature into the nation's cultural life. Of no less importance, however, is its study at the university and high school levels because of education's role in canon formation in and outside the academy. Its study is also responsible for the emergence of a bilingual reading audience, even though Bulgarians read American literature in Bulgarian far more than in English. Still, that readership is progressively composed of students of the English language, whose numbers have been increasing at an unprecedented rate because of a full-scale foreign language program. Language study was launched in the early fifties, very much in the tradition of the American missionary schools set up in the midnineteenth-century Turkish Empire. The implementation of the program led to the establishment of specialized high schools for the study of English, French, Russian, German, and Spanish respectively; these have proliferated to the extent that today in almost every large city in Bulgaria there are one or two. The language program is extended to junior and comprehensive high schools which, in addition to teaching English as a requirement, also offer intensive courses. English is taught to all the students in the institutes of higher learning, in evening courses to adults, and in morning and afternoon classes to preelementary school children; courses are offered in factories and enterprises to any group of people wishing to study English. It can rightly be concluded that the departments of English at Bulgaria's two universities have two principal objectives: first, to produce teachers and translators to meet the demand for training in the English language; and second, to arouse interest in the cultures which have shaped and been shaped by the English language.

Unlike the centuries-old culture of the Bulgarian people—the Bulgarian state was founded in 681—academic institutions as physical entities are of relatively recent vintage, dating back to the last decades of the nineteenth century. Sofia University was founded in 1888, the Department of English Philology in 1928. American literature was introduced in 1949 as a discipline in the required curriculum offered by the English department of Veliko Turnovo University at its founding in 1962. Around the same time American literature began to be taught in the English language high schools. What deserves notice is that education, unlike the more general cultural area which encompasses translation, has proved less susceptible to fluctuations in domestic and international politics. This is particularly true for the study of American literature at the university level. During the early 1950s a narrow, doctrinaire interpretation of Marxism led to the entrenchment of the vulgar sociological approach to literature generally and to literary heritage specifically. This greatly harmed the study of Bulgarian literature, in particular. The teaching of American literature, however, remained unaffected by that tendency, which one can still occasionally hear distantly echoed today. Nor was its teaching savaged by the Cold War atmosphere. On the contrary, American literature was actually introduced during this politically most unpropitious period (when diplomatic relations between the countries were severed), by a Bulgarian-American professor who had been deported from the United States for his leftist views. The stress was, and has been ever since, on the humanistic tradition in American literature. A gravitation to socially oriented and engaged American authors has remained, but so also has the consistent application of the epistemological and aesthetic principles which underlie the Marxist approach to literature. The syllabus of the course on American literature has undergone no change in this respect. It has been expanded, of course, to reflect and encompass the new literary developments of the fifties, sixties, seventies, and eighties. An excerpt from the syllabus may well illustrate the interaction of the five principles of canon formation functioning as criteria for the selection of American authors.

The Post WWI Period (1912–1945) The social-political, intellectual and literary climate of the 20's and 30's. Freudianism and Marxism. Realism and Modernism. The Second Literary Renaissance: The Southern Renaissance, the Harlem Renaissance, the rise of American realist drama. 1. Hemingway (*A Fare-well to Arms*) 2. Fitzgerald (*The Great Gatsby*) 3. Faulkner (*Light in August*) 4. Langston Hughes (poems, plays, short stories) 5. Eugene O'Neill (*Long Day's Journey into Night*) 6. Steinbeck (*The Grapes of Wrath*) 7. Richard Wright (*Native Son*) 8. Albert Maltz (short stories) 9. Clifford Odets (*Awake and Sing*) 10. Lillian Hellman (*The Little Foxes*).

As the brief introduction to the historical period suggests, the approach to the study of American literature is Marxist in at least two basic senses. First, literary phenomena are considered in their sociohistorical context in close relation with the intellectual climate as shaped by prevalent concerns in philosophical and aesthetic thought. Second, implied rather than stated, is the concept of the literary text as a unity of form and content in the dialectical and historical process.

The selection of American authors for the syllabus rests entirely with the academics who teach it and who are thus responsible for the canon formation at the university level. That the reading canon should basically overlap with the academic canon is only logical as there is uninterrupted continuity between the university and the wider culture. Many of the decision makers for the reading canon of the past forty years, with the exception of the oldest generation of editors and translators, are English philology graduates from the two universities, where they acquire their basic knowledge in Marxist aesthetics and methodology.

In terms of academic structure, the Department of English Philology is one of the constituents of the Faculty of Classical and Modern Philologies at Sofia University. The courses in the curriculum are all required for graduation, and while their number is decided by the Faculty Council, approved by the Academic Council, and then put into force by the Ministry of Education and Culture, the content of the courses of study is determined by the academics who conduct them. The History of American Literature is one of the disciplines in the nine-semester curriculum for English philology graduates. It is taught for two semesters, as against six semesters for English literature and one more semester for British civilization. A new project for reform in higher education is under way, and there are very real chances that American literature will be studied an additional semester, either through an extension of the literature course or through a separate course in American civilization. At present all courses, including the one in the history of American literature, are required.

The usual yearly enrollment, excluding the extramurals, varies from forty to ninety students, according to the needs of the country for

English teachers and translators. The tendency at the moment is toward a drastic growth of the student body in the English department. The latest reform in higher education led to formation of a three-stage structure which corresponds to three types of job qualification. In the third and highest stage, in addition to the required curriculum, students are offered optional courses in linguistics, theory of translation, and English and American literature. So far the elective courses in American literature have been in Afro-American literature and American drama. Future projects—courses in Southern literature, native American literature, American folklore, women's literature, and American literary criticism—are intended to respond to new developments in the discipline and to the growing interest of students.

The English Department at Veliko Turnovo University is much smaller than that at Sofia University. The course in the history of American literature for extramurals is taught by a Bulgarian, and its syllabus does not differ greatly from the one offered to regular and extramural students at Sofia University. The syllabus for the regular students, on the other hand, is determined by the visiting American professors who have taught regularly at Veliko Turnovo University since its founding.

Despite the widespread interest in American literature, there are only six academic scholars specializing in the area in Bulgaria: two at Sofia, one at Veliko Turnovo, and three in the Comparative Literature Section at the Bulgarian Studies Institute of the Bulgarian Academy of Sciences. Although four of them hold a doctorate in American literature, none is a full professor. This situation reflects Bulgaria's recent educational history. The academics who founded the various departments in the Faculty of Classical and Modern Philologies during the first several decades of this century received their degrees and professorships abroad. It was not until the 1960s that a system granting advanced degrees and academic titles was instituted in Bulgaria. Even though this system is still in its early stages of development, criteria are stringent; in addition, despite efforts to speed things up, procedures are very slow. Thus, there are only two full professors in the English department, one in linguistics and another one in English literature. The highest title held by an Americanist is that of docent, the last but one in the university hierarchy.

The greatest number of Americanists (approximately fifty) is comprised of historians, sociologists, economists, and political scientists affiliated with the respective university faculties, the Institute of Higher Learning and those of the Academy of Sciences. Still another group is composed of journalists, editors, and professional translators.

Scholarship in American literature falls into two categories, scholarly studies proper and journalistic literary criticism. The first category includes such forms as the literary essay, the article, and the monograph. The most comprehensive scholarly research so far produced in Bulgaria has been doctoral dissertations. These and other scholarly studies are, with few exceptions, written in English and published in the Sofia University Press publications *Philologia, Annuaire de L'Université de Sofia Kliment Ohridski,* and *Sofia University English Papers.* English language scholarship appears as well in collections of essays published abroad, and in conference proceedings published both at home and abroad. Those written in Bulgarian get published in the numerous literary journals and magazines. The only seminal book-length work, which originally appeared in two separate collections of essays and was later published in one volume, is Pauline Pirinska's *A History of American Literature: XIX and XX c.* (1979). Pirinska presents essays on Irving, Cooper, Poe, Emerson, Hawthorne, Melville, Whitman, Dreiser, Lewis, Fitzgerald, Hemingway, Steinbeck, and Faulkner. Despite its rather misleading title, the book is a major contribution to American scholarship in Bulgaria and an indispensable bibliographical aid. It was preceded by Victor Sharenkov's *An Outline History of American Literature,* which is no longer in use.

The volume of journalistic literary criticism is gargantuan compared with scholarship proper. It takes the form of articles and of introductions and afterwords to translated works. Some of the latter lean more toward the literary essay; they vary in length from twenty to sixty pages. Almost every American book that comes out in translation is reviewed in the weekly literary newspapers or in the dailies, most of which carry a page dedicated to cultural events and news. This type of literary criticism is written by literary and drama critics, professional translators, and university Americanists. By writing such criticism, academics find a solution to the problem of audience: they write for students and professionals in English and for a wider audience in Bulgarian. Professional literary theorists and critics, however, are still primarily in the orbit of European literature—Russian, English, French, and German.

By translating, teaching, and writing about American literature during the past few decades of this century, Bulgarian intellectuals succeeded in establishing a permanent place for that literature in the cultural life of the nation, in opening one more window to the world at large. The popularity of American literature equaled and in some cases surpassed that of the more traditionally acceptable European literatures.

Will the interest in American literature continue in the future, as

Bulgaria faces what may be the third great watershed in its modern history? *Perestroika,* which is now sweeping across Eastern Europe, may well prove as important as the liberation of Bulgaria from Turkish domination in 1877 and 1878 and the Socialist Revolution of 1944. On 10 November 1989 the totalitarian regime which had governed Bulgaria was overthrown "from above" by a group of radicals in the Central Committee of the Bulgarian Communist Party. Their action unleashed tremendous political energy in a populace intent upon establishing civil liberties and democratic political practices in the country.

It is widely recognized that cultural policies are contingent upon the political structure of a society. Yet one of the important arguments of this essay has been that, in Bulgaria, there has been an impressive achievement in the study and translation of American literature over a period of forty years, despite the fact that these forty years saw the rule of Stalinist and neo-Stalinist regimes. From this it may be concluded that the grip of totalitarianism was not unrelenting on every sphere of social and cultural life. Another conclusion also presents itself: that while a ruling clique abused socialist ideals by using them for empty sloganeering and demagogy, a great many people continued to believe in these ideals and pursue them as important human values. Bulgarians read and studied American literature because the values they found there were consonant with their genuine beliefs in human freedom and dignity.

Perestroika should only encourage and strengthen this basic belief in human values, and thus it seems reasonable to expect that the promising development of American studies will continue. Indeed, the process of perestroika seems irreversible. Both the self-reforming Bulgarian Communist Party and its opposition, the umbrella organization called the Union of Democratic Forces, are committed to fundamental economic and political reforms, such as introducing a market economy and fostering multiparty government. The two groups differ only in that the former believes true democracy can best be effected by "humane, restructured socialism," while the latter is committed to varieties of "democratic capitalism." The goal of both sides is increased freedom and democracy.

The new directions and new energy which have resulted from perestroika have already affected American studies in a positive way. Three new Bulgarian-American societies have been formed; one of them is the Bulgarian Association for American Studies. The National Assembly passed legislation giving Sofia University full autonomy, thus allowing greater freedom to scholars to pursue the paths of scholarship; almost simultaneously, the English department of that university inaugurated a course in American civilization. Translation of American texts continues apace, and as new Bulgarian-American contacts develop, the translation of heretofore neglected nonfiction should dramatically increase.

Most important, the Bulgarian people are committed to progressing toward the full democratization of their society. That change, like any major social transformation, will not be an easy one. The Bulgarian people are fortunate to have in their own cultural heritage a rich cultural tradition which celebrates human dignity and freedom. At the same time, they are likely to study and borrow from the humanistic tradition which has developed so strongly and influentially in the United States, that tradition of democracy which is not only visible but accessible in American literature. American literature possesses, for Bulgarians, a special contemporaneity. It boldly faces the crucial problems of our modern age, yet at the same time it affirms the worth of the human race and its potential, not only to rise above the untoward circumstances of life but also to change these circumstances for the better.

❧

Progress and Problems
American Literary Studies in China during the Post-Mao Era

XIAO-HUANG YIN

The study of American literature in China is a very recent development. Strictly speaking, it was born only after the end of the Cultural Revolution (1966–1976), with the rapid change of political climate, social fabric, and cultural values in that country during the post-Mao era. The earlier periods were dominated either by a narrow and constraining ideology borrowed from the Soviets in the 1950s or by the xenophobic and anti-intellectual characteristics of the Cultural Revolution in the 1960s. Only in the recent decade have scholars in China been able to develop their studies seriously and to bring to bear an independent Chinese perspective on the discipline.

Of course, this is not to say that the study of American literature remained completely absent in China in previous decades. Translation of Henry Wadsworth Longfellow's poem "A Psalm of Life" in the 1860s shows that even in the nineteenth century Chinese scholars were aware of the literary merits of their American contemporaries. Although they were influenced by the long-standing European bias that American literature was but an appendage to that of Britain, Chinese academics achieved considerable progress in the field. By the time of Liberation in 1949, many major works of American literature had been introduced into China: writers such as Washington Irving, James Fenimore Cooper, Edgar Allan Poe, Ralph Waldo Emerson, Nathaniel Hawthorne, Walt Whitman, Mark Twain, Sherwood Anderson, Eugene O'Neill, and Ernest Hemingway had appeared in Chinese translation and had attracted admirers both in the scholarly community and among sophisticated readers.

The founding of the People's Republic of China in 1949 brought about an abrupt change in the situation. As part of a national program aimed at introducing foreign literature more systematically to the Chinese people, American literature continued to be placed on the official agenda, but it was inevitably affected, alongside American studies as a whole, by the then-degenerating relations between the two countries. While the period saw growing interest in American literature elsewhere in the world, it nevertheless witnessed no corresponding response in China. No more than fifty articles on American literature were written during the whole of the 1950s. Moreover, few of the essays then popular survived the period, for they were too one-sided and too frankly propagandistic to have sufficient literary quality for, or to say anything to, subsequent generations. Similarly, throughout the decade only about a dozen American writers were translated. Reasons for such neglect are not difficult to find.

As is commonly known, China in those years was heavily influenced by the Soviet Union, particularly in the social sciences. Along with many other endeavors, the study of American literature in China was left to Soviet experts, whose ideas were recommended, in the name of Marxist theory, as the standard curriculum for the training of Chinese Americanists. Soviet criticism, then upheld as the ultimate arbiter for determining literary excellence, appears in hindsight more than a bit curious. To the Stalinists, the best American writers were critical realists. Following the influence of the analytic methods of Georg Lukacs, they adhered to the principle that the only criterion for determining literary merit was that of "critical realism," as if realism were something like a crystal ball which could tell good from evil; small wonder, in this context, that only a few American authors were considered worth studying. In practice, the theory divided American literature into two general categories: progressive, because it exposed and denounced the evil nature of the capitalist system; and reactionary, since it defended and praised the decadent American society. In accordance with this definition, only those works judged as critical of American capitalism in one way or another passed the test of political correctness and were introduced into New China: these works either enabled readers to perceive the dark side of American society or upheld the glorious tradition of the American working class. Celebrated writers were almost all from the school of "critical realism." Theodore Dreiser and Jack London, for instance, were two obvious choices. Aside from their proven popularity, they were ideologically "clean," both by virtue of their indignant criticism of the hypocrisy of the

"American dream" and by their sympathetic description of the suffering of the laboring people in the "Dollar Empire."

Such an arbitrary criterion inevitably excluded many American literary masters. For example, despite the fact that William Faulkner had by then emerged as a towering figure in American literature, his works went virtually unnoticed in China because of his alleged conservatism in politics and "decadent tendency" in style. In a similar vein, while Howard Fast and O. Henry were widely read in China during this period, writers of great formal accomplishment such as Henry James and T. S. Eliot were rejected on the grounds that their works did not satisfy the tenets of critical realism. Thus, their works, as well as those of many other distinguished American writers, went largely unread. Measured by such a dogmatic yardstick, even *Uncle Tom's Cabin*, which had enjoyed tremendous popularity in China prior to 1949 because of its profound protest against oppression and injustice, was now considered too humanitarian and too passive to be published.

The fanatic devotion to placing American literary studies at the service of political ends sometimes led to rather surprising selections, as indicated by the translation of *The Scarlet Letter* in 1954. Oddly enough, while publishers were hesitant to publish such realistic works as *Uncle Tom's Cabin*, this "romance" by Hawthorne was translated and brought out in a popular Chinese edition. The seemingly paradoxical phenomenon can be understood through a careful reading of the translator's analytical introduction to *The Scarlet Letter*. "Although Hawthorne is a conservative bourgeois writer," the translator declares in his preface, "he lays bare the hypocritical and ugly essence of religion in America." Interpreted as a sharp exposure of "the evilness of religious regime" and as "a passionate appeal for women's rights," the novel was thought helpful for the promotion of both the antireligious campaign and the women's emancipation movement then under way in China. Albeit hardly consistent with any literary standard of "critical realism" in Western terms, the translation of this classic of Hawthorne reveals that in China major ideological considerations at the time made the work politically acceptable. The publication of *The Scarlet Letter* points out an essential facet of China's American literary studies during this period: no matter what the text under consideration was, it was to be measured by the same yardstick of "realistic exposure," a phrase which denoted a strong denunciation of various aspects of capitalism and an ideologically critical methodology that could lead, at times, to curious conclusions.

Looking back on those years, we can detect a pattern which displayed clearly the general trend that made up the scene of American literary studies then in China: research tended to be politically oriented to an extreme, and literary studies became primarily a means to accomplish an ideological purpose. To be sure, this version of literary criticism was not imposed uniformly throughout the whole period. There were relatively easy and relaxed times such as the Hundred-Flower period in 1956, when Mao proclaimed that the guiding principle of Chinese criticism would be to "let a hundred flowers blossom and a hundred schools of thought contend"; nevertheless, the basic concept of an ideological purity, maintained through critical realism, was dominant.

The split between China and its "big brother," the Soviet Union, in the early 1960s released Chinese scholars from the constraining influence of the Russian brand of Marxism and enabled them to explore a new historicosociological method of criticism of American literature. Unfortunately, when Chinese scholars were just about to break the various bonds of rigid political dogma imposed on them, the xenophobic and anti-intellectual Cultural Revolution broke out, completely obliterating the study of American literature for a whole decade. Ironically, while the disastrous event disrupted any serious research, it ushered forth translations of two American novels, Eudora Welty's *The Optimist's Daughter* and Richard Bach's *Jonathan Livingston Seagull.* Both were translated only in order to be criticized as "typical revelations of the American reactionary delusions." The "optimistic daughter" was denounced because her nostalgia for the old South was thought to be a symbolic and sympathetic gesture for the "confused, decadent, and desperate American society"; and attack on the seagull's "vain attempt to supersede the insurmountable contradictions of the American monopoly" was aimed at stimulating the "greater revolutionary enthusiasm and fighting will of the Chinese people." Such absurdly imaginative interpretations illustrate vividly the catastrophe the ultraleft movement brought on China's American literary studies during those "most revolutionary years."[1]

The year 1976 marked another turning point in modern Chinese history. With the death of Mao, the radical leaders—the so-called Gang of Four—were removed and the decade-long Cultural Revolution came to an end. However, it was not until 1978, when the reform-minded Chinese leaders decided to implement a new policy of openness, that the domestic situation finally allowed for a significant shift in the study of American literature. With the changed political and cultural atmosphere, the discipline rapidly emerged as the center of widespread interest, drawing attention from both academic circles and average people.

Before 1978, no major Chinese university offered specialized courses in American literature or found significant space in its curriculum for the study of any American writers. Since 1978, a wide and growing range of courses in American literature has been taught at both graduate and undergraduate levels in universities and colleges throughout China. Nearly twenty such programs existed in 1982, and there were more than eighty by 1988. The increasing number of both scholarly journals devoted to serious studies and commercial magazines that carried translations of American writing as added attractions to their regular contents enhanced the popularity of American literary studies. In fact, there were more publications in American literature during this recent decade than in any other period in Chinese history. In 1982 alone, less than five years after the change, Chinese Americanists wrote more than sixty critical articles and books; at the same time they translated twenty-one novels, one hundred and fifty-seven short stories, thirty-one plays and movie scenarios, and fifty-four biographies and collections of essays. Furthermore, following the founding of the All-China American Literary Studies Association in 1979, organizations such as the Eugene O'Neill Society, the Ernest Hemingway Seminar, and the William Faulkner Convention were formed, serving as meeting grounds for academics to exchange views and coordinate their research. Indeed, the 1978 to 1988 decade brought about tremendous prosperity for China's American literary studies. To borrow a poetic reference to describe this great progress, the ten years ushered in a "springtime," in which a wide range of works were translated, new dimensions to literary interest were developed, and the voices of sophisticated Chinese critics were clearly heard throughout the country.

The springtime was first evidenced by the publication in 1978 of the first volume of *The Concise History of American Literature,* written by scholars from the authoritative Chinese Academy of Social Sciences. In retrospect, we find that the book is not without weakness. Puritan literature of colonial New England, for instance, was neglected except for a brief description of Ann Bradstreet, mainly because she is "the first woman poet in America." And although James Fenimore Cooper is distinguished as a significant figure in the nineteenth century, he is given less space than Harriet Beecher Stowe. However, these weaknesses are unimportant when measured against the contribution the authors made to the creation of independent and scholarly Chinese-style American literary studies. The true value of the book lies in the fact that it not only is the first critical work on American literature ever written in China, but also represents a major attempt to pass beyond both the influences of the 1950s Stalinist dogmatism and the excesses of orthodox political jargon engendered by the Cultural Revolution.

The traditional mode for producing critical studies of American literature in China was allied to literary translation. Scholars and critics used introductions to Chinese translations as the major vehicle for literary criticism and, indeed, scholarship. There were disadvantages to this manner of engaging in literary criticism, disadvantages which *The Concise History of American Literature* successfully overcame. Although they often contained elaboration on the historical background of a book, translators' introductions were generally inadequate as literary scholarship since they failed to provide readers with a panoramic picture of the development of American literature. In part this inadequacy was owing to the genre, for introductions are circumscribed by their function of explaining the particular book. Thus, these introductions tended to isolate writers from any larger historical perspective, even though an author's position can only be fully understood when it is related to the whole development of the literary and social tradition in which he or she works. Moreover, due to the didactic purpose of most translations, interpretations of a work were made only in terms of the work's significance to Chinese society. In other words, political dogmatism made it difficult for critics to assess objectively and comprehensively the significance of American writers. There was little emphasis on formal and aesthetic concerns. *The Concise History of American Literature* made a major breakthrough and represented a radical departure in this critical tradition: it examined works in their larger American social and literary context, and at the same time it paid attention to formal elements of a work and to its aesthetic achievement.

Covering the period from colonial days to the end of the nineteenth century, the book presented historical orientation and critical reviews of virtually all the major writers in this era, thus providing Chinese readers, for the first time, with the context and the continuity of American literature. By placing American literary figures in a long historical perspective, the book added new dimensions of meaning to the works of American writers. In addition, while the Soviet-modeled dogmatic readings of earlier years had not been completely cast away, they were at least balanced by new historicosociological methodology and by a serious attempt to assess the artistic achievement of the writers of the American literary tradition. Hawthorne, for example, was no longer labelled chiefly as a conservative writer who did not want to change American society. The book devoted a ten-page essay to discussing his unique position as a "psychological anatomist" in American literary history and his influence on later writers. The achievement of Emily Dickinson, whose poems were previously little read and whose name was virtually anathema in China because of her "depoliticized tendency," was elaborated in detail, and her contribution to the creation of a new style of American poetry was thoroughly examined. In a country where criticism is always politically oriented and critical attention is ordinarily guided by considerations of immediate social significance and practical utility, the careful analysis made by the authors of this volume, and their emphasis on the aesthetic values of major American writers, represented a serious effort to move to a more sophisticated stage of criticism and a profound progress toward artistic maturity.

The attempt to break down old conventions, to make a new start on American literary studies on a higher level, led to increased publication of critical works; important among them were: *History of American Literature, Modern American Novelists, Contemporary American Fiction,* and *20th Century American Literature.* These books are typical of American literary studies in contemporary China: they are both of high quality and jointly written by Chinese Americanists at various institutions. Freed from the rigid control of ultraleft dogmatism, scholars were encouraged to explore divergent ways of research. As the old orthodoxy was replaced by new slogans such as "Be bold in creating new" and "Emancipate your mind and liberate your thinking," China gradually witnessed a flowering of schools of criticism, from the old-fashioned Chinese classic approach, to the newly modeled historicosociological methodology, to Western-style deconstructionism. Of course, Marxist criticism has remained the dominant theory, but it has no longer been the only method applied to critical studies. Recognition of the simultaneous existence of a number of schools of criticism and, what may be more important, to recognize their significance for a better understanding of American literature, has marked recent Chinese scholarship. Such an openness is especially significant in China, where schools, movements, and literary theories have never truly flourished.

In addition to the book-length critical works that try to assess the development of American literature from a historical and panoramic angle, there has also appeared a large quantity of short essays published in various scholarly journals and periodicals. Thus, while highly contemporary American writers such as Thomas Pynchon and William Kennedy, or emergent genres like superfiction and experimental realism, fall outside the scope of the book-length studies, short essays have been quick to bridge the gap. Meanwhile, for the first time since 1949, an interest in works written by American critics burgeoned. Shanghai Foreign Language Education Press brought out translations of a set of eight books, under the imprint of the *American Literary History Series*. They include Malcolm Cowley's *Exile's Return*, Van Wyck Brooks's *The World of Washington Irving*, Henry Nash Smith's *Virgin Land*, Robert Ernest Spiller's *The Cycle of American Literature*, Larzer Ziff's *The American 1890's*, Edmund Wilson's *Patriotic Gore*, Richard Pells's *Radical Visions and American Dreams*, and Morris Dickstein's *Gates of Eden*. Aimed at providing Chinese readers with a variety of critical interpretations by American critics, these books are widely used as reference works in Chinese colleges and universities. Not all of them are the best choices, perhaps, but at least the project indicates efforts on the part of Chinese scholars to learn from Western critical approaches and absorb them into their research.

The intense reexamination of American literary studies stimulated a powerful need to reevaluate those American writers who were previously neglected or denounced in China. Faulkner is one representative example. In contrast to prevailing sense in the 1950s and 1960s that he was "a decadent reactionary writer," the *Anthology of Criticism on William Faulkner* (1982) celebrated him as "a literary giant who roots deeply in American soil, draws his creative power from his attachment to the past of his homeland and has deep feeling toward ordinary people." The book examined Faulkner's discovery of "the charm, power, and moral strength in the body and soul of the primary people—Indians, blacks, children, etc." It acknowledged that the Chinese reader would be uncomfortable with Faulkner's descriptions of violence and distorted sexual behavior, but the book went on to assert that Faulkner intended to use these descriptions to undermine received pieties and unexamined social conventions in the hope that such inhuman activities would not happen again. Therefore, in reading him, "we can understand better the essence of modern American society."

It is worthwhile to note that Jewish-American writers, particularly novelists, were being studied with special interest in China. In fact, a specific research project on these writers was listed as one of the eleven projects of the general research program fostered by the All-China American Literary Studies Association.[2] Works by Bernard Malamud, Saul Bellow, Isaac Bashevis Singer, Norman Mailer, and their contemporaries have all been translated and received with enthusiasm. This interest is stimulated partly by the fact that many successful American writers are of Jewish origin and partly by the curiosity of Chinese readers about an ethnic group which is not entirely unlike Chinese Americans.

Yet there is something more behind this powerful interest in Jewish-American fiction, something which is revelatory of deep Chinese literary values and theoretical orientation. A careful examination reveals that what has made Chinese scholars and the reading public enthusiastic about these Jewish-American novelists is that many of them are literary traditionalists as opposed to postmodernists, provided we can divide contemporary American novelists into these two major camps. If their works often strike familiar chords and elicit positive responses from Chinese critics and reading audiences, it is because most Chinese critics and readers are likewise literary conventionalists. They value the level of the primary fiction above any musings about its status; they have a broad commitment to substance and, perhaps, to an eclectic realism. Furthermore, they share with many of these Jewish-American writers a concern with humanism and a commitment to affirming human values. In other words, Chinese scholars tend to place these Jewish-American writers in the context of a coherent, if debatable, overview of postwar American literature. In their eyes, these novelists are important not merely as exemplars of a marginal ethnic group but also because their writings frequently reflect the emerging synthesis of traditional realism and modernism based on Freudian psychology and existentialism in contemporary American literature. In addition, these writers gain additional significance for accepting their role as historians of society: they often reveal the deep influence of social development upon writers' own consciousness.

If the growing publication of critical research is an index to the development of scholarly studies on American literature in the recent decade, the outpouring of translations reflects the increasing popularity of American writers among the reading public. The widespread acceptance of, and admiration for, these translations indicate that American literature in China no longer circulates only among the scholarly community or a small circle of sophisticated readers. It has reached a wide audience. Ranging from classics like Melville's *Moby-Dick* to best-sellers such as Sidney Sheldon's *Rage of Angels,* new or recently reissued translations of American writing occupy a large share of China's book market, a share out of all proportion to the literature of other countries. Authors of "high" literature such as Edgar Allan Poe, Henry David Thoreau, Ralph Waldo Emerson, Henry James, and William Faulkner, who were ignored or untranslated because of ideological considerations or moral reasons, have now appeared in Chinese versions. In fact, one could devote an entire essay to chronicling the classic American writers translated into Chinese in recent years. Although not all readers can fully appreciate this kind of high literature, their enthusiasm for serious American writers, at least in commercial terms, is very impressive. For example, *The Scarlet Letter,* retranslated in 1980, has sold 300,000 copies. Sales of anthologies of short stories by Washington Irving, Edgar Allan Poe, Herman Melville, Ambrose Bierce, Mark Twain, Sherwood Anderson, F. Scott Fitzgerald, Bernard Malamud, and others have all reached high records. In a sense, what Theodore Roosevelt once commented on a poem written by Edwin Robinson may still characterize the feeling of many an average Chinese reader toward serious American literature: "I am not sure I understand it, but I am entirely sure I like it."

In the case of "lowbrow" or popular literature, it is interesting to find that despite sharp contrasts in social systems and cultural traditions, the literary tastes of ordinary people in China are surprisingly similar to their American counterparts. If sales figures are an indication of a writer's popularity, Margaret Mitchell, Arthur Hailey, and Herman Wouk are some of the most widely read authors in China, and translations of their works have been tremendously successful. The reissued translation of *Gone with the Wind* had sales of 600,000 copies. Owing to the perennial love of young people for the war romance, Herman Wouk's *The Winds of War* and *War Remembrances* achieved an extraordinary success in China: translations of the two novels soon became runaway best-sellers. Reprinted several times, they ultimately sold more than two million copies and for a long time remained the hottest books in the country.[3]

The ferment over American literature in many ways can be attributed to the literary periodicals that mushroomed in the recent decade, particularly the rise of commercial magazines specializing in translation such as *Windows of the World, Foreign Short Stories Monthly,* and *Foreign Novels Quarterly.* Popular Western short stories and best-sellers were often first published by these magazines and only thereafter appeared in book form. The *Translation Forest,* founded at Nanjing in 1979, is an excellent example. From the very beginning, this large-scale quarterly was devoted to the entertainment of average readers; its contents consisted mainly of commercially successful Western fiction. It rapidly became an influential vehicle for the transmission of American literary works: the initial four issues carried four best-sellers, two of which were American: Corman Avery's *Kramer versus Kramer,* and Peter Benchley's *Jaws.* This emphasis on popular fiction well suited for a mass audience quickly paid off. While literary critics might question the periodical's standard of selection, they could hardly quarrel with its success and influence: the first issue reached 600,000 copies and by the end of the first year, its circulation rose to 750,000 copies.

An equally impressive aspect of the profound change that occurred during this period was the lessening of censorship. Undoubtedly, a censorship system still exists but it is more tolerant and less often, and less harshly, implemented. With the trend toward liberalization, it seemed less necessary for the publishers to protect the general public from politically or morally "unhealthy elements" contained in American literary works. Although pornographic descriptions remained the target of censorship, much other previously unacceptable material, especially political ideas in conflict with Marxist doctrine, were no longer regarded as "poisoning," thus reflecting the changed ideology and the growing confidence of the authorities during this period. For example, despite the favorable reception of Afro-American writers in China since Liberation, two classics of black literature, *Native Son* and *Invisible Man,* were never allowed to be translated because both contain criticism of, and disillusionment with, communism. Owing to changes in the political climate, the two novels are now available in Chinese editions. Interestingly, though, while Richard Wright and Ralph Ellison's criticisms of communism were acceptable, descriptions of sexual behavior, particularly the incest scene in *Invisible Man,* were deleted from the Chinese translations.

The progress of China's American literary studies, as we have mentioned, was largely the result of the policy of openness and the subsequent political reform which swept over China and touched the very quick of the Chinese consciousness in the past ten years. Meanwhile, the normalization of Sino-American relations also had a profound impact on the development of American literary studies. After being disrupted for nearly three decades, numerous contacts between academics of the two countries once again flourished. Since 1978, some fifty thousand Chinese scholars and students have received education in the United States, while in 1988 alone various academic programs brought about three thousand Americans to teach or study in Chinese institutions. The consequence of this warming of relations was enormous and conspicuous. For one thing, after being closed in for such a long time, once the door was open, people in China rushed to catch a glimpse of the outside world. The stereotypical image of a decadent America declined and gave way to a more varied and objective overview of American society, its culture, and its people. As direct contacts continued, a strong desire to learn more about the United States arose.

Chinese interests in America encompass the political and the social as well as the purely literary or artistic, and, coupled with a curiosity about the actualities of life in the United States, have engendered readings of American literature with new dimensions, some of which are even beyond a literary context. For example, Arthur Hailey's best-sellers have been extremely appealing to Chinese audiences mainly because they are considered reliable sourcebooks packed with priceless ideas about the "American system," information which the average Chinese reader is not likely to find anywhere else. For this reason, Hailey's novels, from the early *The Final Diagnosis* to the recent *Overload,* are all highly recommended in China. After reading *Money Exchangers,* a local Chinese bank manager claimed that "the knowledge contained in the novel on American financial systems is so precious that it should be used as a textbook for us Chinese businessmen."[4]

Ironically, the catastrophically xenophobic Cultural Revolution was also partly responsible for the present widespread interest in American literature. That decade-long tragedy terrified the nation into significantly destroying established patterns of individual belief; its attempt at radically altering ways of thinking and acting transformed the relationship between the people and the community. As a result, traditional values gradually disappeared and the "purified land" of the 1950s was transformed into a drastically changed society which is not altogether different from that of the United States. All of a sudden, Chinese readers, and in particular the intellectuals, realized that the painfulness of alienation, the loss of individual identity, and the other forms of suffering and malaise expressed in contemporary American literature exist, too, in their own lives. In other words, the nightmare of the Cultural Revolution provided the Chinese with a framework within which the complexity of modern American society can be comprehended. For example, the feeling of the absurd is no longer impossible to understand: the confusion and bitterness of the Cultural Revolution enabled Chinese people somehow to discover it in their own experience. How deeply they could share responses to American literature was powerfully reflected in the successful staging of Arthur Miller's *Death of a Salesman* in China in 1984. As Miller himself recognized:

> It was thought that they [the Chinese audience] would never understand the play because there were no salesmen in China, at least since the Liberation. But, as it turned out, they saw a lot of good in Willy Loman. They were

coming out of the Cultural Revolution, when the government was telling everybody that they were all the same and they *better* be all the same, or else. So when Willy Loman says to his son, "I am not a dollar-an-hour. I am Willy Loman, and you're Biff Loman"—in other words, "You are something distinct on the face of the earth"—they were very much for that.

Although the progress of China's American literary studies during the past ten years has been both impressive and exciting, it has not been without problems, some of which are uniquely Chinese. Lack of a unified copyright system has been a continuing source of trouble, frequently causing confusion in translation, particularly that of best-sellers. Three different Chinese editions of Mario Puzo's *The Godfather*, for example, came out in the same year, while at least four of Arthur Hailey's novels, each appearing under several titles, were published by rival publishers competing against each other for sales. Chinese publishing houses, under orders to become self-financing, have found that the easiest way to turn a profit is to give readers what they want, and the Chinese craving for American best-sellers has proved insatiable. As a result, those readers who bought *A Snow Stormy Night at Lincoln Airfield*, *The City of Automobiles*, and *Beyond the Capacity* were surprised to find they were the same books as *Airport*, *Wheels*, and *Overload*. Although the Chinese government has been concerned about the problem, and a copyright law is now in the process of being formulated, it will take some time before the confusion is clarified.

Academically, improving the quality of research has been a serious challenge. The problem is most conspicuous in the study of American poetry. Ironically, though the first piece of American literature translated into Chinese was a poem, criticism of American poetry remains the weakest link in Chinese scholarship, especially when compared to the work done on the other literary genres. To be sure, Walt Whitman, Emily Dickinson, T. S. Eliot, Ezra Pound, William Carlos Williams, Robert Frost, and other major American "muses" have all been introduced into China in recent years and have made a strong impact on both Chinese critics and poets. But perhaps because American poetry, particularly that of the modern period, is so varied and so different from traditional Chinese poetry, the connections between different schools, styles, and voices seem so complex that Chinese scholars hardly hope to sort them out. Or perhaps because poetic tastes require more time to develop, so far no one in China has been able to understand and present a clear pattern to poetic development in America. Judged by Western standards, most research papers on American poetry published in

China are critically naive, often consisting of only introductory-level, factual background and containing no critical insight. With this in mind, we can perhaps understand why not a single Chinese book has yet been written on American poetry, despite the fact that Chinese knowledge of that poetry began over a century ago.

The greatest problem facing Chinese scholars in the past ten years, however, has been the continuing and vexing influence of orthodox political ideology and policy. Although the general political atmosphere improved gradually during this period, "recess" characteristically occurred whenever an ideological movement arose, frustrating efforts by China's Americanists to engage in more scholarly and objective study in the field. For example, the Anti-Spiritual Pollution Campaign—a political movement waged in 1983 to eliminate the "polluting effect" of Western culture, produced harsh criticism of many research projects in American literature. The case of *Catch-22* is illustrative. Heller's novel had been translated and was already in print when the movement began. It was withheld from distribution because some orthodox officials saw in it deep criticism—despite the fact that the book's subject and audience were American—that touched the very quick of the Chinese social system as well. Permission to distribute and circulate the novel was given only after some critics justified its value for the average Chinese reader. They did this by posing three questions which provided a critical approach to the book for the reading public: What is the dilemma of the American capitalist society reflected in the novel? What are the basic contradictions which will lead to inevitable collapse of the Western system? Can you find from reading the novel the features of the monopoly capitalist class in the United States? However, we should not be too quick to blame these critics for analyzing this modern classic as yet another exemplar of propaganda, since this was the only way to have the book published under the circumstances. It demonstrates again how ideology continued to play a significant role in the cultural and social life of China even amidst intensified reform.

The tumultuous events that took place in China in 1989 have brought the ten-year reform to an abrupt end. The crackdown on student demonstrations, the reshuffling of China's leadership, and the consequent nationwide reeducation movement (or "Anti-Bourgeois Liberalization Campaign," as it is called by the authorities) have cast grave doubts on the future of American literary studies in China. Once again, social and political elements are transforming the direction of cultural and academic studies in that nation, and that such transformation may significantly alter Chinese approaches to American literature is most probable. Indeed, the various restrictions newly imposed by the Chinese authorities on academic exchanges with the United States indicate that the springtime for American literary studies in China has come to a close.

However, although it is now too early to predict what possible changes will occur in China, a total regression to the kind of extreme orthodoxy that characterized the Cultural Revolution seems unlikely, due to the drastic changes that have taken place in the past ten years. In addition, the power vacuum created by conflict within the leadership has allowed room for some reform-minded local authorities, especially those in the coastal areas who have reaped tremendous benefits and gained much freedom from the "Open-Door" and decentralization policies, to defy the central government and continue various liberal measures in their areas. For example, despite the newly changed political climate in Beijing, the American Studies Center at the Shanghai International Studies University is continuing its translation project of the "History of American Civilization Series," which includes Sacvan Bercovitch's *The American Jeremiad,* Warner Berthoff's *The Ferment of Realism,* and Daniel Aaron's *Writers on the Left.*

In the long run, although it is highly unlikely that there will arise the same liberal atmosphere for China's Americanists in the near future as it did in the past ten years, the reemergent dominance of orthodox ideology cannot spell total doom for American literary studies in China. Much has changed in that nation since 1978. As a result, it is almost impossible to completely eliminate the legacy of the ten-year reform. Therefore, while political interference will undoubtedly pose serious obstacles in the path of China's American literary studies, research programs in the discipline, including translations, will probably survive, particularly at the local level. It is in this sense that the progress made in the past decade will not be totally lost. Furthermore, having once rushed to catch a glimpse of the outside world, it is unlikely that the blinds can ever be successfully drawn so as to shut out that world. American literary studies in China, having become both broader and deeper during the decade-long springtime, will continue even without the nourishment of the authorities. *How* they continue will be in large part determined, in the future as has been true in the past, by the political climate, by the pressures of—and restrictions on—those ideological demands which shape not only American studies in that nation, but also the progress of Chinese society as a whole.

Notes

1. It is said that there was also a private circulation of *The Scarlet Letter* among a limited audience during the Cultural Revolution, because the book was one of the two favorite American novels of Jiang Qing, Mao's wife and China's cultural czar during those revolutionary years. It might seem absurd that Jiang Qing would make such an exception to her radical ideological tenets, until one recalls that she was at the same time fanatically preaching feminism and that Hawthorne's romance was read in China as a feminist tract. Her other favorite American novel was *Gone with the Wind,* not surprising when one recollects her career as a B-class movie star during the 1930s: *Gone with the Wind* is often considered the most successful B-class movie ever made.

2. The other ten projects are: the development of modern American literature; black writers; Southern writers; political fiction; writings reflecting American social and economic development; modern poetry; drama and movies; critical theory; major philosophical trends in modern American literature; and American literary studies in the Soviet Union.

3. Peter Wright, a British writer, has broken the record. His book *Spycatcher* sold five million copies in China. However, all these figures are less impressive if one realizes that China has a population of 1.2 billion.

4. The example of my own experience may be emblematic of both the desire to know how America works and the degree to which popular fiction like Hailey's is seen as satiating that desire. When I came to the United States to do advanced research, I found myself in the position of needing a car. Accordingly, I went to a car dealer and proceeded to make use of the knowledge I had gained from reading Hailey's *Wheels.* I asked the salesman for an automobile that had been produced midweek, for I knew that American cars produced on a Monday or Friday are likely to be troublesome to their future owners. That a great many Chinese are aware of such "valuable advice" about life in American society is most certain; what is less certain, of course, is whether that advice is always as valuable as its recipient thinks it to be.

ઝ

The American Within
Danes and American Literature

JAN NORDBY GRETLUND

Every Dane has an American relative. From 1868 to 1914 two million Scandinavians emigrated to the United States: 287,000 were Danes. Every tenth Dane emigrated during this period. The large majority were hired farmhands, who hoped to own their own land in the new country. Many of them had been laid off because of America's success as a grain-exporting country. The more the American pioneer farmers produced, the less work there was for farmers in Denmark; so they fired their hired help, who then very often emigrated. They settled in the Midwest, primarily in Illinois, Iowa, Minnesota, Nebraska, and Wisconsin. The Danish immigrants were quickly assimilated into the new culture, and from the beginning there were Danes who helped to shape their adopted culture. Christian Gullager painted one of the early portraits of George Washington, while in a later generation Gutzon Borglum created the Mount Rushmore National Memorial in South Dakota from 1925 until his death in 1941. Ironically, in the 1890s another Danish immigrant had helped to slow the immigration to the United States: Jacob A. Riis's photographs of the New York slums in *How the Other Half Lives* (1890) and *The Children of the Poor* (1892) so frightened many would-be emigrants that by 1910 Danish immigration to the United States had virtually stopped.

Danes have always lived an attraction-repulsion pattern as regard things American. With the Americanization of Danish culture since World War II, Danes have become yet more conscious of the old love-hate affair. There is a growing awareness of the inextricability of the American contribution to Danish life, but there has not been a general fear that Danes would lose their natural characteristics through the influx of American cultural exports. From Don Redman's big-band concert in Copenhagen in 1946 to the recent publication of Bret Easton Ellis's depressing *Less than Zero* in Danish, the American element in Danish culture has grown steadily. To a large extent Danes born in the forties, as I was, were produced by the imported culture. Our cartoons were Donald Duck, Little Orphan Annie, Dick Tracy, and Superman. Our favorite boys' game was cowboys and Indians, and the movies were westerns or Walt Disney productions. Our exciting reading was *The Adventures of Huckleberry Finn* and *The Last of the Mohicans*. The first records we bought were in English, and even though we did not understand the texts we memorized the words. During our teen years we idolized James Dean and Marilyn Monroe, read Henry Miller (in great privacy), and listened to Elvis Presley, Brenda Lee, and Jerry Lee Lewis. Later our hero was John F. Kennedy. And suddenly our food was Kentucky Fried chicken, burgers, fries, and Cokes, and our clothes were T-shirts, sweatshirts, and jeans. TV was full of Bonanza and Laredo, and our language became full of what seemed necessary words: "groovy," "crazy," "cool," and "heavy." Things American dominated our childhood and youth, and as adults we remain in an ambicultural state where most of the concepts in our consciousness are American imports. Surprisingly, the unchecked American influx has not given rise to a strong Danish cultural nationalism. The American within would not allow it.

Before the liberation from German occupation in 1945 there was little inclination to build up a systematic study of American literature in Denmark. Today such study is an integrated part of the curricula at all five Danish universities. It is taught in English departments and departments of comparative literature; only Copenhagen has a chair in American literature. It is taught to students who already have knowledge of English literature. American studies do not exist independently of the departments of history and English. The lecturers are mostly graduates from the sixties, and while there is often a critical attitude to American culture and politics in these departments, there is not the anti-American atmosphere of the prewar years. The emphasis on British culture, history, literature, and (above all) pronunciation is less obvious than just ten years ago. The majority of the students are women, and although they are taught a canon of American literature with an emphasis on classic writers, there is room for the introduction of new names.

The bases for the following evaluation of the situation of American literature in Denmark are surveys of the fiction and poetry taught in secondary schools and at the universities, Danish criticism from this decade in newspapers and in periodicals, and the holdings of public lending libraries. Libraries are important because they are free, well situated, numerous, and their lending rate is impressive. The public libraries buy up to one-third of all books published in translation. No wonder that publishing firms often check with the readers for public libraries before they decide how many copies to print. The preferences of the public libraries help determine the quantity and quality of the presence of American literature in Denmark.

Many Danish readers buy books in English, and most Danish newspapers review American books when the American edition is published. These reviews are often decisive in determining whether a book is translated, as the publishers rely not only on the sales figures from the United States but also on the tenor of these reviews. Academic critics, Danish or foreign, are influential only insofar as the readers for the libraries, the publishers, and the reviewers keep up with scholarly work in periodicals, such as *American Studies in Scandinavia,* which is now published in Copenhagen. Some university scholars also review for the dailies, of course, just as Danish authors often supplement their incomes by reviewing in the papers. They are, of course, particularly alert to new trends from abroad. Several of the best Danish authors also work as regular staff in Danish publishing houses and at the university presses. All in all it is a narrow group of people that determines the canon of American literature in Denmark.

Approximately twenty-two hundred books are translated into Danish every year: more than half are from English-speaking countries, and most titles are American. As it is with publishers in all other countries, Danish publishers invest mostly in novels, rarely in short story collections, and hardly ever in poetry collections. Only contemporary novels are seriously considered for translation. It happens occasionally that an old best-seller is retranslated, but as a rule old translations are not revised or brought up to date. The argument is that if the Danish of the translation is old-fashioned, it is because it reflects the English of the original publication year. Translation is not considered a high art in Denmark. The translator is not highly regarded, is badly paid, and can only count on attention if he does a bad job. There are only about fifteen professional translators in the country who actually make a living by translating for the publishers. It is not an enviable job as most translations have to be done very quickly. One professional translator recently revealed that to translate Richard Adams's *Watership Down* he had been given eleven days! Translating is a popular hobby in Denmark, so it often happens that the amateur translator makes the rounds of the publishing houses with the translation of a favorite book. Yet if it is accepted, it is one of the exceptional cases where a translator influences the publisher's selection process. Only rarely does a translator reach the position where he can choose the books he would like to translate, for instance Mogens Boisen who, allowed the choice, became the translator of several English and American masterpieces. He even managed to make his retranslations of Joyce's *Ulysses* a common cause, and many readers submitted suggestions for improvements.

Publishers will, of course, choose books that are topical and fit into the current debate, books that will probably sell. At times they publish authors for what they consider idealistic reasons. But when a reader for a Danish publishing house recommends a translation of a promising young writer, the advice is often taken simply to prevent competing publishers from investing in the new talent. It is considered an investment even though the first publication is sure not to sell. The money invested and apparently lost in the initial failures of John Irving and Jean M. Auel in the Danish market has since earned many times over. A regular first edition is cautiously published with twelve hundred or fifteen hundred copies; if the publisher is convinced that he has a best-selling book, he may print five thousand copies. And he hopes the public libraries will take one thousand of them. The Danish book clubs are associated with various publishers, who not only sell their own books, but also buy from competing publishing houses. But this is usually after they have seen how well a book does in ordinary sales.

Various fashions in criticism such as Marxist or deconstructionist criticism have had little influence on what is published in Denmark. Feminist critics have been able to get a number of women writers into print, mostly in small editions and by small publishing presses. A certain demand *has* been created, and all Danish publishing houses try to find good women writers. The major critical interest is biographical and historical; it offers prospective readers the basic information they look for. All critical schools have been represented in Denmark, but the publishing world acts as if nothing has happened in criticism since the days of Georg Brandes. The fashions of criticism are of academic interest only, and so, it seems, is the popularity or unpopularity of United States foreign policy, at least when we speak of the reception of American literature in Denmark. The most trenchant criticism of America and American writers that is available in Danish often has its origin in publications by American critics, whereas Danish professors and politicians have had little influence on the reception of American literature in Denmark. Yet, despite constant American efforts to market new writers, the canon of American literature in Denmark is stable in its choice of masters, and only new talent of the rarest kind can hope to qualify for a place among the favored few.

In the Danish version of the canon, Edgar Allan Poe and Mark Twain are the two great names among classic American authors. In the late seventies and early eighties several new translations of their works appeared. The new interest in Poe is mostly focused on his literary theory and on his philosophy. The academic interest is now in the so-called other Poe, who spoke of individual identity, disintegration, and transcendence as exemplified in *The Narrative of Arthur Gordon Pym* and *Eureka.* So it is ironic that these two works have not appeared in new translations whereas the stories are translated again and again. The most recent Mark Twain publications in Denmark are *Pudd'nhead Wilson* and *The Mysterious Stranger.* Traditionally it has been Twain the humorist who is best known. In many ways Danes have reduced Twain and sent him to the children's room. But Twain hardly ever wrote for children: he was a skeptic and saw man as a fool and a con-man. It is the old embittered Twain, the misanthrope who saw life as a grotesque dream and humankind as a useless and futile idea, who is now the object of critical attention in Denmark. Perhaps it says something about many Danes today that our interest is now mainly in the darker Mark Twain.

T. S. Eliot was formerly regarded as a classic American poet whose poetry is a record of his journey from doubt to faith. A Danish critic once visited Eliot in England and told the poet that the interest in Eliot in Denmark was found primarily in Christian circles. With a little sigh of resignation Eliot replied, "Oh, yes of course, the religious-minded." He might have been more pleased with the Danish interest in his poetry today, where it is the doubting poet that gets the attention. The sympathy is with the tortured questioner at Margate Sands and not with the almost transfigured "preacher" of "Little Gidding." The modern Danish reader will identify with the tragicomic Prufrock-Eliot rather than with the poet who found peace in his religion. Most of Eliot's poetry was already translated in the forties and fifties, but it seems that every so often there is a demand for new translations of his work, as if the Danish of older translations tends to become dated. In 1984 Bo Green Jensen published an excellent Danish version of Eliot's greatest poems.

In *Makers of Modern Culture* (1981) the critic Geoffrey Moore describes how the European reaction to Hemingway still fluctuates between uncritical admiration and overt hostility. It is possible that you have to be an American to be able to appreciate Hemingway's quest for self-knowledge, his initiation problems, his "separate peace," and his fatalism. Although he lived most of his life in other parts of the world, Hemingway always remained a distinctly American voice, and it is as such that he still has a Danish audience. The old translation of *For Whom the Bell Tolls* was republished in 1984; one of our best novelists, Klaus Rifbjerg, has completed with his wife a new translation of *The Sun Also Rises,* and Poul Borum, a fine poet, has produced a highly acclaimed translation of the first forty-nine stories. Every scrap by Hemingway that can be found seems to find its way into print. The Danish press watches the process and records its publication. In the case of Hemingway the translations appear quickly, usually within a year of the American publication. The Danish reviews from 1986 and 1987 have reported on the publication of the translations of Larry Phillips's collection of Hemingway on writing, Hemingway's report for *Life* on the bullfighting season of 1953 called *The Dangerous Summer,* and on the publication of his youthful efforts from 1919. Hemingway is still seen as the master stylist who reintroduced Mark Twain's simple declarative sentence as an ideal. His preoccupation with style and bullfighting is accepted by most Danish critics and seen as his attempt at coming to terms with the existential questions that haunted him. The stories by the young Hemingway have not been well received. One critic argues that if he had continued to write as he set out to do, he would never have become famous. When Alfred Kazin visited Copenhagen in the fall of 1987, he argued that Hemingway never really wrote a *novel.* Mr. Kazin is wrong in several respects, for Hemingway wrote some fine novels, but he did not have the courage to publish one of his best, *The Garden of Eden.* The enthusiastic reception by the Danish press of the translation of this recently published novel was in large measure based on Hemingway's anticipation of the present debates on sexuality and gender. Hemingway's problems of sexual identification seem to speak directly to the concerns of the Danish reader.

As a Danish critic has said, to understand Fitzgerald it is necessary to realize that he represents something specifically American to an even greater extent than Hemingway. This may be why Fitzgerald has never enjoyed a similar popularity in Denmark. The point of departure for all of his art, that the American yearning for riches and recognition finally petrifies and brutalizes, has so far appeared more removed from the problems of Danish everyday life than Hemingway's concerns. Fitzgerald's popularity has fluctuated with the presentations of filmed versions of his fiction, such as the Hollywood production of *The Great Gatsby* and the TV film of *Tender Is the Night.* Since he is considered a flawed genius in Denmark, it is not surprising that most of the gossipy "biographical" confessions of the last decades have found their way into Danish. Despite occasional doubts about his relevance to Danish life, despite awareness of his aesthetic shortcomings, Fitzgerald's two major novels have been accorded a permanent place in the canon of American literature in Denmark.

Nathanael West was Fitzgerald's contemporary and the two were acquainted. Yet their achievement differs considerably. West's cold, clinical, and abrupt style is too peculiar for him to become popular in Denmark, so in spite of the relative success of the 1980 translation of *Miss Lonelyhearts,* it was difficult to find a publisher for a translation of another of his masterpieces, *A Cool Million.* But it has finally appeared. These two "delayed" translations have demonstrated to many Danish readers that West is a writer of importance to the eighties. There is a line in American literature connecting Nathanael West to several major modern prose artists in America. But Joyce Carol Oates, Barry Hannah, Raymond Carver, Jayne Anne Phillips, and Daniel Curley did not learn from West in direct line. Their grotesque view of the world and their frightening conclusions came to them by way of Flannery O'Connor.

Many would-be writers seem to have listened to Flannery O'Connor when she said, "For the almost deaf you have to shout and for the almost blind you have to draw large and startling figures." Although less than one percent of the Danish population is Roman Catholic, Flannery O'Connor's religious fiction is highly regarded in Denmark. She is a writer about whom it is impossible to generalize on the basis of period, region, or religious persuasion, and her reputation in Denmark is not based on these. She tries to recall us to our largely forgotten relation to the world and to each other. Even atheistic Danes of the eighties have recognized the peculiar power of her vision. Most of her stories have been translated into Danish during this decade. And, perhaps as a result of the showing of John Huston's film *Wise Blood,* this excellent novel is now being translated.

Flannery O'Connor did not want her mule and wagon to get "stalled on the same track the Dixie Limited is roaring down," as she once said when asked about William Faulkner's influence on her, but she always acknowledged him as the master novelist of the South. William Faulkner's novels have not all been published in Danish, and the ones that were published appeared in an order entirely unrelated to the original American publishing sequence. There was a good deal of interest in Faulkner in Denmark after he was awarded the Nobel Prize, but the increased visibility in the press was not enough to get *A Fable* translated. It is surprising that *Sartoris* has not been translated; it is depressing that nothing from the Snopes trilogy has appeared in Danish; and it is incredible that *Absalom, Absalom!* remains untranslated. The publishing omissions are even more surprising because several works of a lower grade, such as *Soldier's Pay, Knight's Gambit,* and *The Reivers,* have appeared in Danish.

The first Danish publication of a novel by Faulkner was *The Wild Palms* in 1939, and it is the first translation of that novel anywhere. The strangeness which sometimes marks the translation of a novel from one culture to another may be illustrated by the book jacket of the 1965 edition of *As I Lay Dying.* The cover of this edition by an anonymous artist, who probably wants to remain unknown, shows Addie Bundren's coffin on a prairie schooner, and the focus of the drawing is on a figure dressed in a ten-gallon hat and wearing cowboy boots! The most recent Faulkner publication is *Light in August,* which appeared in a new edition in 1981. This novel has always been the most popular novel by Faulkner in the Scandinavian countries. But since 1969 only this novel and *The Reivers,* which became known through the movie, have appeared in new editions. It is tempting to see the disappearance of the South from the headlines in the seventies as an explanation. With the Vietnam War in progress, full coverage of the civil rights battles in the Danish dailies stopped. It was no longer fashionable to discuss the South, especially as the racial situation improved there. Today only *Light in August* is in print in Danish, and only a decided effort by the publishers will make it possible to keep Faulkner in print in Denmark. That a publishing policy is badly needed becomes clear from the brief and inadequate entry on William Faulkner in *Lademanns Leksikon* (1982 edition), the most popular Danish encyclopedia: "American author, whose characteristic, psychologically penetrating novels and short stories about tragic, seedy, depraved figures of the American South are deeply pessimistic."

The history of the reception of Walker Percy's novels in Scandinavia is instructive and sometimes amusing. The Danish edition of *The Moviegoer* was the first Scandinavian appearance of Walker Percy's work. Is it possible that national pride was tickled by the overt reference to "the Danish philosopher" in the epilogue of the novel? Percy himself had called his first three novels "a gloss on Kierkegaard," so a favorable

Danish critical reception might have been expected. But the Danish response to Percy's first novel was anything but favorable. One of the most influential reviewers called his contribution to the general denunciation of Percy "New Orleans Spleen," and he seems to have done lasting damage with the following statement:

> A Southern writer may offer us almost anything—decadence, depravation and total insanity, indeed . . . he may be completely disgusting, as long as his book reflects this indefinable will to survive and endure. The only thing we cannot accept, is that he throws in the sponge and gives up. . . . The best thing about Southern novels is that they fan the fire of a century-old rebellious spirit against a pompous and somewhat hypocritical Yankee moralism. . . . What is left in the way of a rebellion in Binx is a somewhat cowardly and inaccurate irony, which only serves to underline that the final surrender has taken place. (Ole Storm, *Politiken*, 29 September 1964, *my translation*)

This review is quoted here not only because it illustrates the relative failure of *The Moviegoer* in Denmark, but also because the tone of this review and of others like it reveals that Danish critics expect new Southern novels to conform to the classic Caldwell or Faulkner patterns. If they do not, the critics react strongly. As a consequence it has for years been impossible to publish another Walker Percy novel in Denmark, a circumstance happily transformed by the recent translation of his latest novel, *The Thanatos Syndrome*.

Joyce Carol Oates is highly successful in Denmark. Her many portraits of monomaniac neurotics and her attempts to enlighten us about psychological anomalies have won her a secure place in the minds of Danish readers. Her novels from the sixties and seventies such as *Expensive People*, *The Assassins*, and *Crossing the Border* have in the eighties appeared in Danish in rapid succession. And she is so prolific that her Danish publisher has decided not to publish every book she writes. Nevertheless, *You Must Remember This* and *Marya* have recently appeared. While a majority of Danish reviewers recognize that her plots are tiresome and predictable, they also recognize her remarkable psychological acuity. And they realize that, as a woman writer, she has explored sister solidarity.

Joyce Carol Oates is not the only American woman writer who receives extended critical attention and has a wide reading audience in Denmark. Some women writers, such as Anne Tyler, Gail Godwin, and Shirley Ann Grau are now quite established in translation; others such as Ellen Gilchrist, Bobbie Ann Mason, and Jayne Anne Phillips are getting an audience. But none of these is as successful as Sylvia Plath, who died in 1963, and Ursula Le Guin, who is as productive as Joyce Carol Oates. Almost all of Le Guin's futuristic fiction has been translated: the latest are *The Lathe of Heaven, The Eye of the Heron,* and *The Compass Rose,* which in Denmark became two volumes of stories. Her warnings against a polluted, totalitarian future are tremendously popular with the customers of the Danish public libraries. Sylvia Plath is not popular in the same sense, but there is much serious interest in her work and in that of her friend Anne Sexton. Most of their poems have appeared in translation, and Danish critics are doing a good job of trying to save the two poets from sectarian women and groups of potential suicides. Most of Plath's short prose from *Johnny Panic and the Bible of Dreams* appeared in Danish in 1982, and thirty-seven of her poems have been included in a new Sylvia Plath biography in Danish by Thomas Bredsdorff, titled *The Sudden Change.* An important argument in this biography is that Plath's poems are not simply case sheets of a potential suicide, but that she used her mental illness creatively and managed to give expression to universal existential problems in her poems.

In frequency of translations into Danish only John Updike can rival Joyce Carol Oates and Ursula Le Guin. It seems that every tenth year Updike takes time off from his more ambitious efforts to check in with Harry Rabbit Angstrom: *Rabbit, Run; Rabbit Redux;* and *Rabbit Is Rich* have all appeared in Danish. The trilogy is deservedly famous for its portrait of the United States of the last three decades, and Danish readers also recognize the echoes of unrealistic dreams in an emotional ice age. A recent novel by John Updike in Danish is *The Witches of Eastwick;* it has been suggested by some, especially the Danish publisher, that it is some sort of women's novel, but this is misleading. The target in this novel is anybody who denies the wonder and mystery in life in order to serve some cause. The plot is so simple that it had to become a movie. This is certainly not true of Updike's twelfth novel, *Roger's Version,* the most recent in Danish translation. In spite of the satirical scenes in the department of theology and the sexual acrobatics on a mattress in the attic, it is doubtful whether Danish readers will suffer through the congested theological discussion with its many Latin quotations. Updike's *Trust Me* and his epistolary novel *S.* are scheduled for publication in Danish, but as in the case of Joyce Carol Oates, the publisher is worried that the saturation point may have been reached for Updike's fiction in the Danish market.

Kurt Vonnegut's latest novel in Danish is *Galapagos.* It is yet another end-of-the-world novel warning against the scientist who tries to manipulate the natural selection process. The novel does not live up to Vonnegut's idiosyncratic, irritating-yet-irresistible masterpieces such as *Mother Night* and *Slaughterhouse-Five* or the later *Slapstick* and *Jailbird,* all out in Danish. Vonnegut may well be the closest thing to Mark Twain that we have today, as American and Danish critics are fond of pointing out, but it is the Mark Twain of the final years, a writer who constantly had to try to avoid writing self-parodies that Vonnegut resembles today. To find equals to Updike's and Vonnegut's humor, satire, realism, and pessimism, we have to turn to the Jewish school of American novelists. Isaac Bashevis Singer, Saul Bellow, E. L. Doctorow, Bernard Malamud, Norman Mailer, Joseph Heller, and Philip Roth have all had most of their books translated into Danish. Norman Mailer can no longer count on a Danish translation of his new books as a matter of course, whereas Joseph Heller still can, which is a bit surprising as Heller's work has deteriorated from his *Something Happened* and *Good as Gold* to the most recently translated *God Knows.* The latest translation into Danish of a work by Saul Bellow is the rather pessimistic collection of short stories called *Him with His Foot in His Mouth.* All in all this collection has not been received as favorably in Denmark as the translations of Bellow's great novels *The Dean's December* and *Humboldt's Gift.* His *More Die of Heartbreak* appeared in Danish in the fall of 1988. E. L. Doctorow's most recent Danish publications, *World's Fair* and *Lives of the Poets,* are equally disappointing for an audience that has come to expect the quality of *Ragtime, The Book of Daniel,* and *Loon Lake.* Danish critics consider the new collection thought-provoking, but primarily with regard to the form of the short story and the artist's discussion of his own art. For most Danish readers this is too little and therefore disappointing for a writer of Doctorow's stature. It is a pleasure for his Danish audience that Philip Roth, with his latest account of Nathan Zuckerman's career, *The Counterlife,* seems to have stopped diluting his material. The new novel is a celebration of the creative imagination. The experiments with perspective and plot are perhaps too many for one short Zuckerman novel, and in basic entertainment value the new novel fails to live up to Roth's classic achievement of *Goodbye, Columbus* and *Portnoy's Complaint,* which were both popular in Denmark, but *The Counterlife* is considered by Danish critics a promising change in Roth's recent career.

There are two other distinct groups of American writers who are read and discussed in Denmark. The Beat Generation writers constitute one of them. From 1955 when he read his poem "Howl" at The San Francisco Revival and up to the present, Allen Ginsberg has been well known in Denmark as madman, guru, and poet. He has toured Denmark with his poetry readings and has helped keep the Beat poets in print. The most prominent Danish literary intellectuals such as Poul Borum, Dan Turell, and Bo Green Jensen have paid homage to Allen Ginsberg, Gary Snyder, Jack Kerouac, Kenneth Rexroth, Kenneth Patchen, Lawrence Ferlinghetti, Robert Stone, Ken Kesey, and William S. Burroughs. What appeals to some Danes about Ginsberg's poetry is his openness, his objective humor, and his hallucinatory honesty. "Howl" is a poem of just twenty-two pages, but this poem and Jack Kerouac's novel *On the Road* became the manifestoes of a generation in Denmark, as well as in the United States. There is clearly something appealing to a modern Danish consciousness about a poet who sees Walt Whitman steal melons in a supermarket and hears William Blake's voice through the afternoon traffic in Harlem. Gary Snyder's poetry has also influenced many Danish poets. Many of his poems from *Riprap and Cold Mountain Poems* and *The Back Country* have been translated into Danish. Their readers in Denmark try to come to terms with the Beat poets' apparent rejection of Europe; at the same time some critics see the Beats as supporting themselves comfortably on European poetic traditions. It is in the nature of poetry that it is unusual if it sells well, so most of Ginsberg's and Snyder's poems have appeared in Denmark in little magazines and literary periodicals. William S. Burroughs's *Naked Lunch* finally made it into Danish in 1984.

Robert Stone is a somewhat younger member of the Beat Generation. His war novel *Dog Soldiers* won him a Danish audience, and his most recent novel, *A Flag for Sunrise,* is perhaps the fullest account of how the defeat in Vietnam, disguised in the novel as Central America, became the definitive loss of American innocence. The novel was translated immediately and was well received by the Danish press. The most recent translation of a work by a writer from the Beat group is of Lawrence Ferlinghetti's confessional poems. In these he seems less pessimistic than Stone, less driven than Burroughs, less self-conscious and more sentimental than Ginsberg. These Beat Generation writers still have a Danish following.

The final group of American writers who are widely read and discussed in Denmark is black Americans. It is a tradition that good Afro-American writers are published in Danish. For years the scene was dominated by black male writers such as Richard Wright, Ralph Ellison, and James Baldwin, but during the last decade black women novelists have become popular. Toni Morrison, Alice Walker, and newcomers

Gloria Naylor and Ntozake Shange totally dominate this area of publication in Danish editions. The greatest success has been *The Color Purple*, and this is not only because of the movie. Alice Walker is successful because she does not write traditional protest novels about saintly blacks and evil whites. She writes of problems with which a Danish reader may easily identify. In *The Color Purple* the problems are within the community, the family, and ultimately between men and women. The success of *The Color Purple* has made it possible to publish a translation of *Meridian*, Walker's earlier novel about the changing civil rights movement, and her short story collection *You Can't Keep a Good Woman Down*. These stories focus on crucial situations in the relationship between every possible combination of races, old and young, man and woman. And they offer the unique perspective of universal existential problems, which has enabled black American literature to keep its Danish audience.

American literature is, without serious competition, the single most important foreign literature in Danish. If we look at the individual writer, the Danish interest is easily understood. The Danish reader is fascinated with Poe's disintegrating individual, Twain's humorous bitterness, Eliot's tortured questions, Hemingway's initiation problems, Faulkner's preoccupation with the past in the present, Plath's and Oates's quests for identity, Updike's and Ginsberg's searches for genuine emotions, Walker's troubled families, and Roth's humorous satire. With the impressive variety of universal interests represented here it is impossible to point to one unifying factor that would explain why Danes find these American writers particularly appealing. In general it seems that life in the somewhat boring, homogenous everyday of Denmark has created a need for accounts of individuals in extreme and marginal "what-if" situations. The likes and dislikes of Danish readers are finally decided by how useful a book is in the universal, daily quest for self-knowledge and self-definition, and in that respect American literature has proved particularly valuable to many Danes.

The canon of American literature as seen from a Danish perspective seems to be stable in its choice of masters and schools. Edgar Allan Poe and Mark Twain are the traditional classics. The modern classics are T. S. Eliot, Ernest Hemingway, William Faulkner, Sylvia Plath, and Allen Ginsberg. Joyce Carol Oates, John Updike, Philip Roth, and Alice Walker are the best-selling, quality American writers of today. If we add peculiarities such as the lingering popularity of John Steinbeck and Henry Miller, and the fact that at the end of 1987 John Irving's *The Cider House Rules* and Jean M. Auel's trilogy were the only American books on the Danish best-seller lists for fiction, we only need to qualify the canon outlined above by mentioning that new talents such as Raymond Carver, David Leavitt, Jay McInerney, Louise Erdrich, and Pat Conroy are out in new translations. And Danish publishers have recently brought out new books by Joseph Heller, Jayne Anne Phillips, Marge Piercy, and Reynolds Price. The impression made by the new writers will modify the canon and alter it, if ever so slightly. But apart from the occasional new writer, there is an obvious canon of the most widely read, the most widely studied, the best received and the best-selling American writers, which reflects very well the Danish sense of what American literature is. An impressive supply of American literature is always available in translation in Denmark. The American within every Danish reader demands it.

American Literature in France
Pleasures in Perspective

MARC CHÉNETIER

You will be part of the flavor of the fruit
—RENÉ CHAR

As I write these lines, it has been approximately a century and a half since Alexis de Tocqueville first wondered about the destinies of American literature and the attraction it might exert upon a French public. Published in 1835 and 1840, *De la démocratie en Amérique* underlined his concerns in chapters 22 to 24, endeavoring to discern "the literary characteristics of democratic times," "some sources of poetry among democratic nations," and "why American writers and orators often use an inflated style." He understood that "amongst such nations . . . literature will not easily be subjected to strict rules, and it is impossible that any such rules should ever be permanent," concluding upon his "fear that the productions of democratic poets may often be surcharged with immense and incoherent imagery, with exaggerated descriptions and strange creations; and that the fantastic beings of their brain may sometimes make us regret the world of reality."

History indeed has its ironies and little did Tocqueville suspect—a good seer, prophetlike, will, as a matter of course, overcome the apprehensions that might restrain him from giving voice to his visions—that such reprehensible absence of "rules," such attraction for "the new," such word-painting oratory and exploration of dreams would indeed become the central attractions of the literature of the United States for the French public. Now, each year when the Paris Book Fair opens, a greater number of contemporary American literary works in translation are displayed than ever before. The fascination, obviously, goes on unabated.

The word *fascination* is one I choose for its illuminating as well as blinding overtones: focussed on the object of desire, the eye selects what features have attracted it to feed upon; whatever surrounds it is blurred, as well as traits one might otherwise not overlook. What I am describing here is love, a feeling logic has a hard time hampering. I rather hold, in effect, that France and the United States, politically hammered out from comparable crucibles but culturally born from far too different ancestries in far too different cradles, historically united by the strongest of links but philosophically divided by the chasm that separates Descartes from Cotton Mather and methodological doubt from fideism, rather than made kin by a shared Enlightenment, hardly stand a chance of ever really understanding each other. But love each other they can, and do, passionately, as only periodic anti-French feeling in the United States and anti-American waves in France can prove. Tiffs demonstrate care. And the lover *will* be berated for admiring the clothes the object of his adoration positively does not like to wear.

"I am talking projection here, exoticism is what I am talking," Stanley Elkin might put it. And, sometimes as Whitmanian as can be, the French, in their supercilious reasonings, are not beyond bearing with contradiction. At the very heart of French suspicions concerning the United States, there lies an incontrovertible attraction for its cultural expressions. I am fairly sure American literature is not where most French readers would like to live, but they love the thrills of repeated visits. So that, pushing the paradox to the extreme, one might say, borrowing one's polarities from Philip Rahv, that in France, the "red-skin" literature of the United States is an object of fascination, and the "paleface" literature one of understanding. Come moments of awareness of cultural and political differences and the French at large will fall back upon "un-American" literature (Melville, James, Eliot, most modernists, Nabokov), that which is not considered indigenous to the soil; come moments of communion in the unrolling of history, and a dose of the American exotic will be in order (the hard-boiled detective novel is an all-time winner, followed by Steinbeck, Hemingway, Kerouac and the Beats, Burroughs, Miller, Bukowski . . .). Agreed: schematic views are a bother; "But I have promises to keep, / And miles to go before I sleep."

The above, of course, is in some sense true of French public opinion in general, however *that* is measured. A substantially different story holds sway when it comes to intellectual assessments, critical and academic. Tocqueville, Jean-Jacques Ampère (*Promenade en Amérique,* 1855) and Philarète Chasles looked upon the literature of the United States as evidence for their respective observations of a society gradually coming of age. Soon, however, more strictly literary measurements took place that signalled an originality of French reactions. Marcus Cunliffe, his usual witty self, mentions the presence in world literature of two contemporary writers: a Frenchman by the name of Edgarpo and an American better known as Edgar Allan Poe, vituperated in his own country for his light-headed and gratuitous "tintinnabulations." Edgarpo, much admired by Baudelaire and by Mallarmé, for whom no one could be *guilty* of engineering "abolis bibelots d'inanité sonore," later praised by Paul Valéry, this most intellectual of French poets, stands, somehow, as an icon of what I might call the "Frenchness" of critical approaches to the literature of the United States. I am, indeed, loath to generalize in an exaggerated fashion here; but it seems that, by and large, what Tocqueville feared most is what the French love best: the free linguistic exploration of an imagination unfettered by the real as they know it. The literature of the United States tends to appear as a reservation for phantasms and the unexplorable, a space (crucial word, this, for any approach to the United States by a French person) which the word can channel in ways our ordinary literary discourse does not afford. On the whole, Americans resent this vision of Poe, because it has little to do with the American *experience*, a word far less sacred over here than over there, most often carrying a totally different semantic load. This most American of literary "inventions," the romance, is read in the same terms and with the same kind of appetite; and Poe's reputation in France (early risen thanks to Baudelaire, then to Marie Bonaparte, traced by Célestin Cambiaire and Léon Lemonnier, enriched by Valéry and Lacan, deepened and steadily unfolded by the untiring efforts of Claude Richard and the more recent breakthroughs of Henri Justin) hardly has anything to do with the mythological context which accompanies him in the United States. Poe, in France, for all his being a popular writer, is a writer's writer.

Which invites the following generalization, contrary, naturally, to the first one I proposed: in *critical* terms, United States literature in France is, with exceptions, steadily appraised in terms of its strictly *literary* qualities rather than in terms of its alleged relevance to any sort of *sociological* or narrowly *cultural* reality. Witness the remarkable fate of Melville and Faulkner: Giono's translation and endorsement of *Moby-Dick* in 1941 did, indeed, come in the wake of the gradual rediscovery of an author praised for his most exotic work. But as early as the 1910s and 1920s, in French circles, *the* book by Melville to read was *Moby-Dick* rather than *Omoo* or *Typee*. Faulkner, out of print in the United States by

1940 if *The Sound and the Fury* was what you wanted to read, was transformed from a regional hick writer into a novelist of Nobel stature
under the influence of Maurice-Edgar Coindreau's translation, relayed
by Sartre, Claude-Edmonde Magny, and André Malraux. Exoticism may
well have remained the name of the game, but it was Faulkner's *writing*
that launched his reputation here, then in the United States, leaving
lasting imprints on the tradition, as we shall see. It was most often, in
other words, French writers or highly literary translators—Coindreau
taught the French symbolists for over thirty years at Princeton—
praising American writers that launched the critical reputation of these
Americans, however wide their appeal was to the general public. Few
today care a fig about Hemingway's rather hazy *nada,* or his half-baked,
would-be existential stands. But what he and Gertrude Stein did to the
sentence remains in all minds. The quality of French critical assessments
of United States literature in general has much to do with their subsequent critical reputation, and what I have just underlined for two "living
pillars" (J.-J. Mayoux) of the American tradition would serve as well for
Nabokov and Henry Miller.

American literature in France became more widely known between
the two world wars and much can be drawn from that fact. Expatriation
had placed French and American artists side by side, political alliances
had played first against and then with the grain of a cultural *rapproche-
ment.* The criticism that emerged then was largely couched in terms of
bewildered discovery. Léon Bazalgette, Charles Cestre (who held the
first chair of American literature at La Sorbonne), Marcel Brion, Le
Breton, Valéry Larbaud, René Taupin and his celebrated *L'influence du
symbolisme français sur la poésie américaine de 1910 à 1920* (1929), all introduced segments of American literature which had particularly drawn
their attention; and even if their appraisal was more than lightly colored
by Wilsonian idealism, their attention more often than not fell on the
literary features of these works rather than on the image of the country
they hailed from. Come the end of World War II, the pattern held.
Simone de Beauvoir could publish, in 1947, in the *New York Times Book
Review,* an article entitled "An American Renaissance in France" which
connected such a renaissance to the liberation of the country; meanwhile, her companion, Sartre, in *Situations,* spoke of Faulkner and Dos
Passos in uncompromisingly philosophical and literary terms. Claude-
Edmonde Magny's ground-breaking *L'age du roman américain,* appearing
the following year, was entirely couched in aesthetic terms, examining,
among other factors, the impact of the cinema on literary forms. Surely,

there were critics, like André Maurois, or Henry Peyre ("American Literature through French Eyes" came out in the *Virginia Quarterly Review* in 1947) for whom the recent military and political events made all the difference, and such scholars as had their formative years during the war—Cyrille Arnavon, Roger Asselineau, J.-M. Santraud, Claude Pérotin and others—saw their outlook profoundly shaped by their experience. This did not keep them, and specifically Arnavon and Asselineau, from demythologizing their literary approach at a time when the "myth and symbol" school was rising. America may always be a place in the mind rather than a place of real interest in the French imagination; myth, however, rarely was the approach that literary scholars used to gain access to that place.

On the whole, then, and before I come to more recent particulars, the taste of the French public, shaped by journalistic views, tends to be attracted by the anti-intellectual tradition in American literature while French criticism and academic life either feed more generally on authors that are closer to continental literary preoccupations or consider other American writers from an angle less sociological, cultural, or mythical than theoretical and aesthetic.

Which does not mean that French scholars of the literature of the United States have overlooked such dimensions of it as have most often drawn the attention of American criticism itself. Panoramas in bold strokes were painted, on the eve of the most recent period, by M. E. Coindreau (*Aperçus de littérature américaine*), C. Arnavon (*Histoire littéraire des Etats-Unis*, 1953), Jacques Cabau (*La prairie perdue: histoire du roman américain*, 1966), J.-M. Santraud (*La mer dans la littérature américaine*) and others. Nor is there any dearth—given the ancient French tradition of the writing of *thèses d'Etat* that often imply work over eight to fifteen years—of impressive monographs, from Asselineau's massive *L'évolution de Walt Whitman* to Laurette Véza's *La poésie américaine de 1910 à 1940*, via such dissertations as Jean Normand's on Hawthorne, Guy-Jean Forgue's on H. L. Mencken, Robert Silhol's on Sinclair Lewis, or Bernard Poli's analysis of Mark Twain, to name only a very few. The more recent publication of Maurice Gonnaud's thesis on Emerson by Princeton University Press, or André LeVot's magisterial biography of F. Scott Fitzgerald (Doubleday), or the reprint of Jean-Jacques Mayoux's *Vivants Piliers*, only confirms this point. But the latter three books, in particular, stand out as specifically French approaches to authors abundantly commented upon in the United States, marking, as they do, a strong distancing from American scholarship—however impeccably documented and argued they may be—in favor of more widely understood literary and philosophical frameworks that tend to counteract the accent of American exceptionalism that often hovers over the images of these writers. Both Gonnaud and LeVot are now retired from academic life and Jean-Jacques Mayoux recently passed away; but the generations of scholars they trained, directly or indirectly, their enduring presence as masters at the hinge of two periods in Americanist criticism in France, indicate the nature of a shift that can be diversely traced and that defines by and large the present situation.

Broadly speaking, studies concerning the literature of the United States in France underwent a profound change in the late 1960s, and this change took two forms which should not necessarily be seen as distinct.

On the one hand, I take as a symptom of the new mood the publication of several of Pierre Dommergues's works (*Les écrivains américains d'aujourd'hui*, 1965; *Les USA à la recherche de leur identité*, 1967; *L'aliénation dans le roman américain contemporain [1940–1965]*), and as a symbol the publication date (1968) and title of the work of Marianne Debouzy (*La genèse de l'esprit de révolte dans le roman américain, 1875–1915*). There is, clearly, in the thematics of these works, more than a sign of the times and, however dated they may now seem, such books point to ideological concerns in tune with the period in which they were written. (They triggered, if the whole story be told, rather vivacious reactions, and the academic world was rife with expletives in the late sixties. Slaps were heard in the corridors of La Sorbonne. Duels, however, were already passé. Thus will fashions indeed save lives. . . .) The leftist overtones of their work signal a shift in the tonality of American literary studies from mitigated veneration to critical stance, a shift not unrelated to the passage from postwar Americanophilia to more critical attitudes informed by the political problems and overseas commitments of the United States in the 1960s, from Cuba and Santo Domingo to Vietnam. This is only part of the story, however, as in terms of critical methods, both Dommergues and Debouzy camp on rather traditional grounds despite the attention they give to themes rapidly coming to prominence in American as well as French national preoccupations during the 1960s. The accent, then, falls more willingly on dissenting views within American literature than on the presentational or the hagiographic; it still remains largely a criticism of ideas.

This is not, on the other hand, what the late sixties and the seventies had fundamentally in store for literary Americanism in France. By the time Kennikat Press brought out I. & C. Johnson's *Les Américanistes* (1978), it had become abundantly clear that the new critical tools of the sixties and seventies had been amply put to use in the field. Once past the trauma of 1968, which often left the French Americanist community divided and sometimes sorted out political and ideological approaches to things American, a more important and lasting split occurred which, largely born from the first, had to do with ideological conceptions of the literary object and its handling. In other words, the evolution then undergone by the community of literary Americanists had far more to do with methodological approaches than with altering one's stance from varying degrees of the thuriferous to varying degrees of the rabidly critical. What *must* be understood here is that cultural and methodological radicalism were often offshoots of, or inspired by, political and ideological choices, with enough exceptions to make the general rule stick. Barthes, Ricardou, Genette, Kristeva, Brémond, Todorov, Foucault, and many others made no sense—even in a country long devoted to *explication de texte!*—if one was not, shall I say, *publicly privy* to their ideological makeup and the historical circumstances of their surfacing to fame. One will hopefully find in this remark enough reasons for the sense of utter puzzlement that dawns on the French academic in the United States when he or she is made witness to wall-to-wall debates on deconstruction and poststructuralism that are divorced from the ideological environment which presided over their development and do not seem to affect in the least, from what evidence is available, the ideological and political behavior of the academic community. Deconstruction and the marketing of a career make for hilariously funny bedfellows . . .

Which leads me to mention the varying types of attraction that American literature has for French students. It is, I suppose, a component of the overall attraction of an exotic America that makes students most often go for the margins of the culture. In this, they tend to follow a trait of French journalism and certain American views of American studies. It is, is it not, infinitely more attractive to discuss contemporary fiction, black, native American, or Chicano culture than to try and come to terms with the infinite complexities of, say, the Wasp mentality, in the light of a long and even more alien tradition that one would then have to master, realizing painfully that the apparently closest aspects of the culture are not necessarily what they appear to be. Both coasts tend to attract students' (and journalists') attention more than, say, the Midwest. Enough Scarlett O'Haras in crinolines remain in the unconscious to make the South fairly interesting to newcomers in the field. On the whole, interest naturally goes where the clichés lie. Asked to discuss a particular aspect of this black writer's work or of that woman poet and, therefore, faced with the rather predictable demand of his or her professor for evidence of literary competence, as opposed to more or less spontaneous arousals and inarticulate enthusiasms, the student will, more often than not, reapportion his interest; he will train his eye onto the multiple components of the culture and the indispensable tools of the literary trade, keep his or her desire for specialization for years when the sheer sociological or cultural interest of his or her first subject of predilection can be served by decent methodological equipment.

What is it, anyway, that the French student of American literature is taught? With increasing autonomy in the pedagogical dispositions of individual universities in a still heavily centralized country, generalization becomes more and more hazardous, but enough remains in common to attempt this minimal sketch. To begin with, since there is no such thing as a major in American studies, *a fortiori* there is none in American literature at French universities. All American literature is taught within departments of English within which, much too often, the ex-colonial situation goes on unabated. However, for many reasons, including the superior cultural pressure exercised by the United States, American literature tends in places to acquire a status close enough to that of British literature. The latter still dominates the national *concours* that qualify teachers, but with a rough ratio of one-third of the authors on the syllabus, American literature has now come a long way. Furthermore, the place recently acquired by living American authors—a fact unthinkable as recently as twenty years ago—seems to point to further developments.

All students, before they receive their Bachelor of Arts, will have had at least a few credits in American literature properly said, whatever the university. Proportions, however, may vary, and emphasis be placed on survey courses in the early years of one's studies or on specialized units nearer the end of the curriculum, or on a combination of both. Clearly, when given a choice, more and more students turn to American literature, and it even becomes hard at times to convince them that English literature might come in handy as part of its background. Syllabi will also vary from place to place and moment to moment but if this can be some indication, looking up the table of contents of two recent French anthologies (*American Trails: An Anthology of Representative Writers*, edited by Deflaux, Martin, Royot & Guiguet, 1970; and Françoise Grellet's recent

Time Present, Time Past: An Introduction to American Literature, 1987) one is not exactly in for surprises, should that necessarily be considered a good thing. The first comes in two volumes that respectively correspond to the periods 1620 to 1850 and 1850 to 1910; Jack London is the last author represented. Its composition points out the prevailing conviction that, whatever twentieth-century literary studies might be undertaken, a strong sense of the literary tradition is an indispensable starting point. The irony, as we shall see, is that the most voluminous and visible part of French research now going on in the academic world tends to revolve around twentieth-century authors; but the fact remains that no student is ever permitted to launch directly into a specialty in the twentieth century without having been abundantly exposed to earlier periods of the literature of the United States.

The second book mentioned above was published to sighs of relief as the first anthology that, first, uncompromisingly framed all authors within their aesthetic, philosophical, and historical contexts and, second, included authors up to the present day without omitting older authors in order to make room for the new ones. One might assert that today American literature, with varying accents being placed on this or that period depending on the interests of the teachers involved, is taught from the Pilgrim fathers to Donald Barthelme, or Washington Irving to John Irving. Clearly, however, neither time nor staff allow as complete coverage as might be desired. The recent development of survey-like courses is an attempt at bridging the gaps too often found in the coverage of the corpus between nuclei of overspecialized units.

The consensus, in other words, is fairly general as to what authors must be known if students are to be given any chance at all of getting some sort of overall view and some insight into the major characteristics of the American tradition: Puritanism, the revolutionary period, the transcendentalists, Hawthorne, Melville, the various types of realism from Twain to James, modernist poetry, some representatives of the novel between the two world wars. . . . The list, up to some ten years ago, usually stopped some time around Faulkner. It will be made plain by the following developments that the situation has been somewhat altered and that Françoise Grellet's book is but the symptom of wider-ranging phenomena.

"The house of fiction has many windows," and one's outlook on the literature of the United States as it exists in one's own country is sure to depend heavily on one's own experience. Rather than try and convey an objective view that would camouflage what I really know under what I would be tempted to wager, rather than insist on the (quite real) all-round completeness of French research on American literature (see "French Contributions" in the last ten volumes of *American Literary Scholarship*), I will hereafter attempt to describe what areas of contemporary research and development seem to me most representative, if not necessarily most useful.

It appears, in effect, that whatever excellent traditional work is done by French researchers in traditional areas, the specificity of French contributions lies rather in their methodological implications and discursive innovations. I stand convinced that Jean Béranger's work on the colonial period, Bernard Vincent's biography of Thomas Paine, Jean-Marie Bonnet's panorama of American criticism to 1837, Judith Stora-Sandor's study of Jewish humor or Daniel Royot's studies of American humor, Claude Pérotin's work on antislavery writers, as well as many other books I have no space to mention, are among the pieces of work the international community of Americanists might very well benefit from, their documentary precision being matched in most cases by the clearest of expositions. I do believe, nonetheless, that recent as these works may be (all were published after 1970), they could by and large emanate from the pen of American colleagues, and that their methodology is on the whole a prolongation of sound, time-hallowed principles of thoroughness and lucidity. By the same token, the careful research accomplished in some new areas by such colleagues as G.-M. Sarrotte (on gay literature), Marcienne Rocard (on Chicano literature), Jean Méral (on Paris in American literature), for all its precision, does not offer a vision of its field that differs significantly from that of their American counterparts. In a different sector of the methodological spectrum, Viola Sachs's imaginative revisiting of the works of Melville, Hawthorne, and Faulkner, drawing on cosmology, numerology, the occult, and symbology sometimes reads as an attempt at out-myth-and-symbolizing the myth and symbol school.

No, on the whole, these are not the pieces of research that make our American colleagues exclaim, using a by now well-worn semantic formula that lumps together "crazily theoretical," "somewhat zany," and "perfectly irrelevant": "This is very French," meaning, roughly, "You can expect anything from people who will read Poe, but not much good will come of them." It is, in the United States, more and more widely admitted that continental theories of the last quarter of a century may legitimately affect American literary studies; the usual effect of such an acceptance, however, is somewhat distorted, for French academic eyes at least, by the pragmatic rage that seems to seize our American colleagues every time a new theory emerges, the question tending to become: "How do Lacan, Barthes, Foucault, Derrida—choose one—*apply* to the novel or poem X by writer Y," as if such had indeed ever been the question. The peculiar idio(t?)syncras(z?)y attributed to French critics often proceeds from the fact that whatever new theoretical notions they have developed or ingested over the years have often been assimilated to the point of profoundly changing one's viewpoint and approach, even one's personal mode of discourse, but that they do not necessarily or automatically appear as such in the critical work itself. There is not *one* footnote in Philippe Jaworski's *Le Désert et l'Empire,* the most impressive reading of Melville to be done in France in the recent period, even though it is a period that saw the publication of books by Régis Durand, Viola Sachs, and others on the question, as well as a double issue of *Delta* (Montpellier) on "Bartleby the Scrivener." A perfectly integrated critical culture needs not resort to compulsory theoretical name-dropping. There isn't much more in the way of a critical apparatus in Pierre-Yves Pétillon's *La Grand-Route;* still, this highly subjective flight over the land of Washington Irving, Whitman, Bellow, Pynchon, and others stands in my mind as one of the most brilliant and penetrating pieces of literary criticism in the last few years. Voice, again, and intellectual passion, are substituted for academic role. Or take André Bleikasten's *The Most Splendid Failure,* to me the best—bar none—study of *The Sound and the Fury* ever published: method is all in this wonderfully clear book and Lacanian ideas loom large, but Lacan is nowhere to be found, stylistically or by means of quotes. While the latter book satisfies all the formal requirements of the traditional academic publication, for its lightness of style and subtlety of nuance it lies much closer to the French tradition of the essay. My last example of this integration of theoretical thought and vitally personal involvement is also the latest to be published. In 1987, a small publisher in Aix-en-Provence (Alinéa) brought out a small volume by Claude Richard entitled *Lettres Américaines,* an astonishing meditation on the role played by signs and letters in American literature, be they Hester Prynne's *A* or Poe's purloined document. Nourished by contemporary philosophy and beautifully written, it stands as a wonderful illustration of the most original and interesting contribution French criticism can offer. Fittingly enough, if my loop is to be looped, it is written by a man who spent over twenty years of his life exploring the thought of Edgar Allan Poe, whose complete works he is now editing for Laffont.

Needless to say, such endeavors, among which I should also place dozens of similarly inspired articles, are often forcefully resisted from within the very country in which they emerge, traditional views always being more easily accepted than unsettling ones. But they also signal a transformation of the French Americanist landscape, a transformation I shall now report on as I saw it take place.

In 1967, the Association Française d'Etudes Américaines was created in Paris, on the impulse of such figures as Roger Asselineau, Sim Copans, and Jeanne-Marie Santraud. In 1976, the Association gave itself a journal, now in its fourteenth year of publication, the *Revue Française d'Etudes Américaines*, which I have the honor of editing. Between these two dates, membership grew from a few dozen to 250. Today members number somewhere between 350 and 400. They represent all aspects of American studies but close to half can be said to be dealing with literature. The first issue of the *Revue*, masterminded by A. LeVot, was dedicated, rather symbolically in retrospect, to "The Contemporary American Novel," with articles on Burroughs, Crawford, Brautigan, Nabokov, Coover, Reed, Hawkes, Vonnegut, O'Connor, and Purdy. The very same year, the first issue of *Trema* came out of the Université de Paris III, while A. LeVot and I were still teaching there; it dealt with contemporary American literature and was followed, one year later, by another issue on the same field. This was also when Yves LePellec edited the issue of *Entretiens* (Rodez) dedicated to the Beat Generation. Over these years, the rise of the study of contemporary American fiction in France was spectacular. Even journals originally dedicated to Southern literature (*Delta*, in Montpellier, founded in 1975) or to other literary concerns (*Ranam* in Strasbourg) repeatedly provided space for analyses and presentations of contemporary literature. Today, from *In'Hui* (Amiens) to *TEL* (Paris VIII), from *Delta* to the *Revue Française d'Etudes Américaines*, and from *Caliban* (Toulouse) to *Fabula* (Lille), most academic journals regularly include contemporary literature. To someone who knew the situation in 1972 and 1973 and contemplates the scene today, the evolution is nothing less than staggering. Centers for research on various aspects of American literature have sprung up all over France, newsletters and journals have increased in number, the most recent advances in critical theory manifest themselves in the works of specialists of all literary fields. Michel Fabre's work on black literature is known worldwide; Geneviève Fabre's book on black American theater was translated into English and received great acclaim, as have Marie-Claire Pasquier's

French publications on American theater in general. In poetry, the students of Laurette Véza—recently retired, whose works on Pound, Williams, and others designate her as the best French specialist of modern American poetry—have carried on her work (F. Delphy on Dickinson, M. C. Cunci on Rich, J. Ollier on Williams, J. Kerblat on H. D., I on Lindsay). J. Darras, Ph. Mikriammos, and others each contribute efficiently to the field, hailing from other quarters. The French school of Faulkner studies is in full bloom with a team of internationally known specialists: André Bleikasten, Michel Gresset, François Pitavy, Monique Pruvot, Jean Rouberol. The heirs of Maurice Gonnaud (Roland Tissot, Michel Granger, Yves Carlet) are bringing fresh new views to nineteenth-century studies; those of André LeVot (Noëlle Batt, Maurice Couturier, Pierre Gault, Claude Grimal, and I among many others) pursue their exploration of the contemporary scene in fiction. Science fiction has found the most eloquent and theoretically sophisticated of advocates in Toulouse, where Gérard Cordesse teaches. The very approach of "minority writing" is being profoundly renovated at the hands of Elizabeth Béranger (Djuna Barnes), D. Pitavy (Eudora Welty), and Joëlle Rostkowski (native American writers).

I must stop before the temptation of longer lists takes hold of me, and be content with the following affirmation: American literary studies in France are in better shape than they ever were, for all the institutional trouble they have to put up with. Revisitings of the tradition take place everywhere without ever getting bogged down in cosmetic debates on the canon. In the tradition of French literary criticism, writers are assessed on their merits rather than on some vague affirmative action approach that would reghettoize portions of a literary history more and more conceived, in the United States, as a patrolling of the borders. No field of investigation is barred, and women and minority writers are routinely integrated into curricula with no particular difficulty. One does not teach Djuna Barnes or Grace Paley to fill a quota, but because they are so very good. One does not praise Clarence Major or Ishmael Reed for being good black writers, but for being artists of the written word. "Au poète, on ne demande pas ses papiers." This is not only because minority writers reinforce the potential taste for the American exotic that may be found in teachers and students alike. There is enthusiasm, pleasure, and intellectual excitement in reading and rereading classics and newcomers alike for whatever enriches the heritage of the human mind, rather than what will promote this or that parochial and fleeting preoccupation. Enthusiasm tends to be contagious, and although I have no doubt that the economic and political situation of the United States in the Western world does just as much for the appeal of its literature, the momentum of such academic work, I suspect, has not been without major influence. For this, also, has profoundly changed.

Should you have asked anybody on a French street, twenty years ago, to name two American authors they knew, ninety-five people out of a hundred would probably have answered Hemingway or Steinbeck or both. No doubt the name of Faulkner would have crept into the list often enough, and there would have been the occasional Twain or Jack London. On the whole, the average man or woman in the street would have wondered whether there *was* an American literature outside of Hemingway. Back in the 1940s, Maurice-Edgar Coindreau had nearly single-handedly introduced the modernists to the French public, and many a Southern writer since. Faulkner, Dos Passos, Flannery O'Connor, and many others (Caldwell, Goyen, Capote, Styron, Humphrey, Chappell, Foote, Price, H. Ross Miller) can be considered as Coindreau creations for the French public; these were the times when only Gallimard and Le Seuil cared enough about contemporary American fiction to take— uneven—risks to promote such unknown newcomers as Gaddis, Malamud, Roth, and McCullers. Today, publishers fall all over one another to steal the newest newcomers from their neighbor's grip. It is a most recent phenomenon, one for which some of us in the university take pride in having been partly responsible, however difficult it may be to assess the relative factors that made this surge and such *engouement* possible. Let us simply notice that translation has progressed by leaps and bounds in this field and that publishers have a hard time finding as many quality translators as they need these days.

This may well be too much of a good thing, for speed unfortunately sometimes becomes of the essence; I could not begin to count the translations that have been organized burials. Something of the atmosphere of the American publishing industry has taken over French publishing, and not the best part either: this week's new translation pushes out last week's, and there is hardly time for a book to be given a chance before pulping time comes round to free some space in publishers' warehouses. Today many translations are just as good as lost on a public that used to consume its American literature in small doses and deal with highly and durably visible authors.

However that may be, attention needs be drawn to the recent initiatives of publishers who either had been keeping away from American

literature until recently (Flammarion, Laffont, Fayard, and others having added their efforts to those of Gallimard and Le Seuil in particular)
or just recently came into existence (Alinéa, Actes Sud, Rivages, Maza-
rine, Quai Voltaire, among others). Christian Bourgois and Maurice
Nadeau for the last twenty years, and Hubert Nyssen (Actes Sud) for the
last ten, have been actively promoting international literature and particularly that of the United States. Which does not necessarily mean that
what is being translated is necessarily either very representative of the
new trends in America or excludes translations from texts of the past
that had so far been neglected. Among the forty-odd titles the members
of the jury of the Maurice-Edgar Coindreau Prize—established in 1982
to reward "the best translation of an American book" in the spirit of the
discoverer it is named after—have to read each year, there are just as
frequently still untranslated works by Thoreau, James, Faulkner, John
Fante, or Djuna Barnes, as there are first novels published in the United
States in the preceding two years or at nearly the same time as their
French translations. In 1985, the jury of the Prize organized debates and
readings at the Musée d'Art Moderne in Paris on the occasion of the
crowning of the translation of Elkin's novella, "The Bailbondsman" by
Jean-Pierre Carasso. Attending this occasion were Grace Paley, Shelby
Foote, Edmund White, and Toni Morrison. Elkin was ill and could not
come. Fifty people were expected to attend. More than five hundred
showed up. In 1986, the American Book Fair organized in Aix-en-
Provence around Coover, Ashbery, Koch, Baldwin, Jayne Anne Phillips,
Jerome Charyn, Robert Steiner, and a few others gathered close to two
thousand people. Every reading given by an American writer coming
through Paris these days fills the—admittedly smallish—reading room
of the Village Voice bookstore, in the Latin Quarter, or the lower-level
auditorium of the Centre Pompidou. Paris, always a city favored by
American literary expatriates, is also a frequent meeting place for those
who reside in France and the summer literary travelers who come from
all over the United States.

So that the public image of American literature is indeed slowly
changing. There are fads and fashions of course. Bukowski makes it big
with the young one season and Alison Lurie the next. Unexpectedly,
translations of Grace Paley sell upward of fifteen thousand copies.
Jerome Charyn and John Hawkes have more readers in France than in
the United States. American fiction need not be "popular fiction" to be
popular. Bellow, Updike, André Dubus, Joyce Carol Oates, and Styron,
using rather traditional forms, tend of course to be read more widely,

but the works of Toni Morrison, Paul Auster, Robert Coover, or Thomas Pynchon are making surprising breakthroughs. A number of classical American writers so far ignored in favor of the "big five" (Dos Passos, Fitzgerald, Hemingway, Steinbeck, and Faulkner) are being reprinted (McCullers, O'Connor); others are being translated for the first time extensively: William Carlos Williams's poetry and prose are practically available in toto now; Pound's *Cantos* came out in translation in 1986, triggering a vast array of articles and reviews; the fifth novel of Willa Cather in three years came out in October 1988, and its publisher (Ramsay) intends not to stop until the complete works are out; Delta published in 1986 a bilingual anthology of the L=A=N=G=U=A=G=E poets of which there is no equivalent in the United States. Numerous texts of Henry James so far unpublished in French are seeing the light of day. New translations of Melville are attempted. There is hardly one publisher today that does not have a list of "its" American authors. This does not mean, unfortunately, that agreements have intervened to systematize and organize the translation of what is still missing. Publication tends to go on in a happy-go-lucky way that leaves huge gaps in what is available to the French reader. Gaddis's *The Recognitions* was published by Gallimard in the early sixties. Now Albin Michel intends to publish *Carpenter's Gothic*, but no one is in sight to do *JR*. The competition can be very steep to publish the latest hot item from the United States (Kathy Acker or Susan Minot) and no taker steps forward for the much-needed translation of the far more important but more austere works of Joseph McElroy. Even within the last twenty years, however, many publishers have seemed to "wise up," to awake to the fact that rather hasty translations of major works had been done sloppily in the sixties and early seventies, in the first rushes of interest; they seem ready to undertake, by and by, a number of fundamental retranslations of recent fiction. Heller's *Catch-22* has come out in a new version, and so has *The Catcher in the Rye*. Coover's *Pricksongs & Descants,* butchered in the early seventies, will probably be retranslated soon. William Gass's *In the Heart of the Heart of the Country* will appear in a new version in 1989; Le Seuil has just republished improved versions of Pynchon's novels, and so on. Parallel to this movement, more and more critical books are published in the contemporary field and find their way to a nonacademic readership: Pierre Gault's *La Parole Coupée* (Hawkes), Maurice Couturier's *Nabokov,* Claude Lévy's *Saul Bellow,* Claire Bruyère's *Sherwood Anderson,* Asselineau's work on Hemingway, Claude Richard's on Poe, and the books put out by the French Faulknerians (Gresset and Bleikasten in particular).

Whereas there used to be two or three bookstores selling American books in Paris in the 1960s, sizable collections can now be found in at least half a dozen specialized stores. On the whole, things, for the French literary Americanist, are looking up.

There are ironies too, of course. American best-sellers dearly bought by French publishers will very often flop while ignored writers will, in oenological terms, "travel well." It does take some time, except where such academics as are specialized in the field happen to be on hand, for contemporary fiction to integrate into university curricula; but the osmosis between public and academic audiences is growing. Indeed, one of the first tasks some of us university people have when we get our first batches of students is to destroy the clichés that have been gathered from more and more extensive but hasty media coverage; to give the students, whatever the literature they are studying, a sense of place, a respect for distance, a feeling for the relative, a sense of perspective on the pleasures and ravishments involved. These are our duties as teachers. To transform the power of exoticism into less transient intellectual and aesthetic foods. To propose questions where there have seemed to be answers. To transform enthusiastic *liseurs* into lucid *lecteurs*. While the former will occasionally be *nos semblables*, only the latter can really be *nos frères*.

Stepping out of Hitler's Shadow to Embrace Uncle Sam?

Notes toward a History of American Literary Studies in West Germany

HANS-PETER WAGNER

Those who have not understood the past are condemned to repeat it.
—JORGE AGUSTIN NICOLAS DE SANTAYANA

Truth! stark naked truth, is the word, and I will not so much as take the pains to bestow the strip of a gauze-wrapper on it, but paint situations such as they actually rose to me in nature, careless of violating . . . laws of decency.
—FRANCES HILL to her correspondent in John Cleland's *Memoirs of a Woman of Pleasure*

It is not things, but opinions about things, which trouble men.
—EPICTETUS

For most Germans America is, initially, a state of mind conditioned and shaped by fiction, films, hearsay, and wishful thinking. Many eventually get to the United States and are able to modify their ideas, many others continue to derive their personal images of America from *Dallas* and *Miami Vice* and from dreams and myths that, more often than not, have more to do with their own psyches than with what the Puritan settlers called God's own country. Like so many others born in the late 1940s or early 1950s, I did not grow up with TV. When TV finally reached my parents' household in the early 1960s, America had already taken a distinct shape in my mind: Karl May's noble Apaches and evil Comanches, and his German superman, Old Shatterhand, had done a magnificent job in conjuring up, before my mind's eye, a huge and unexplored country that was beautiful, wild, mysterious, and full of promise.

It is, therefore, hardly surprising that my first encounter with a true American proved a disappointment. I had just begun with English in school, at the age of thirteen, when the U.S. Army, performing maneuvers in the Saar area, moved as close to my parents' house as is possible in such mock wars. When I came home from school, hundreds of army tents had been pitched in the fields and meadows which, at that time, served as an adventure playground for my friends and me. This was the chance of a lifetime to see a true Indian; so, after a quick lunch, I rushed to the nearest tent and approached the first soldier I saw. He was white, probably a Southerner. Hiding my disappointment, I decided to ask him some questions, casting a few of the new (British) English words I had learned into the mold of German syntax. As far as I remember, we engaged in the following conversation:

"How do you do?"
"Hi."
"Live you in New York?"
"Sure do."
"Live you in a skyscraper?"
"Sure do."

I was at the end of my tether. So the soldier decided to save me from embarrassment. Handing me a piece of chewing gum, he asked *me* a question.

"You got a sister?"

Unfortunately, and to my utter dejection, I did not have a sister, but I did recommend to him a girl I had adored from afar, providing him with her name and address. Of course, later on, I could not forgive myself for betraying her in such a cheap way, although, as far as I know, the soldier and some of his friends merely went up and down her street calling out her name, much to the astonishment of the girl's parents. I enjoyed the Wrigley's gum the soldier gave me; it was the first symbol for me of an America I did not yet know.

I have recounted this story because I believe that history affects our lives, be it the personal history of one's childhood or the seemingly more important sociopolitical history of one's country. This means that my account, in the following pages, of American Literary Studies in West Germany (hereafter ALS) can only be a personal one for which I am prepared to take full responsibility: I write, on the one hand, as a

"Saarlander." The Saarland has always been on the fringe of Germany, and I have been in turn a semi-French citizen, a citizen of a temporarily independent European state, and a citizen of West Germany; hence, perhaps, my wariness of national pride and feelings. And I write, on the other hand, as a member of the German postwar generation who acquired his knowledge of the war, and of Nazism, in a painful process that led to an estrangement between parents and children, between politicians and postwar citizens, and, in our context, between university teachers and students (Greiner, Schneider). I shall return to this point in the following pages.

Dealing with ALS in West Germany, I find myself faced with a welter of issues which, when seen together, conjure up the image of Hydra in Greek myth: there are just too many heads to be dealt with, and when you think you have successfully exhausted one, many others have grown beside it. Since I am not Hercules, it seems to me that I should be modest and confine myself to those issues which need clarification: the way that Hydra was conceived, how it could grow its heads, and how it keeps on living. I also feel that I should say a few words about the discourse generated by the Hydra, not least because institutions tend to write their own histories and invent their own myths. That is to say, I want to address myself not to the contents of ALS (which, as several attempts in the past have made obvious, can be a convenient way to avoid some very uneasy issues), but rather to the limits, concepts, and structures, both self-imposed and imposed from outside, which have determined, and continue to determine, those contents in very decisive ways. Hence I cannot avoid talking about history and historiography, about ideology, politics, and pedagogy/didactics, and about the impact these have had on my subject.

I

To understand contemporary ALS in Germany, one must turn to Adolf Hitler's Reich that was to last a thousand years but, fortunately, came to an end in 1945. The period of Nazi rule in Germany (1933–1945) has been neglected and even shunned by those German Anglicists and Americanists who taught during that time and, in the past two decades, wrote about it. It is one of the bitter ironies of the postwar history of ALS in Germany that a few Americanists who either were Nazis or had assisted Nazism by remaining silent and "adjusting to the system," also assisted in the launching of *Amerikanistik* after 1945. But West Germany has seen, tolerated, and finally accepted the return of ex-fascists in politics, too: former Nazis became upright democrats in 1949, as the example of the late Chancellor Kiesinger illustrates.

As there has been a tendency in German politics over the last five years—this has not been the first time—to make the public less conscious of what happened between 1933 and 1945, I should like to state here what is rarely admitted (see, however, the critical accounts by Aust; Giordano; and Mitscherlich), and even more rarely stated, by older German Americanists: those 55 percent of German academics who were not ousted by the Nazis between 1934 and 1938 showed an amazing lack of moral and intellectual honesty. Their lack of integrity served as an unfortunate example: after only a few years of Nazi domination the great majority of German university teachers obediently served the new creed (Finkenstaedt, 1975, 1983; Lehberger; Schottländer; Skard). Sigmund Skard has dealt with this period in a most authoritative manner that relieves me of the obligation to provide further sad details of the treachery and the delusion of German intellectuals; and Hans Peter Bleuel, in his sociopolitical study of German professors between 1900 and 1933, has provided convincing explanations for this development.

Something important, however, needs to be added here, not least because even younger German Anglicists, who did not study or teach during the Nazi period, tend to exculpate their predecessors. What German academics did (or one perhaps should rather say, what they did not do) in the Third Reich may be understandable, but it remains unpardonable as long as the persons concerned lack the little courage it would take today to confess publicly to their errors and misjudgments. A power of good could have been done with simple public statements in the form of articles. Such statements admitting guilt or error would have eased the pain the postwar generation suffered because of the obstinate silence of their fathers and teachers in a generational conflict that had no precedent in history. These fathers and teachers possessed not only the strength to lay in ruins an entire continent, to bring death and misery to millions of people, to eradicate an entire culture, and to approach the apocalypse as closely as possible. They also possessed the even more astonishing strength to clear away the debris; to build new houses, factories, and schools; to create new families in the traditional way; to father children, to drill and educate them in the old spirit; and to reinstitute the old authorities and morals—and they did all that as if nothing had happened and as if what had happened did not require something completely different (Greiner).

In his history of English philology in Germany, Finkenstaedt, who was born in 1930, argues that he prefers not to mention names in his chapter on the Nazi period as many persons are still alive and that he will open his archives at "the proper time" (293). He provides an implicit apologia of Nazi *Anglisten* by asking: "Who among the tenured [German] lecturers in English who did not experience the Third Reich would want to throw the first stone against the students of 1933 who later became professors? He who does/dares should at least pray that he be spared similar decisions" (168). I certainly do not intend to stone elderly gentlemen who happened to study or teach under Hitler, were too deluded or cowardly to oppose the Nazi terror, returned to their jobs in the late 1940s, and have now retired as professors emeriti. But I cannot excuse intellectuals who tolerated racism, supported a totalitarian system, and by letting the Nazis get on with their inhuman business can be held responsible, even if only indirectly, for the killing of six million Jews, twenty million Russians (of these some seven million were civilians), five and a quarter million Germans, and four and a half million Poles. After all, Hitler's henchmen, both those in the "regular" army and the SS, could go on killing only as long as they were abetted in their crimes by the civil servants (Bleuel, Müller); and the concentration camps kept on functioning as long as the so-called regular army kept on fighting. What cause did those many "innocents" and "upright soldiers," such as former Chancellor Schmidt and the late president of the Free State of Bavaria, Franz Josef Strauss, fight for? I have not heard a satisfactory answer. Two of my uncles died in the criminal war Hitler started: my uncle Hans, whose name I bear, was killed in Russia in 1943. He was nineteen years old. My uncle Luitpold died of hunger and diarrhea at the age of thirty-three in a Russian prisoner of war camp in 1946. The Russians merely practiced what the so-called regular German army had done with Russian prisoners of war in the years before—it is only recently that the crimes of parts of the German *Wehrmacht* have been unveiled (Wette).

If some professors, along with other intellectuals, had at least been more honest, I could now travel abroad without the feelings of guilt that haunt me every time I speak to a foreigner and speculate on the suffering of his or her family during the war. (See Schneider's comments on "being a third-generation German," and also Greiner.)

The chapter about the history of German professors of *Anglistik* (English philology) during and before the war still needs to be written. For after the silence (Galinsky) and the exculpations and explanations (Blanke), what we need to admit at long last is that, as far as the German side was concerned, there was nothing honorable about the war or about the pitiful behavior of deluded and fearful intellectuals. Hitler's wars were criminal, by every standard. Equally criminal were the academics who tried to adapt to the system and preached its ideology to their students. Some of those who have survived and even returned to their professorial chairs probably know why they have dropped their Nazi publications from the more recent editions of *Kürschner's Gelehrten Kalender*. It is high time, indeed the proper time, for Professor Finkenstaedt to open his archives, for those concerned have remained silent, and it is unlikely that they will have an epiphanic change of mind.

Until very recently, historical accounts of the development of the Federal Republic of Germany have neglected the crucial role of the postwar years up to 1949. When Skard wrote in 1958 that "West Germany adapted itself with amazing efficiency to a democratic political life, parallel to its economic recovery," and that "There was in powerful circles . . . a willingness to write off the past and to begin afresh," he was not quite aware of the ambiguity of a statement whose tragic dimension became obvious in the wave of terrorism in the 1970s. The (left-wing) terrorists, mostly people born after 1940, reacted violently and brutally against the quickness and readiness with which the "reconstructors" turned away from the past while using the reconstruction of the country as an excuse for their often total lack of remembrance, regret, and shame (Aust; Wagner; Schneider).

In connection with the rise of ALS after 1945 it is of some interest to have a look at the political aspects of what has been termed "reeducation." Recent studies suggest, and partly confirm, what many clear-eyed observers have suspected for a long time and what has been drowned by the false rhetoric of the democratic jargon so quickly adopted by the new German leaders: reeducation did not work. It failed in all three sectors or zones of what became West Germany (Borchers; Bungenstab; Gehring; Niethammer; Peitsch; Taper).

The reasons for the failure of reeducation are manifold and complex, and I must confine myself to what seem to me to be the more important causes. There was, to begin with, the naiveté of American officers and authorities who believed that democracy could be ordered and imposed or enforced. They imagined that changing, by way of free elections and reeducation, an authoritarian and hierarchical system that had existed before the Nazis would produce democratic minds (Taper). This naiveté gave way to more realistic power politics as Germany became strategically even more important for the United States in the Cold War that began with Truman's doctrine in 1947. It was in this period that the American secret services protected former members of the Gestapo such as Klaus Barbie, ex-Nazis such as the journalist Werner Höfer, and generals who had been in Russia (O'Toole). By 1949, the American zone in Germany propagated a concept of democracy that equated the democratic way of life with the American way of life. The initial idea of a true democracy was thus sacrificed in the ongoing battle between Russian communism and American capitalism (Borchers).

The attempts on the part of the Allies to reeducate the Germans met with a population that was fed up with ideology. After all, one had had a firsthand impression of what strict adherence to an ideology could produce. Most Germans were more interested in surviving and getting on in life, thus proving right Bertolt Brecht's dictum about the priority of natural instinct over morality.

Around 1950, Alfred Kazin, a New York Jew, spent some time in Cologne as a Fulbright professor in *Amerikanistik*. His autobiographical report about German academics and the failure of reeducation is worth reading. Kazin's recollection may be biased and inspired by spite, but he has recorded German features that can still be found today: the refusal of the war generation to regret or repent; the authoritarian and hierarchical structures of German universities, and the repression and psychic deformities they produce; the return into teaching positions of former Nazis; the obstinate silence about the war; and the desperate efforts to forget by looking ahead. Kazin writes:

> The war was over. The war was not to be mentioned. Not a word was said by my students about the war. They were busy getting ahead on the magic road of *Amerikanistik,* and with determination that had made their elders the despair of everyone but other Germans, they spoke and wrote the American language with ease, sparkle, and even humor. . . . [T]hey were like other nineteen-year-olds in Minneapolis, Cambridge, Washington Square. *The war did not exist.* History as it pushed along just removed the past.

With the permission of the Allied authorities, most German universities were reopened in 1946 and 1947. Sigmund Skard's observations about this period are correct when he argues:

> University leaders were preoccupied with practical difficulties and had little time for constructive thinking. A great part of the residual staffs were elderly men, swamped with students and overburdened with work; they naturally felt

content if they were able to re-establish the conditions which they knew from their younger days. The same was largely true of the personnel of the new Ministries of Education; nowhere did the radical reformers come to power. During the latter half of the 1940's the universities in West Germany largely returned to the pre-Nazi pattern of organization, as did German secondary schools and German society generally. (P. 303)

Gustav H. Blanke, apparently unimpressed by the reeducation he underwent as a prisoner of war in the United States, wrote in 1986 that in the postwar years one realized on the German side that the reeducation measures would neither produce democracy nor prevent the re-institution (especially in the universities) of former Nazis. Professor Blanke's phrasing seems to imply acceptance and approval of that historical fact. A few outspoken Nazis like Friedrich Schönemann were prevented from returning to the university. Schönemann, the director of the influential Amerika-Institute at the University of Berlin from 1936 to 1945, propagated Nazi ideology in the field of American studies. He did not make it back to a chair—but when he died he did get a laudatory and exculpating obituary in the pages of *American Studies* (Hölzle).

But a sizable number of former Nazis, or faculty with Nazi sympathies, returned and took a crucial part in the shaping of ALS in the 1950s. For obvious reasons, they were scalded cats as far as politics was concerned and therefore tried to keep politics and ideology out of their lives and teaching. The apolitical attitude had a certain history in Germany, especially among the *Beamten*. The result, in practical teaching, could be termed a flight into aesthetics. Even before New Criticism began to make its impact in Europe in the late 1950s and early 1960s, there had been a tradition called *explication de texte* which focussed more on structural and formal aspects and tended to neglect ideological dimensions. So New Criticism was the best thing that could happen to these people: interpreting works of literature exclusively in the ivory tower of self-contained literary criticism (the closed world of the work of art; aesthetics instead of sociopolitical dimensions; literary history instead of or without the real history) became rather fashionable in many places, and two generations of students were trained if not drilled according to an approach that called itself *explication de texte* or close reading. It had the advantage of saving the teacher the trouble of considering his own past and that of the text, and of saving the students the trouble of questioning the politics of their texts and teachers.

When the students of the late 1960s turned against the age-old structures of the German university system, their aim was for more democracy and the abolishment of authoritarian hierarchy as it had been practiced before and under Hitler. Their slogan, "Unter den Talaren Muff von tausend Jahren" (Under your gowns there is the stench of a thousand years), was specifically directed against those professors, some of them Anglicists and Americanists, who had managed to get back into teaching positions during the 1950s and against the sudden expansion of the universities in the early 1960s. However, the student protests were, in the long run, as ineffectual as the attempts of some of the Allies to introduce reforms in schools and universities. Change occurred in the *content*, not in the *structure*, of ALS: some professors reacted to student protest and pressure, and to the demands of younger colleagues, and changed their lectures and reading lists. In most cases this meant modernizing the canon, making room for recent American literature (Lang). The political force of the student movement, initially organized somewhat haphazardly in the APO (extra-parliamentary opposition), was channeled into dead ends like left-wing terrorism or, in the case of the "march through the institutions," aborted by the *Radikalenerlass*, the ruling of the German Supreme Court in the early 1970s barring communists from politics and administrative life; it has reemerged, considerably weakened, in the new Grüne Partei with its self-destructive wings of fundamentalists and realists who seem to have been more concerned with infighting than with practical politics.

It took some time for ALS to be recognized as at least valuable if not equal beside or within existing English departments. Although around 1947 most universities began introducing ALS, some of them on an impressive scale, no organizational change was made in the departments. Nevertheless, the institutional organization of ALS was decisively influenced by the politics of the Allies in the three zones of occupation.

In the British zone, both the German faculty and the British authorities were more interested in establishing the pre-1933 English department than in new and independent *Amerikanistik-Abteilungen*. British English and British literature were given preference, and ALS was entrusted to the *Mittelbau*, to American guest professors, or to German professors with a background in English literature.

In the French zone, where I grew up and studied, independent *Amerikanistik* departments emerged in the universities due to the absence of German Anglophilia and to the French insistence that the example of the Sorbonne be emulated. As early as 1918, a chair for American language and literature had been created at the Sorbonne. From the very beginning, the *Amerikanistik* professors in the French zone—in

Tübingen, Mainz, Freiburg—were considered equal to their *Anglistik* colleagues, and they also participated in the state exams, which was not always the case in the British zone.

It was in the United States-controlled zone that American studies as an interdisciplinary field flourished best, especially in the independent Amerika-Institutes in Berlin, Erlangen, Munich, and Frankfurt. Hans Galinsky has provided a brief discussion of the development in the American zone that also takes into account the fact that American authorities "abstained from interfering with the pre-1919 oriented curriculum of German junior and senior high schools, whose concept of English was as one-sided as that of most noteworthy university departments of English":

> The availability of eminent German refugees, having returned to professorships of political science, sociology, and philosophy or cultural history, imparted to American Studies at Munich, Frankfurt and Berlin an impetus, zest and interdisciplinary breadth unparalleled elsewhere. (Galinsky 1974, 6)

Professor Galinsky's survey would be more complete had he added to the "availability of . . . German refugees" the availability of former Nazis.

The consequences of Allied politics in the zones are, as Galinsky rightly remarked in 1974, "still with us today," even though the interrelations of the three types of organization (that is, the Amerika-Institute, with its interdisciplinary approach; the "British" American literature professor with a primary training in British literature; and the independent *Amerikanistik* department) have overlapped and coalesced in the past two decades.

The names of a few important people in postwar *Amerikanistik* ought to be mentioned here. Ernst Fraenkel had been persecuted in Germany, and he returned to Berlin, now an American citizen, to work at the Freie Universität in what became one of the first important centers of American studies, the John F. Kennedy-Institute. Equally influential were Walther P. Fischer and Arnold Bergsträsser; they attempted interdepartmental and interdisciplinary approaches, which were for the most part disliked in German universities. The call for such an integrated method, mostly from the ranks of younger scholars, was supported by the American Anderson Report which in 1950 suggested the establishment of interdisciplinary institutes for the study of American culture. As early as 1946 such an institute was founded at the University of Frankfurt and has continued to thrive. Others followed: the Amerika-Institutes in Erlangen (1947), Munich (1949), Berlin (1952, transformed into the JFK-Institute in 1963), and Mainz. In the late 1960s, the Amerika-Institute absorbed some of the student protest and offered classes that included and considered politics (often with an anti-American stance); and there were some attempts to introduce democratic patterns among the body of lecturers and professors who initiated these courses. But these institutes have been quite exceptional in the German academic landscape, for in the majority of German institutions of higher learning *Amerikanistik* is attached to, or part of, the English departments. Normally, there is one full professor who teaches mainly American literature, and in some cases also subjects that belong to ALS, such as *Landeskunde* and history.

The founding of the German Society for American Studies in 1953 has of course boosted the rise of *Amerikanistik,* and especially the interdisciplinary approach. The annual meetings of the Society, which welcomes contributions by foreign scholars, have proved that it is a much less exclusive organization than the German *Anglistentag* which admits only professors or people with professorial qualifications (Finkenstaedt/ Schröder; Moltmann). In 1955 there were eleven chairs for *Amerikanistik* in Germany; by 1980 each institution of higher learning that offered *Anglistik* also had a professor teaching mainly or partly American literature.

The role of *Amerikanistik* in German universities remains dependent on a number of issues that are still developing and on some problems that have not been resolved. To begin with, there is the structure of the university itself. Despite a series of reforms in the 1960s and 1970s, German universities have changed little during the periods of political upheaval; their tendency to authoritarianism and their conservatism have survived and led to an isolationism that is regrettable in a democratic society.

More often than not, *Amerikanistik* is geared to, or considered to be a smaller section of, *Anglistik.* Excepting the Amerika-Institutes in Berlin, Erlangen, Frankfurt, Mainz, and Munich, it is English philology that often determines the teaching and, as far as criticism and literary theory are concerned, even the contents of *Amerikanistik.* The factual-minded whose interests lie in the area of who teaches what where, will find useful information on ALS in Germany, including publications and periodicals, in Finkenstaedt's *Neuer Anglistenspiegel* and in his *Informationen,* published each term.

II

If history and politics have had a decisive influence on ALS, so have the institutional organizations and structures of the universities that govern and often determine the actual contents of teaching and research. In order to understand how *Amerikanistik* functions in Germany, we must look at the training and the professional careers of faculty members, at canons and canon formation, and at exams. It will become obvious that these issues have political dimensions, too, and that they relate to, or depend on each other in a number of ways.

The training of German *Amerikanisten* implies a certain danger which is due to the various levels of dependence that are inherent to a hierarchical and basically nondemocratic system which has its roots in the nineteenth century. After a brief period of democratization in the 1970s, which saw the creation, but also the final abolishment of the newfangled position of *Assistenzprofessor* (comparable to the American associate professor), we are today back at square one in that the full professor is in complete control of his or (rarely) her subject and *Mitarbeiter*. This German word means coworker or helper, and the situation is in fact such that every person below the professor is, as Professor Finkenstaedt has put it, a "mini-monad," that is, someone who is there but does not really count. It is the professor who sets the papers and asks the questions in the state exams; and it is the professor who is all-important in the doctorate. Professors appoint and dismiss their mini-monads, and they actually decide on the careers of their *Mitarbeiter* by controlling the *Habilitation*, the postdoctoral scholarly thesis and examination which serve as the final qualification for an academic career.

This concentration of authority in the hands of the professor creates dependence which often proves detrimental, especially in the areas of teaching methods and research. Heide Ziegler, who survived her years in the *Mittelbau* (a word with a true hierarchical ring to it, suggesting the middle part of the ivory tower) as an *Assistentin* and is today herself a distinguished professor, has described her personal experience of downright tyranny that seems incredible to an American or British reader but is still possible in German universities (Ziegler). Comparing the ways that American and German universities select and train their future faculty members, Harvard professor Carl J. Friedrich rightly criticized a number of features which prevent independent teaching and research; these include the dependence of the *Mittelbau* on the professor, a dependence that reaches from seemingly insignificant details (photocopying, approval of lectures abroad) to the approach chosen in literature classes and in the doctorate and the *Habilitation* (Friedrich, Gerhard, Wenke).

It is hardly surprising that such a hierarchical system often leads to subordination on the part of the *Mittelbau*. The American tenure-track system, despite its publish or perish syndrome, at least seems to generate a degree of personal and professional freedom. The long and back-breaking German way up to the *Habilitation* normally implies that publications outside one's limited field are neither asked for nor appreciated; and as the *Habilitation,* like the doctorate, is usually controlled by one professor only, its value outside the specific university will always be questionable.

Professors share with some members of the *Mittelbau* the professional tag *Beamten;* that is to say they are civil servants. As such they are required to support the constitution of the Federal Republic. If conservatism and authoritarianism have prevailed in German universities, and if too many German faculty members remain apolitical in the bad sense, the so-called *Beamtentum* is certainly one of the reasons for this situation.

Created in the nineteenth century (in Bavaria and Prussia), this system of civil "servitude" was supposed to guarantee an efficient state administration. Meanwhile, however, the civil servants have become the most powerful professional group in the country. Since they control the state parliaments, it is virtually impossible to abolish the system. The disadvantages of the *Beamten* status, as far as ALS are concerned, are the following: Since *Beamte* are supposed to be objective (neutral) in their professional capacity, they tend to be apolitical or conservative. The verdict of the German Supreme Court of May 1975 made it impossible for members of the Communist party (which is tolerated in West Germany) to become or stay *Beamte.* This verdict and the federal *Radikalenerlass* also demonstrate a peculiar interpretation of the German constitution. Whereas in France, communists can even participate in the government, in Germany this would be unthinkable. Since *Beamte* depend on evaluation by their superiors, subordination and obedience often rule the field where critical attitudes, freedom of choice, and individual decisions should hold sway. Finally, since *Beamte* are not allowed to go on strike, being "servants of the state," it is very difficult to change regulations and conditions without running into crucial personal problems (Wunder).

Given such conservative conditions and hierarchical structures, it is indeed surprising that, since the 1960s, there has been some change and innovation in ALS. The German university system may have weathered the storms of the student movement, but the intellectual and ideological influence of that movement, although quickly banned from politics, has made itself felt in a number of German universities. To begin with, a younger generation of teachers and faculty members, some of them "'68ers," jockeyed into their professional positions in the 1970s when jobs were still available. Some of them were able to breathe new life into the field of ALS: they tried new methods and approaches, and they shifted the attention of the German scholarly world to the modern and contemporary period in American literature. Admittedly, there is still inbreeding in various universities; there are still (left-wing) closed shops in some of the Amerika-Institutes; and a few traditional schools survive which are ruled by a handful of distinguished professors. But ALS has today become a rich field, both in teaching and research, which is much less conservative and much more diverse than its older sister, *Anglistik*.

As for the exams, the central problem was formulated as early as 1922 by Max Weber, who regretted the growing bureaucracy as a result of the interference of the state in university exams (Fraenkel, 66). In the German federal system the educational authority is vested in the state governments which have developed different regulations for the university examinations. Meanwhile, the orals in literature are exclusively in the hands of professors; the *Mittelbau* is virtually excluded. This creates a problem in that whereas members of the *Mittelbau* teach literature classes and literary theory, the regulations make it obvious that only professorial opinions are relevant. Students, unfortunately, are thus well advised to adhere to professorial views and to ignore any dissenting perspectives of younger lecturers, for these may prove suicidal in the final examination.

The regulations for the final exams differ slightly among the states with a conservative government, and more decisively between the states with a social-democratic government and a conservative government. Although many literary scholars in Germany disregard this aspect, or consider it of little importance for their work, it is obvious that ideological concepts of the two big parties in West Germany can be found as a mirror reflection, even though at times slightly distorted, in the *Lehramtsprüfungsordnung,* the regulations for the state exams.

There are two spheres of interest in American literature in Germany, that of the popular market, frequently despised and ignored by academics, and that of the universities. I feel unable to comment on the first, not because I despise it but because I find it too complicated an issue to be dealt with in a few sentences or even in an article. Suffice it to say that most American best-sellers are translated, within a year, into German. The spectrum of American literature in German translation is almost as wide as the market in the United States, ranging from popular western novels and science fiction to contemporary writers cherished by middlebrow and highbrow audiences (e.g., Oates, Updike, Singer, Vonnegut, John Irving, Erica Jong, and Paul Theroux) and the postmodernists catering to a select group of intellectuals (e.g., Abish, Ashbery, Barth, Brautigan, Coover, Federman, Gaddis, Heller, and Pynchon). More information about the beginnings and growth of American literature in German translation can be found in books and articles by Bungenstab (1971), Frenz, Galinsky (1986), Gehring, Peitsch, Price, and Schmitt-Kaufhold.

As to the canon of American literature as it is taught at the university, it is essentially the holder of the chair in American literature who decides what is put on the reading list in his or her department. He or she usually considers the state exam regulations in which preference is given to American literature of the nineteenth and twentieth centuries and may or may not respond to the suggestions made by the *Mittelbau* and the students. Still, the reading lists of the universities often, but not always, reflect the personal predilections, the temperament and the prejudices of the professorial heart and soul.

It is unfortunate that the wave of vastly interesting and helpful studies we have seen in the field of didactics over the past ten years should have such a pitiful echo on the practical side, that is in the teaching of literature at the university. English and American studies continue on well-trod paths. Given the structure and institutional organization of the German university, such valuable attempts in the field of didactics have been doomed to remaining theory-restricted: published in scholarly journals and doctoral dissertations, they have little or no effect on teaching and curriculum in the universities.

Thus the teaching of and the research on American literature at the university level in West Germany remain intricate subjects whose problems are rooted in politics, history, and the structures of academe itself. It is difficult to suggest solutions and alternatives, but I hope to find some ideas in the articles by my colleagues and friends in this volume. Like the narrator in Sterne's *A Sentimental Journey,* I suspect that "they order this matter . . . better in France."

Works Cited

Aust, Stefan. *The Baader-Meinhof Group: The Inside Story of a Phenomenon.* Translated by Anthea Bell. Topsfield, Mass.: The Bodley Head, 1987.

Blanke, Gustav. "Zur Entstehung der Amerikanistik im Nachkriegsdeutschland." *Gulliver* 20 (1986): 78–85.

Bleuel, Hans P. *Deutschlands Bekenner: Professoren zwischen Kaisserreich und Diktatur.* Bern: Scherz, 1968.

Borchers, Hans, and K. Vowe, eds. *Die zarte Pflanze Demokratie: Amerikanische Reeducation in Deutschland im Spiegel ausgewählter politischer und literarischer Zeitschriften (1945–49).* Tubingen: G. Narr, 1979.

Bungenstab, Karl-Ernst. "Die Ausbildung der amerikanischen Offiziere für die Militärregierungen nach 1945." *Jahrbuch für Amerikastudien* 18 (1973): 195–212.

Finkenstaedt, Thomas. *Kleine Geschichte der Anglistik in Deutschland.* Darmstadt: Wissenschaftliche Buchgesellschaft, 1983.

———. *Neuer Anglistenspiegel.* Augsburg: Universität Augsburg, 1983. Contains biographical and bibliographical information on German Anglicists and Americanists.

———. "Zwischen Diktat und Oberseminar, oder: Das 2. Jahrhundert der deutschen Anglistik." In *Wissenschaft zwischen Forschung und Ausbildung,* edited by Josef Becker and Rolf Bergmann, 153–66. Munich: Vogel, 1975.

Finkenstaedt, Thomas, and Klaus H. Gradinger. *Fachstudienführer Englische Philologie (Anglistik/Amerikanistik).* Grafenau: Lexika-Verlag, 1978.

Finkenstaedt, Thomas, and Konrad Schröder. *Englische Philologie: Anglistik und Amerikanistik.* Wildstein und Haunstetten: Privately printed, 1983.

Fraenkel Ernst. "Akademisches Prüfungswesen in Deutschland und in den USA." *Jahrbuch für Amerikastudien* 12 (1967): 61–73.

Frenz, Horst, and Hans-Joachim Lang, eds. *Nordamerikanische Literatur im deutschen Sprachraum seit 1945.* Munich: Winkler, 1973.

Friedrich, Carl J. "Auswahl und Ausbildung des akademischen Nachwuchses in Amerika und ihre Bedeutung für die deutsche Hochschulreform." *Jahrbuch für Amerikastudien* 12 (1967): 36–47.

Galinsky, Hans. "American Studies in Germany." In *American Studies in Transition,* edited by Marshall Fishwick, 232–52. Philadelphia: University of Pennsylvania Press, 1964. Reprint. Boston: Houghton Mifflin Company, 1969.

———. "American Studies in Germany: Their Growth, Variety and Prospects." *American Studies International* 13, no. 1(1974): 3–10.

———. "Contemporary Prose of the American South: Its German Reception and Influence." In *Studien zur englischen und amerikanischen Prosa nach dem 1. Weltkrieg: Festschrift für Kurt Otten zum 60. Geburtstag,* edited by Maria Diedrich and Christoph Schoneich, 242–55. Darmstadt: Wissenschaftliche Buchgesellschaft, 1986.

Gehring, Hansjörg. *Amerikanische Literaturpolitik in Deutschland 1945–53: ein Aspekt des Re-Education-Programms.* Stuttgart: Deutsche Verlags-Anstalt, 1976.

Gerhard, Dietrich. "Development and Structure of Continental European and American Universities—A Comparison." *Jahrbuch für Amerikastudien* 12 (1967): 19–35.

Giordano, Ralph. *Die zweite Schuld oder Von der Last Deutscher zu sein.* Hamburg: Rasch und Rohring, 1987.

Greiner, Ulrich. "Sohne und ihre Vater. Uber die Studentenbewegung als Konflikt der Generationen." *Die Zeit*, 29 April 1988, 55–56.

Hölzle, Erwin. "Friedrich Schonemann." *Jahrbuch für Amerikastudien* 2 (1957): 283–85. An obituary.

Kazin, Alfred. *New York Jew.* New York: Knopf, 1978.

Kürschners Deutscher Gelehrten-Kalender. Berlin: De Gruyter, 1941 and 1987.

Lang, Hans-Joachim. "H.J.L., Journalist: Rückblicke statt einer Bibliographie." In *Myth and Enlightenment in American Literature*, edited by Dieter Meindl et al. Erlangen: Universitätsbund Erlangen, 1985.

Lehberger, Reiner. *Englischunterricht im Nationalsozialismus.* Tubingen: Stauffenburg, 1986.

Mitscherlich, Alexander, and Margerete Mitscherlich. *Die Unfähigkeit zu trauern.* Munich: Piper, 1967.

Moltmann, Günter. "25 Jahre DGfAS." *Mitteilungsblatt der DGfAS* 25 (1978): 5–10.

Müller, Ingo. *Furchtbare Juristen: Die unbewältigte Vergangenheit unserer Justiz.* Munich: Kindler, 1987.

Niethammer, Lutz. *Entnazifizierung in Bayern: Sauberung und Rehabilitierung unter amerikanischer Besatzung.* Frankfurt: Fischer, 1972.

O'Toole, Thomas. "U.S. Used Many Ex-Nazis Sought for War Crimes." *Washington Post*, 28 March 1983. Reprinted in *Gulliver* 15 (1984): 165–68, with additional commentary and bibliography by D. Hoerder.

Peitsch, Helmut. "Literaturpolitik in der Britischen Zone." *Gulliver* 20 (1986): 86–112.

Price, Lawrence M. *The Reception of United States Literature in Germany.* Chapel Hill: University of North Carolina Press, 1966.

Schmitt-Kaufhold, Angelika. *Nordamerikanische Literatur im deutschen Sprachraum nach 1945.* Frankfurt: Lang, 1977.

Schneider, Peter. "Hitler's Shadow: On Being a Self-conscious German." *Harper's*, September 1987, 49–54.

Schottländer, Rudolf. *Verfolgte Berliner Wissenschaft.* Berlin: Edition Hentrich, 1988.

Skard, Sigmund. *American Studies in Europe: Their History and Present Organization.* 2 vols. Philadelphia: University of Pennsylvania Press, 1958.

Taper, Bernard. "Heil Free Elections." *Harper's Magazine*, February 1949, 29–37.

Wagner, Peter. "'Utopia Now!' Terrorism in West Germany: Causes, Targets, and Consequences." *Quinquereme: New Studies in Modern Languages* 3, no. 1(1980): 64–75.

Wenke, Hans. "Akademisches Prüfungswesen in Deutschland-Tatbestände und Probleme." *Jahrbuch für Amerikastudien* 12 (1967): 48–60.

Wette, Wolfram. "Erobern, zerstören, auslöschen. Die verdrängte Last von 1941: Der Russlandfeldzug war ein Raub- und Vernichtungskrieg von Anfang an." *Die Ziet*, 20 November 1987, 49–50.

Ziegler, Heide. "Herr Pozzo und seine Knechte." *Sprache im technischen Zeitalter*. March 1985, 76–81.

ঽ৯

(Mis)Understanding America's Literary Canon
The Greek Paradigm

SAVAS PATSALIDIS

To write something meaningful about the large and still unexplored topic of the introduction and reception of American literature in Greece, one has to be wary of the many pitfalls embedded in the terrain of the project. For one thing, such an exploration should not be conclusive; nor should it set any limits to the study of American literary performance in Greece. Nor should it tame the difference of its heterogeneous material in order to provide or promote a finalized proposition about the organic unity of Greek readership. Rather, it should be deconcentrating. Thus, the principal aim of this essay is to move beyond closure in order to locate some of the literary and nonliterary factors that made, and still make, the task of canonizing American literature in Greece an unsettled affair, a textual *ludo.*

Although the first works of American literature were translated much earlier (a Greek version of Poe appeared in the late 1870s) and even systematically (between 1900 and 1935 Emerson, Whitman, Twain, Thoreau, and Stowe were translated), it was not until the implementation of the Marshall Plan in 1947 that American literature and American culture in general started making their presence felt in the Greek market. More specifically, on 26 February 1947, Secretary of State George C. Marshall sent a memorandum to President Truman saying among other things that the situation in Greece was "desperate" and that immediate steps had to be taken "to extend all possible aid to Greece . . . to resist communist pressure from the Soviet satellite countries of the North."

This decision signalled the end of British domination in Greece and the beginning of an active American intervention.

The Americans came to Greece at a time when Greece was still suffering from the consequences of its civil war. The people were severely divided, both economically and ideologically. The losers, mainly leftists, were under systematic persecution. The victors, "drunk with power and American dollars," in the words of Loukas Axelos, did their utmost to propagate their own ideology of "normality" as an alternative to Marxist propositions of "abnormality." To this end, the newly introduced rhetoric of the "American way of life," with its emphasis on opportunity for all, free enterprise, and success, proved to be an ideal weapon in the strategy of local politics. In the name of an American-style democracy the State urged its salaried workers to implement its moralistic prejudices and canonize its schemes of interpretation. Using as its arsenal an obsolete, ethnocentric jargon mixed with undigested and distorted elements from America's sociopolitical discourse, the local nomenclature taught people to be satisfied with their lot, carry out orders, think piously, be patriotic, obey their king, be good Greeks and good Christians. As dictator Papadopoulos plainly put the case in 1967, no one would be allowed to counterfeit or exploit cheap and forbidden speculations which (1) disturb or could disturb public order, (2) propagate subversive theories, (3) defame Greece nationally or touristically, (4) undermine the healthy social traditions of the Greek people and their ancestral habits and customs, (5) touch upon the Christian religion, (6) attack the person of the king, the members of the royal family and the government, (7) exercise a noxious influence on Youth, or (8) exercise a distorting influence on the aesthetic evolution of the people. As for America itself, it was portrayed as a land of promise and also as an ideal host for anyone willing to work there. Thousands of unemployed Greeks were encouraged to emigrate in search of the American dream. Those who were left behind moved to Greek urban centers in search of better living conditions or, in the case of hard core leftists, they were forced into exile or to the margins of society.

Given the dominance of this American-inspired sociocultural reality and ideology, it was only natural that American cultural products moved overseas freely, and steadily penetrated the social body of Greece. Music, movies, dance, cheap romances, spy stories, and other commodities, ranging from clothing to hardware, were the powerful salesmen for the rhetoric of the American way of life. Their typology came to challenge the local reality with a set of new standards that gradually affected not only the taste and needs of the public but also the heterogeneous orientations of local producers and tastemakers. Tempted by the commercial success of the imported cultural products, Greeks started catering to the new petty bourgeois of the urban centers by concocting their own hellenized versions of the American adventure story, love story, and so on. The new Greek-American immigrant even became, in the years between 1950 and 1970, the hero of numerous movies, mainly comedies. His cinematic portrait frequently indicated a particular type of person: successful, rich, cosmopolitan, honest, progressive, open-minded, good-hearted, generous, and a little eccentric and naive. He was placed in the foreground by local filmmakers as an exemplar of the American dream, the person who went "there" and "made it" and now, like another *deus ex machina,* was back home to resolve the family conflicts and restore happiness. In his presence, all visions of "difference" entered the paradigm of "resemblances."

In addition to the direct and/or indirect promotion of America's subcultural products, there were serious publishing houses like Galaxias and Fexis that turned, for the first time, to the cheap paperback format in order to promote and distribute to a wide readership classics of American and European literature. In less than a decade, dozens of major and long neglected American authors were translated into Greek and numerous playwrights had their first Greek productions. William Faulkner, Sherwood Anderson, F. Scott Fitzgerald, Henry Miller, Thornton Wilder, Tennessee Williams, Henry James, Arthur Miller, Lillian Hellman, and Ernest Hemingway entered the canon, gaining visibility and attracting some minimal attention.

Yet unfortunately, the American literary canon, despite its appeal and promising financial prospects, hardly received proper academic and critical attention. The members of the conservative academic community proved unable or unwilling to account for something new and living. United under the umbrella of classical philology, they showed little concern with what most men and women thought, read, or wrote at a particular time. In fact, they showed profound contempt for any form of current literature and theory. Their policy was to keep "true" art insulated from the market in order to resist its commercialization and commodification. Popularity, in their minds, was equated with low quality. For them the classics were the true banner of our communal identity, the reservoir of images and archetypes repeatedly applied to new situations and circumstances. They never tried to see that the new and the unknown could be significant in ways other than those that characterize "normal" and "legitimate" masterpieces. Thus, within the confines of such critical standards, it was inevitable that American literature remained, for quite some time, outside the parameters of the nation's official cultural life.

For decades there was hardly anyone to provide a logical and coherent picture of the literary production of the United States. Greek scholarly and academic acquaintance with American literature was limited to the occasional visits of American authors like Tennessee Williams and Henry Miller to Greece or, more important, to the personal odysseys of artists like George Seferis, Cosmas Pilitis, Karolos Koun, and Marios Ploritis. This small group of interested artists helped make the presence of American authors felt in Greece, in the process widening through international discourse the range of our writing and our understanding of international poetics. It is doubtful, for example, whether Williams would have become a local celebrity and the most influential of foreign playwrights without the sensational theatrical productions mounted by Koun with the help of translations by Ploritis and Nikos Spanias. Without Seferis, neither Eliot nor Pound would have been translated in the thirties and forties, at a time when the romantic poetics of Costis Palamas still reigned supreme. As Yiorgos Savidis says, "It is no shame to admit that . . . without Eliot the development of Seferis would have been much different in the same way that without Seferis the development of our poetry would have also been different."

As already mentioned, neither Seferis nor anyone else involved in the promotion of American literature in Greece was a professional critic or an Americanist. Whatever these people chose to translate and promote was in accord with their personal needs and tastes rather than with a well-organized plan. Their selections were mainly novels, poetry, and plays rather than theory or criticism. That explains, to a certain extent, the schizophrenic trajectory of American literature in Greece. While Eliot's poetry, for example, was translated in the 1930s, the Greek reader had to wait for well over four decades to acquaint himself with Eliot's literary theory. William Carlos Williams, on the other hand, although Eliot's contemporary and an important poet, remained on the margins of Greek discourse for many years. Only after the deterioration of Eliot's poetic influence on the local canon did Williams's "anti-Eliot" aesthetics make its presence felt. And that happened shortly after the discovery of the Williams-inspired Beat poetry in the midseventies.

In short, what I am trying to stress here is that the mode of discourse our "mediating" artists wielded could provide access to one kind of reality only by delimiting some other. And since very few readers had easy access to international bibliographies, people interested in the study of American literature had to rely on their assumptions about what kind of subjects great or marginal American literature discusses, or what values it considers worth emulating. What people read imprinted itself upon the mind of the reader, turning him or her into a part of a particular cultural economy.

Nevertheless, in the early sixties a canonical interpretation of American literature began to emerge not unlike that propagated in American universities. The first amateur critics of American literature seemed to agree that the discourse of Twain, Cooper, Hawthorne, Melville, Emerson, Whitman, Longfellow, Hemingway, and Faulkner embodied what certain Americanists consider the characteristic ideological grounds of American exceptionalism: the distinctive American literary tradition of the romance, the role of the frontier in American imagination, the ideological power of the Puritan covenant, and the consumer culture of the "people of plenty." Andreas Karantonis, for example, a critic whose central role in canonization was analogous to the role of Matthiessen in the United States, described Twain as a true American who expresses the spirit of the frontier at the same time as he propagates a new style of poetics and modern discourse. Like all Americans, the critic observed, Twain respects and reveres his native tradition; yet, he is smart enough not to get caught in it. Any limiting factors or dense patterns of cultural history are playfully subverted and replaced by an Adamic *parole* whose borders are guaranteed no more. Hemingway, on the other hand, is understood to be a unique giant, "just like all the great men of the U.S." The New World, Karantonis noted, "that produced new ideas also produced a new type of writer: the macho-writer, the complete Man-writer," who nowhere manifests himself better than in *The Old Man and the Sea*. As for Whitman, the Greek critic claimed that the American bard of democracy provided us with a spirit of adventure that we, as Europeans, lack. He flirted with the infinite, the open, the untried. His stamina, omnivorous and relentless, moved him and his art beyond the centered cultural activities and institutions to the limitless and everpromising frontier, a movement that in many ways resembles the recent trip to the moon.

In addition to Karantonis there were other critics who used American literature in order to praise the country itself and its democratic ideals. Kostas Papapanos, for example, argued that literary America gave us the image of the *hard worker*, the unsatisfied man who is always trying to better his life, making his living conditions more comfortable by using the teachings of the nation's founding fathers as his guidelines; the *idealist worker* who saved Europe twice from the clutches of anarchy and violence; the *ideologue* who runs from country to country ready to sacrifice his life for the freedom of others; and finally, the *humanist* who taught us a lesson: "Man can be destroyed but not defeated," just like the Old Man of Hemingway.

Limited in quantity and poor in quality, Greek criticism of American literature did nevertheless try to project a particular image of the United States that was no different from the State's rightist rhetoric. The United States was understood to be a country close to paradise where freedom, collective genius, simplicity, romance, the work ethic, and Adamic innocence reigned supreme. Our critics' empiricist appraisals disguised real divisions and serious social problems. America surfaced as a homogeneous, white, middle-class, suburban society of contented consumers who suffered, if at all, from the spiritual malaise of too much consumption. These critics paid little or no heed to the agitations of the 1960s—the antiwar movements, the black freedom movement, and all the other counterculture phenomena—as they likewise paid no heed to the experimentation going on in literature by authors like John Barth, Rochelle Owens, Thomas Pynchon, Allen Ginsberg, LeRoi Jones, Megan Terry, and many others.

It would certainly be very difficult to argue that any *logos* can be so absolute and absorbent as to cover the whole spectrum of cultural activity in any country, nor did it do so in the post–Civil War Greece. Admittedly, there were a few movements that operated clandestinely from within the core of the traditional Left, but they were too unfocused to disrupt the workings of the hegemonic network and its sign-producing mechanisms. Even in the literary field, where there was a concentration of a significant mass of leftists (authors, critics, book distributors, and so on), the movement of ideas was minimal. The few voices that were heard from the Stalinized Marxism of the Communist party were too "loud" to convince anyone, or too deeply committed to the idea of socialist realism to appreciate anything noncommunist. The communist Left usually portrayed the United States as a militarist, aggressive country whose mechanisms "sacrificed every trace of humanism to the altar of its hegemonic and technocratic ambitions," as Depoudis put it. Its monolithic litanies about the "evils of capitalism" were no more convincing than the ethnocentric rhetoric of the official purveyors of democracy.

Whether or not one agrees with the critical readings of this period is not the issue here. The few samples I have chosen are not meant to exhaust the whole spectrum of discourses but rather to show, very briefly, the failure of the Greek critical *logos* to produce an indigenous epistemic structure, a native and well-argued discourse that would question, or at least examine, protected judgments and the teleology of readings and requisite conclusions. By validating the earlier assessments of other critics or by aligning themselves with the order of things manifested in the modes of discourse that the State or a particular ideology approved, local critics isolated themselves from the actual living conditions that lie behind any literary activity, showing, in return, a serious lack of theoretical self-consciousness. It never occurred to them that criticism as such might be a problem. As it never occurred to them that their ideal image of the great literary works, the storehouse of cosmic vision and unaging prophecy, might be in need of some rethinking and original reshuffling.

In sum, what was needed at the time was a *mundus inversus,* an anastrophe of literary "theology" that would open the well-guarded aeolian flasks and produce new possibilities for the rediscovery of the excluded, the reexamination of the slighted or the established, and the recasting of the heretical and noncanonical. In the light of these one can understand why the year 1974 was a historical turning point. It not only signified the restoration of parliamentarism with the collapse of the seven-year dictatorship but it also allowed to surface numerous discourses that ravaged the authority and cultural dominance of those small groups of people whose performative patterns and centered discourse played a disproportionate role in the formation of the local order of things.

The first years following the ousting of the colonels were as erotic and vibrant as they were commercially profitable, fashionable, and inflationary. Those who missed the revolution of the sixties thought that the time had come to separate themselves from that constrictive referent, the preexisting sociocultural matrix, and to develop a new Marcusean sensibility necessary for social change. After years of praising order, younger Greeks felt that they could now rehearse with various forms of disorder. The euphoria of the times obviously favored the radical breakup of the inherited modes of thinking and the moralistic thou-shalt-nots of the past. The Right was, for the first time in its history, pushed to the margins of society. The Left was back, stronger than ever. But as usually happens in analogous cases very few, either from the traditional Left or the New Left, knew what to do with the possibilities of an order divorced from the established referent and from its earlier discursive practices. More leftist intellectuals were dragged into endless debates about political and cultural decolonization and "third worldism" while rushing, at the same time, helter-skelter, to welcome everything that arrived from abroad. Unable to confront the protean reality of the new cultural *ludo*, they gave themselves up to an uncritical consumption of the ready-made diet.

There was no analysis of the channels through which new ideas entered our lives. People simply fell into camps following one rhetoric or another. Even philology lost its academic innocence and embraced the undigested rhetoric of the political platform. The various publishing houses, on the other hand, having for the first time an easier access to the potential public of art and the international book market, did everything they could to impose the spell of commodity fetishism on art, even that art which more than any other challenged the values and traditions of our conservative culture. Within a couple of years the market was flooded with books covering a wide spectrum of discourses including antiauthoritarian texts, espousing feminist, neo-Marxist, structuralist, anarchist, and postmodernist perspectives and values. The question of whether this display window of pluralism and leftist erotics was strategically weighted with particular intellectual risks seemed to concern only a small minority. The majority was simply content to work on the edge, constantly transgressing the "bounds of decency," the tranquilizing schemata of official discourse. For every new, unsettling discovery there were hundreds of ambitious conquistadors ready to invest their money or their names in order to appropriate a promising literary or cultural activity.

This is not to say that I lament a "paradise lost." Far from it. After all, at no other time in the history of Greece has there been such an exciting literary dialogue with such an active readership, such a renewal of earlier practices, and such a total embrace of news. What I wish to stress and criticize here is first, the practice of many inexperienced members of the Greek literary community who, in their effort to cast across the textual plateau their own "progressive" (mis)understanding of literature, often misdirected the urge to encounter foreign literatures, in the process driving the unprotected reader to mangled understandings and unwarranted confusion; and second, our personal failure as intellectuals to connect radical strategies and popular culture in a critical, aesthetic, and political project. In our enthusiasm to overrun the borders of reference and foreground our pluralistic discourse, we created a vacuum into which the dominant social values and practices—profit making, commodification, and consumerism—steadily intruded their shaping powers, in the process robbing the rhetoric of our effort of its arsenal. The problem of course is not new. It had been foreshadowed by Herbert Marcuse who wrote, back in 1964: "The absorbent power of society depletes the artistic dimension by assimilating its antagonistic contents. In the realm of culture, the new totalitarianism manifests itself precisely in a harmonizing pluralism, where the most contradictory works and truths peacefully coexist in indifference." For the last fourteen years we have been confronted by a mass media network that openly co-opts any form of "anti" activity in its search for the new and the marketable. It has come to the point now that it is difficult to discover who is imitating whom. There is no better index to confirm this promising and also deleterious aspect of the new literary liberation than the trajectory of the American novel and poetry in the Greek market, to which I shall now return.

The uninterrupted presence of American culture in Greece suffered a brief setback between 1974 and 1976. Following the collapse of the dictatorship many Greeks blamed the United States for supporting the colonels and the Turkish invasion of Cyprus. Communists, socialists, anarchists, and even a sizable portion of democrats joined their forces against American imperialism. This anti-Americanism, epitomized in the poststructuralist slogan "We belong to ourselves," had as a result the temporary marginalization of the American literary work. Indicative of this is the fact that in that period about twenty American books were translated, mostly nonmainstream, an extremely small number compared to what would follow.

As the decade wound down, however, we witnessed a diminishing of political interest and, as a result, a neutralization of anti-Americanism and a renewed interest in American cultural products. The generation of scholars and artists created by earlier sociopolitical and cultural realities had, by that time, reached retirement age. The younger people, disillusioned by their political and cultural leaders, and disappointed by the inflated rhetoric about decolonization and third worldism, were in need of a new space to express themselves, more diverse and colorful, and less politically oriented. Responding to this shift in perspectives, publishing houses and translators began promoting, en masse, American literary and nonliterary material.

Starting with the translations of Ginsberg and Plath in the midseventies, well over four hundred new titles, fifteen anthologies, hundreds of reworked translations, thousands of cheap romances, and multitudes of mainstream, nonmainstream, and commercial authors entered the Greek market to challenge previous literary histories and reading habits. In the field of drama alone about three hundred plays were produced over a period of fourteen years and numerous American companies and artists were invited to perform and work here. The movie and television industries went even further: they totally embraced American productions. For the first time since 1947 the cultural heritage of the United States was traveling with much speed across the country, reaching a broadly based and heterogeneous audience. Artists like Shepard and Mamet, unknown in the seventies, began gaining visibility as playwrights right after their debuts in the movies. Bukowski, hardly respected a few years ago, has become since the mideighties a best-selling author; and likewise American singers, composers, fashion designers, and others have become best-sellers. The English language, on the other hand, established itself gradually as the nation's most important second language. I know of no other European country that runs so many classes in English. Statistics show that in each four-member family there is at least one student of English, which means one prospective consumer of America's cultural products.

If we accept what Yuri Lotman says about each text containing in itself the image of its audience that actively affects the real audience by becoming for it a normalizing code, we can see that this sudden inflow of American literary material alters the consciousness of the Greek audience by becoming, in some strange and certainly confusing way, the norm for its changing image of itself. To put it another way: postwar American literature powerfully touched the existential space of a significant segment of the Greek readership in such works of fiction as Burroughs's *Naked Lunch, Junkie, The Queer,* and *Ah Pook Is Here!;* Bukowski's *Love Is a Dog from Hell* and *Women;* Vonnegut's *Cat's Cradle* and *Slaughterhouse-Five;* Plath's *The Bell Jar;* Pynchon's *The Crying of Lot 49;* Mailer's *An American Dream* and *Armies of the Night;* Brautigan's *Trout Fishing in America;* Robbins's *Even Cowgirls Get the Blues;* Morrison's *Song of Solomon.* Likewise, the Beat poetry of Ginsberg, Corso, and Ferlinghetti and the drama of Shepard, Rabe, Feiffer, and Mamet penetrated and transformed Greek consciousness. In the poetic space opened up by these artists the Greek reader found fertile ground for sowing his own feelings of entrapment and disillusionment over life. As the Greek poet

Nana Isaia has said, Plath's haunting nightmares and her narrative of despair came to challenge but also enrich the canon of the Greek "Me Generation" at a time when it needed a way out of the "exciting confusion" of the midseventies. It is no exaggeration to claim that after Eliot and Pound no other American discourse has influenced the Greek canon as much as the discourse of anger found in Plath, Ginsberg, Kerouac, and Bukowski. No other contemporary novelist has been so extensively translated as Burroughs, whose novels provide the most extreme expression of anarchic rage in contemporary literature. His reception, like the reception of many contemporary American artists, is an important index to the idiosyncrasies of Greek society in its time of crisis.

While for the Greek reader of two or three decades ago reading American literature was a somewhat guarded search for the typology of the American dream, for the contemporary reader who is more informed, more widely traveled, and more aware of the complexities of the American way of life, such totalizing interpretations can no longer suffice. Today any form of closure undergoes severe questioning. Both the contemporary reader and translator are eager to learn more about the United States and its polymorphous literary performances. America is no longer thought to be just middle class, white or anglophone; it is also seen as Hispanic, native American, black, Greek, female, lower class. It is, in other words, a cultural text cluttered with numerous subtexts, each one trying to strike some form of balance between its marginality and mainstream discourse. Therefore, recently published anthologies like *Fuck You: Underground Poetry* (1982), *Negro Poets* (1982), *American Gay Poetry* (1982), *The Poetry of Indians* (1984), *On the Trail of the Wind* (1984), and *Carriers of the Dream Wheel* (1987), along with recently introduced writers totally ignored by the standard histories of American literature (like the Greek-Americans H. M. Petrakis, Charles Jarvis, Stratis Haviaras, and Nicholas Gage, among others), should be seen as attempts by Greek translators to challenge the rhetoric of the canonical literary history of the United States, to make the unaware readers confront a reality they cannot normally see in their ordinary, day-to-day living. In other words readers, instead of being protected against dissemination, are now driven to a multiplicity of texts and codes where the legitimacy of the canon is no longer the issue. Hemingway's "macho types," Burroughs's "wild boys," Shepard's "transformational characters," Baraka's "angry nationalists," Kazan's "restless immigrants," and

Ellis's "young drifters" are all given a chance to be heard, to have their own audience.

As one cannot find a better example of this promising as well as labyrinthine literary play than in the three anthologies of contemporary American verse recently published by three contemporary Greek poets, a brief summary of their contents is in order. The first anthology, published in 1979 by Alexis Traianos, includes forty-five representative poets of contemporary America, most of them published for the first time in Greek. Among them there are five women (Bishop, Plath, Rich, Sexton, and Wakoski). The second anthology, published four years later by Katerina Angelaki-Rook, reduces Traianos' original selection to nineteen. It drops, among others, Wakoski and Bishop, and adds Ai and Levertov. It introduces Kinnell to the Greek public and keeps Ashbery, Corso, Lamantia, Levine, Lowell, Merwin, Bly, Wright, Simic, Strand, Hugo, and Justice as the "best voices" of contemporary American verse. Finally, the third anthology, assembled by Socrates Skartsis in 1987, increases the number of representative poets to eighty-one. Writers totally unknown to the Greek and, as far as I know, to the American public are anthologized: Brigham, Contoski, Frazer, Raybin, Torregian, Morgan, and many others. Poets in the other two more restricted anthologies are, surprisingly, dropped from this one: Kinnell, for example, and Justice. Older figures like Edna St. Vincent Millay and Emily Dickinson are, curiously, brought back and placed in the context of contemporary poets like Julia Vinograd, Louise Gluck, and others. Finally, Bishop reappears and Ai disappears. Merrill is totally ignored. Charles Olson receives minimal attention while Creeley is highlighted as the major representative of the Black Mountain School.

What is most interesting in these ventures is the significant presence of women poets. Although the anthologists have different notions of excellence and value, the fact that fourteen women are now included in anthologies of modern American verse, as opposed to three (Dickinson, St. Vincent Millay, Moore) in editions published in 1958 and 1962, testifies not only to the increased visibility of women writers in the United States but also to the increase of interest in women's literature in Greece. In the last fifteen years many Greek women poets and novelists have also started moving, or have already moved, toward the center of literary discourse, opening up a new territory that is now in need of new standards of evaluation. Their presence in the midst of a formerly masculine domain not only gives rise to new sets of poetic values but also stands as a challenge to the logic and limits of "phallic" discourse. In the light of this information it is quite understandable why Simone de Beauvoir and Doris Lessing are so popular, as it is equally understandable why the presence of Plath, Rich, and Levertov is felt in almost every anthology and in the majority of literary magazines.

This analysis could clearly be greatly expanded, but these suggestions must suffice; it is hoped that they reveal, at least in a schematic way, the direction in which contemporary American literature in Greece is going. Since 1975 contemporary American literary discourse has enjoyed the strengths and has suffered the weaknesses of our pluralistic modes of operation. At no other time in the past has there been such a dramatic increase in newcomers. Within the last decade or so most of America's major contemporaries have entered the nation's official culture and have attracted serious critical attention. And there is strong indication that there will be more to come. The practice of our mediators has helped close the gap between America's recent art scene and our acquaintance with it. At the same time, however, it has led to an overabundance of formlessness and vulgarization that tends to undermine not only established discourse, but all discourse. The absence of any coherent standards, save the idiosyncratically individual or the commercially profitable, has created a serious vacuum which, unless we try to fill it with a continuing critique of our practices, threatens to envelop all of us.

Having recognized the profusion of literary texts, and the diversity of new approaches generated in contemporary Greece, one may wonder about the role and even presence of classic discourse. What happens to the "great" American books brought to eminence by earlier critics? Have they disappeared as the ideals of the established pedagogy have weakened, as the literary canon has exploded?

If we accept the assumption that repeated translations, references, citations, inclusion on university reading lists, reviews, and articles are indices of value, then we must accept that the American authors celebrated by the classic discourse of past decades show an impressive continuity and stability, both in the market and in academe. The literary magazines of Greece, for example, welcome more and more scholarly articles on classic American authors. With the exception of French literature, no other literature has had as many special issues by local literary magazines as American fiction, poetry, and drama have had in the last five years: a total of fifteen that includes, among others, issues on Hemingway, Poe, Fitzgerald, Steinbeck, Tennessee Williams, Faulkner, Eliot,

and Pound. Another indication of the enduring popularity of the traditional canon is the numerous belated translations that obviously help
close up the gaps in the canon of American literature. *Babbitt,* for example, was translated for the first time in 1976; *Absalom, Absalom!* and *The
Jungle* in 1980; *Light in August* and *U.S.A.* in 1982; and *Sister Carrie* in
1987. One should also point out that many masterpieces translated into
Greek thirty and forty years ago have been reworked and retranslated in
the last fifteen years. *A Farewell to Arms,* for example, translated four
times between 1953 and 1968, was translated five more times in the
years 1971 to 1986. *For Whom the Bell Tolls* was translated five times
between 1947 and 1958 and six times in the years 1971 to 1986. *The Old
Man and the Sea* underwent three translations between 1954 and 1960
and six since 1971. The same phenomenon holds even for the "difficult"
Faulknerian oeuvre: there has been more than one recent translation of
The Sound and the Fury, As I Lay Dying, and others. *The Great Gatsby, Nexus,
Plexus, Sexus, The Grapes of Wrath, A Long Day's Journey into Night, A
Streetcar Named Desire, Leaves of Grass, The Waste Land,* Pound's *Cantos,*
and dozens of other works have been rediscovered by new translators
with new ideas about the problematics of translation, people who still
find in these works not only pleasure but also values worth updating.

If statistics are a reliable gauge of the endurance and modernity of
writers, we can claim that Faulkner, Steinbeck, Pound, Tennessee Williams, Arthur Miller, Twain, Fitzgerald, Henry James, Jack London,
Poe, Hemingway, and O'Neill, among others, are still read and still
considered modern and marketable. Of course, no one can be sure how
long these artists will hold their ground in Greece. After all, it was only a
couple of decades ago that Karantonis thought of Marquand as an
excellent writer; today he has dropped from sight. When cultural activity ceases to inject life into a particular work by looking into it for new
values and possibilities, then inevitably the work loses its vital textuality,
its voice, and becomes just another library item.

What may of course strike the reader of this essay as unorthodox is the
fact that its discussion of literary trends focuses upon the role translators, anthologists, editors, and publishing houses play in canon formation, while it has almost ignored the role of academic institutions and
their contribution to the institutionalization of literature through the
curriculum, methods of teaching, and scholarship.

Founded about thirty-five years ago, the English departments of both
Thessaloniki and Athens (with a present population of thirty-six hun-

dred students and eighty teachers) were for well over twenty-five years under the managerial control of the departments of Classics, the British Council, and the American Cultural centers, unable to set their own independent programs or run their departments in ways they thought best. As a result, these departments remained mere bystanders throughout the fifties, the sixties, and especially the turbulent seventies: they had little access to, and no influence on, the literary game that was under way all around them. Any university activity concerning American literature was conducted either by non-Americanists or simply by enthusiasts with limiting or limited knowledge of American literature, and was hampered further by limited access to updated bibliographies. As the seventies were winding down, however, and enrolled students were swelling to unprecedented numbers, the government removed the departments of English from the managerial control of the departments of Classics; later, the government changed the Chair system, thus allowing more holders of doctorates into academe. These changed policies resulted in the dramatic renewal of university curricula in general and the English departments in particular. It also led to the creation, by the Department of Thessaloniki, of the first American studies program, one launched with new orientations and ambitious future plans. Certainly this freeing of repressed energies will not lead to the elimination of standard texts like *The Sound and the Fury, The Scarlet Letter, Moby-Dick, Benito Cereno, The Sun Also Rises, The Waste Land, A Glass Menagerie,* and others, for they are still an inseparable part of the new syllabus. Now, however, their presence is challenged by the presence of other discourses recently introduced, like Ethnicity and Literature: The Greek-American Paradigm, Ethnic Discourse in American Literature, Afro-American Drama, Underground Theater, and Film Studies.

Most significant of the new courses may be those dealing with writing by women. Despite the fact that 95 percent of the enrolled students and well over 60 percent of the department's professors are women, until recently there were no courses on women's literature. Presently there are six courses available that offer a powerful challenge to conventional male-dominated discourse. A brief survey of these courses is informative of what is occurring in Greek academe at the present moment.

Two courses on contemporary American women writers have as their premise that since 1965 women writers and, more recently, black women writers have produced the best and most important poetry and prose in North America, and perhaps throughout the English-speaking world. One course examines writers like Paula Marshall, Toni Morrison, Gloria

Naylor, Joyce Carol Oates, Adrienne Rich, Alice Walker, and the Canadian Margaret Atwood; the other concentrates on Maya Angelou, Gwendolyn Brooks, Rita Dove, Nikki Giovanni, and Audre Lorde. A third course examines the characterization of women and gender in drama by examining the sociopolitical conditions in which that drama was written and performed. Yet another course on fictional autobiography investigates gendered self-reference from Charlotte Brontë to Maxine Hong Kingston. A course in feminist poetics proposes that the confrontation of academic feminism and poststructuralist discourse has resulted in a radical deconstruction of patriarchal language, while at the same time recognizing the resistance of black, lesbian, and Marxist feminists to a theoretical organization as a weapon of male hegemony. These new courses insist that women and other marginal groups no longer be "colonized" voices, that they cease being heard only on the periphery of mainstream discourse. Women are seen as subjects of history as well as men.

The idea of literature has changed radically all over the world in the last two decades, in approaches to the text, author, meaning, circulation, production, and consumption. What our departments have lately realized is that, to be useful at all, they have to keep pace with these new discourses. The controlling authorial intentions, the solidifying references and representations that guided earlier Greek critics and professors through the paths of literary discourse, no longer provide the same reassurance. Literature has to be rethought in the light of the new developments, so that new possibilities for defining a literary canon—especially a foreign one—and its present utility emerge.

One cannot help noticing the efforts of local Americanists to find new contexts to guide the reader through the perplexing network of American literature. Studying the effects of the commodity form on culture, or how ideology mediates between texts and institutions, or how the authority fetish sets boundaries on future action—all emergent perspectives in contemporary Greece—both questions many ideas deeply rooted in our former understanding of American literature and challenges earlier practices. Furthermore, the fact that the American way of life is neither rejected nor celebrated, but simply reexamined in good faith is a positive sign. It points toward a more constructive dialogue between foreign texts and their local recipients. It creates new possibilities for the formulation of a native critical *logos* that will certainly strengthen us in the teaching and promotion of foreign literature.

This is not to claim that the emergence of this young "Americanist managerial class" is any form of instant panacea. There is still anarchy and confusion in the field. Yet the fact that there is now scholarly criticism of American literature united by a set of questions rather than by a set of answers is promising; also the fact that more and more Americanists are asked to work as advisors for publishing houses that specialize in American literature is probably the first step toward a more organized and informed introduction of American literature in Greece. During this exciting period when the reexamination and reorganization are beginning, however, the contours of our literary activities will remain unclear, their geographical boundaries unspecified, and their ability to gain access to the magic of foreign signifiers unpredictable.

᷂

The Counterlife
Israeli Perspectives on American Literature

HANA WIRTH-NESHER

To live in Israel is to be reminded regularly that one inhabits a failed paradise, that one is banished from Eden. Few societies have had such messianic expectations of their new nation; few communities have felt so deeply the pangs of a lost utopia. Only a society that has enormous dreams for itself could be so utterly devastated when men and women appear to be merely human. Unless perhaps this is always so for a newly independent nation whose political independence has been accompanied by a social and cultural revolution. This was the case for Zionism, and this was the case for the United States of America. In both enterprises, sacred and secular time converged as the founders believed the new nation to be fulfilling a divinely ordained destiny. The continuing quest in Israel for a national literature had its parallels in an earlier stage of America's development, and this affinity accounts for some of the deep interest in American literature among Israelis.

Before pursuing the place of American literature in the Israeli consciousness, it is important to place contemporary Israeli attitudes toward American literature in a historical context. Most pertinent in the historical framework is that the majority of the first Jewish settlers in Palestine were from Eastern Europe. Moreover, Zionism itself was in large part an Eastern European socialist movement, with its roots in Russian culture. The major waves of immigrants in the early part of the century, the founders of the infrastructure of the new state, were to a great extent from Russia and Poland, with a minority from Germany and the Austro-Hungarian Empire, the home of Zionism's ideological father, Theodore Herzl. As a result, the most powerful secular cultural forces in the nascent state were Russian, a fact reflected in Israeli folklore, music, theater, and literature. Translations of Dostoevsky and Tolstoy were the mainstay of literary life in the new settlement, to the extent that a heavily Russian-accented Hebrew was a requirement on the stage of Habimah, Israel's national theater. Hebrew writers tended to derive their literary models from Russian authors, with the exception of pockets of resettled German Jews who continued to prefer Heine.

English language and culture were nevertheless present in Palestine in the form of an occupying force under the British Mandate. Although the English were regarded as a colonial power that had to be resisted and overthrown, they left their mark. Until recently, demonstrated knowledge of Shakespeare was required on the high school matriculation examinations, and the only officially sanctioned pronunciation for the schools and the media was British.

Both Russian and British cultural influences began to decline in the late 1950s and 1960s, the Russian as news of the Stalin purges embittered even the most orthodox members of kibbutzim, as the emigrants from Eastern Europe grew older, and as the Six-Day War brought about the severing of political ties with the Eastern bloc. The dominance of the United States as a source of political protection and economic aid diminished the British influence. The image of the ugly American began to give way to the fact of America the benefactor, accompanied by an interest in American culture which has been increasing from year to year. Major literary journals have sponsored special issues of translations of contemporary American literature, and each publication is accompanied by significant media coverage. Jewish-American literature is of particular interest, of course: the death of Bernard Malamud in 1986 occasioned a special program on prime time television on the phenomenon of Jewish literature in America; Haifa University sponsored a three-day conference on Saul Bellow that same year.

As Israel continues to be a country of immigration, American literature in Israel is taught largely by emigrants, often from English-speaking countries. To cite Tel Aviv University as only one example, Pound and Eliot are taught by a former Australian; Dos Passos, Twain, and Alice Walker by former Americans; Poe by a former Russian; Bellow by a former Briton; and Whitman, Hawthorne, and Faulkner by native Israelis with some training in American universities. It is difficult to discuss an indigenous approach to American literary studies, given the fact of such diversity of countries of origin or education. As a young, developing, and very small country, Israel has neither the critical mass nor the resources to support very much doctoral study in English or

American literature. Therefore, most of the faculty teaching American literature in Israel today are either American immigrants or native Israelis who studied in America at some stage of their careers. Furthermore, the teaching of American literature as a separate tradition is a more recent development than the teaching of English literature, in part because the founders of English literature departments in Israel tended to be British or British-trained, and their attitudes were decidedly Anglophile. A curious phenomenon, for example, is that Israeli scholars have produced a significant corpus of critical studies of Henry James, yet in very few cases do these works treat James as an American writer. Instead, he is treated as either a Christian moralist, in the Arnoldian or Leavisite tradition, or as a formal innovator, in the tradition of Prague formalism and structuralism. American literature is taught in each of the five major universities, and there are at least two full-time Americanists in each of these departments. In addition to courses in American literature in the departments of English, American texts are also studied in translation in departments of comparative literature and in American studies programs in Jerusalem and Tel Aviv.

The American literary canon taught in the Israeli university classrooms, therefore, reflects a familiarity with current trends in American literary scholarship and does not differ significantly from the teaching of American literature in the United States. At the introductory level, students are presented with a wide range of authors and critical approaches, including women and Afro-American writers who have only recently been accorded a place in American literary anthologies and literary histories. At the advanced level, budgetary constraints in recent years have prevented libraries from amassing significant collections of minority and women writers, so that seminar and term papers still tend to focus on more traditional figures in American literature.

Furthermore, even before students reach the university, they are exposed to American literature with the mandatory reading lists distributed by the Ministry of Education to prepare high school students for their matriculation exams. In place of the Shakespearean plays which were the sine qua non of these examinations a generation ago, today teachers and students may choose from a list of texts, of which Shakespeare's dramas are only one option. For the past several years the majority of the authors on this national reading list are American; among them are Baldwin, Malamud, Steinbeck, Thurber, Dorothy Parker, Philip Roth, Stephen Crane, Flannery O'Connor, Frost, Tennessee Williams, Susan Glaspell, and Arthur Miller. The only British writers of fiction are Joyce and Lawrence, and the only other English writers apart from Shakespeare are two Irishmen, Shaw and Beckett. Predictably, authors enshrined in an official Ministry of Education syllabus continue to maintain a place in the readerly canon, but not always in the scholarly and academic one as well. Arthur Miller has enjoyed great popularity among Israeli readers and theatergoers but not so in the university classroom, whereas the opposite has been true for Henry James, who enjoys continuing prominence in the university curriculum but is not widely read despite available translations. The presence of Glaspell, Roth, and Baldwin is testimony to Israeli awareness of an American literary canon that has begun to include women, Jews, and blacks, all of these authors having been added to the mainstream white male literary tradition sometime in the 1960s and 1970s.

In several cases, it is worth noting the particular choice of texts. For example, Arthur Miller's play *All My Sons*, which is read widely and has been studied in the high schools for at least the past twenty years, is the story of an arms manufacturer whose defective products may have been responsible for the deaths of many of his country's soldiers. Although he has been exonerated by the courts, the shadow of guilt haunts his life as does the fact that his own son is missing in action. Apart from its wartime theme, which is all too familiar to Israelis, the play raises questions about collective guilt, loyalty to the community, and sacrifices of sons by their fathers. As these themes are echoed in indigenous Israeli literature, it is not surprising to find this play inscribed in the Israeli curriculum. Of equal interest is a story like Philip Roth's "Eli the Fanatic," which treats satirically the attempts of an assimilated upper-middle-class Jewish community in suburban America to deny its Jewish identity. When Eli Peck finally dons the black caftan of the religious Holocaust survivor, he is branded by the traumatic history of the Jews, accepting as his own the same collective destiny that has shaped and continues to shape Israeli consciousness. These are both clear instances of texts that speak directly to Israeli educators, although their readings of these works are molded by their own experiences rather than by those of the American authors and their public.

Most of the classic American texts are available in translation, including many abridged children's versions which remain popular, such as *The Adventures of Huckleberry Finn, The Adventures of Tom Sawyer, Uncle Tom's Cabin,* and *Little Women.* Since mandatory reading lists for English language and literature matriculation exams are identical for both the Hebrew and the Arabic school system, Israeli Arabs tend to be familiar with, and readers of, the same American literature as that of Hebrew-speaking Israelis. Moreover, many of the books that have been translated into Hebrew have been translated into Arabic as well, among the most popular being works by Hemingway, Steinbeck, Faulkner, and Hawthorne, as well as the popular novels of Pearl Buck, Harold Robbins, and Howard Fast.

American literature has not only become a pervasive presence in the educational system, it has also begun to influence the works of indigenous Israeli writers, just as Russian culture once did. In the fictions of Amos Oz and A. B. Yehoshua, for example, Faulkner's works are a dominant force both in literary strategies, particularly the multiple narrative point of view and the Gothic strain, and in theme. Faulkner's investigations of the place of the individual faced with the tragic burden of history, of one group identity threatening that of another, are compelling for both Jewish and Arab novelists, and for their readers. Yehoshua has acknowledged his debt to Faulkner, in part through his gratitude to translators of Faulkner's works into Hebrew; likewise the Arab Israeli writer Ghassan Knfani has acknowledged his debt to Faulkner in *The Return to Haifa*. Furthermore, literary critics in Israel have noted the imprint of Eliot and Pound on Nathan Zach, of Lowell and Ginsberg on Meir Wieseltier, of Wallace Stevens on Dan Pagis and Ted Carmi. Simon Halkin's landmark translation of *Leaves of Grass* in 1952 has had a profound effect on Israeli literature, in part because the spirit of folk revival and egalitarianism and the interweaving of the personal and the national voice seeking to create a new social order struck familiar chords among Israeli poets in a postrevolutionary society aiming for a national renaissance often linked with the visions of Labor Zionism. The influence of Walt Whitman on Uri Zvi Greenberg, for example, is the subject of a course at Everyman's University. More recently, translations of Raymond Carver have been received enthusiastically by Israeli writers; Nathan Zach's translation of Allen Ginsberg's "Kaddish" this past year received nationwide attention; and a long-awaited translation of Plath will undoubtedly leave its mark on Israeli poetry.

When it comes to the influence and the study of American literature in Israel, the single most significant factor is that the country is a society of immigrants in the process of forging a national identity. The diversity of countries of origin in a society based on an ingathering of exiles is a major factor in Israel's attempts to define its *own* national literature. The creation of a national literature where it cannot simply be taken for granted in an evolutionary sense also has a bearing on attitudes toward the national literature of America, another society which self-consciously fashioned for itself a literary tradition that would set it apart from other canons. Research conducted in Israel on American literature often seems inspired by just such parallels, so that it is not surprising to find an interest in historical romance in American literature, on the question of how a nation conceives of its history one or two generations removed from its founding. This sensibility lends an air of immediacy to Israeli readings of Emerson, Jefferson, and Hawthorne. Moreover, as Israel's sense of its own destiny is shaped by both secular and religious forces, so that sacred history is part of its national symbology, Israeli students of American literature are drawn to the early stages of the nation, to the two strains of Puritan sacred historiography and democratic humanism.

Israel's status as a multicultural country of immigrants where many of the university faculty engaged in teaching American literature are themselves emigrants from English-speaking countries has meant that American studies in Israel differ little from American studies in the United States. Yet, Israeli concern in one area of American literature is atypical, and that is the approach to Jewish-American writing, because it casts Israeli cultural questions into stark perspective. For Israeli students of American literature, the question of how Jewish-American literature fits into the American canon is inextricably interwoven with the question of what constitutes Jewish literary history. The definition of Jewish literature is a prerequisite for meaningful discussion of both Jewish-American and Israeli literature.

The discussion of what constitutes an Israeli literary canon has its roots in the multilingual experience of the Jewish people in the Diaspora and the *kulturkampf* between Yiddish and Hebrew, between universalism and nationalism, between secularism and religion. As the definition of a Jew continues to be a source of contention in Israel, so the definition of a distinctively Jewish literature is equally contentious. Attempts to define an Israeli literature have had to come to terms with Jewish culture, and these various positions regarding a national canon have a bearing on the reception of American literature as well.

Three models of literary self-definition in Israel will suffice to demonstrate its diversity. The first, formulated by the poet Yonatan Ratosh, is a plea for differentiating Hebrew literature from Jewish literature, including Jewish literature written in the Hebrew language. According to Ratosh, Jewish literature had always been multilingual and concerned with Jewish religion and the fate of Jewish people. Because it lacked national territory, a shared national history, and one national language, it had always been and would continue to be a literature of immigrants. For Ratosh, the new national literature must be written by self-declared Hebrews, not by Jews, and this nascent Hebrew nation now sharing a common territory would constitute a radical break with Diaspora Jewish cultural life. Respect would continue to be accorded to the Hebrew works in the Jewish tradition, as long as one understood that they were not part of the new canon of Hebrew national literature. The goal of the national literature would be the liberation of the Hebrews, children of the homeland, from the value system of the Jewish generation of immigrants.

In contrast, the only viable national literature envisioned by Baruch Kurzweil was one that located itself on the continuum of the traditional religious Jewish way of life. Kurzweil's canon of literature for the new nation consisted of writers in whose works he perceived a longing for an earlier spiritual world and an acute skepticism about the secular culture born of Zionism. For Kurzweil, the new Hebrew literature advocated by Ratosh was national suicide bred by deliberate amnesia. The only literature worth sanctioning in the national canon were works that documented Jewish culture and literature "in terms of a myth of a lost paradise."

Finally, Dov Sadan attempted a synthesis of these two in his conviction that the new national literature would go beyond the modern secular experiment by returning to and adapting the old religious tradition. For Sadan, modern Jewish literature consisted of several elements, among them a national literature but also Jewish literature in many European languages. But the latter was doomed to extinction, and only the literatures of Jewish languages would eventually compose one corpus. National redemption for Sadan would mean the union of the secular national consciousness with the Jewish spirit from which it had emerged.

These three models of national self-definition are significant in several respects. First of all, a generation or more removed from the war of independence and the founding fathers and mothers, Israel finds itself in a position similar to that of America in the early nineteenth century as it attempted to define for itself a culture independent from that of its mother country, England. Emerson's words of warning that the success of the national experiment cannot be taken for granted strike a responsive chord among an Israeli readership, and his plea for a separation from the past also finds a sympathetic listener: "We have listened too long to the courtly muses of Europe." But when Emerson defined the

American scholar by upholding the primacy of the sanctified self, his one strong voice gave expression to the national cultural identity: "Our day of independence, our long apprenticeship to the learning of other lands, draws to a close." As is evident, Israel, with its competing models of what makes up its national literature, has not found one such voice. There is interest, then, in America's quest for its own Americanness at the time that its founding fathers died, a situation parallel to Israel's own; yet there is also awareness of the greater diversity of voices vying for the soul of the new nation.

To understand how such theories of national cultural self-definition influence the perception of Jewish-American literature in Israel, one needs first to examine prevailing attitudes on the same subject in the United States. Most definitions of Jewish-American literature by American critics since the early 1950s have been attempts to assimilate a set of texts into the established definitions of the *American* canon. Taking their cues from Mathiessen, R. W. B. Lewis, Chase, and other scholars who offered theories about the distinctiveness of American literary history and culture, these critics at times portrayed Jewish-American literature as if it were the very archetype of American literature, the very essence of the majority culture. If American literature is perceived to be essentially revolutionary, the Jewish-American literature is identifiable when a Jewish writer shows an "ultimate concern" in creating a wholly new structure of belief. According to Irving Malin, it would seem that a religious impulse linked with individualism and antitraditionalism is the mark of Jewishness. That would make Emerson a model of Jewish-American writing. If the essence of American literature is located in transcendentalism, then critics have argued that Jewish-American writers are "crusaders hoping for a transcendent ideal."

Continuing in this religious vein, some critics, in order to achieve a place in the center for Jewish-American literature, have portrayed Jewishness as the very essence of America's major religion, Christianity: Theodore Solotaroff, for example, identified as distinctively Jewish the theme of suffering leading to purification. In the works of Bellow, Malamud, and Roth, he observed "conversion into the essential Jew, achieved by acts of striving, sacrificing, and suffering for the sake of some fundamental goodness and truth in one's self that has been lost and buried." Variations abound of this strategy of accommodating a minority literature to existing mainstream frameworks. If American literature is perceived as containing regional literatures as part of its canon, then Irving Howe, for example, categorizes Jewish-American writing as such a regional literature, similar to that of the American South. For those critics subscribing to the melting pot theory of American culture in the Diaspora, Jewish-American literature is defined as a transient social and historical phenomenon, a documentation of the immigrant Jew's conversion to other passions—communism, capitalism, and secularization. For Allen Guttmann, assimilation into the American dominant culture was inevitable and imminent.

Finally, moral perspectives often dominated beginning with Malin and Stark's landmark essay in 1964 which depicts the Jew as an existential hero and a modern Everyman, who, by virtue of his victimization and suffering is an apt symbol for all of humankind. Robert Alter, consistently a dissenter regarding these models of Jewish literature, has argued that it makes no real sense to speak of "the Jewishness of a writer who neither uses a uniquely Jewish language, nor describes a distinctively Jewish milieu, nor draws upon literary traditions that are recognizably Jewish."

These differing concepts of a corpus of Jewish literature, and more specifically Jewish-American literature, then, affect which works will be included in the canon. In America, the moralistic model would be more inclusive, while the sociological one would limit Jewish-American literature to that literature which deals exclusively with the question of immigration and assimilation. In the recent *Harvard Guide to Contemporary Writing*, Marc Shechner is most inclusive in his survey of a canon he simply refuses to define. He admits that neither Jewish writer nor Jewish fiction is an obvious or self-justifying subdivision of literature, and therefore he claims that in his chapter on that subject he is chronicling a "historical fact"—that many American novelists happen to be Jews—and that the concept of the Jewish writer is a "convenient shorthand for a feature of the literary consensus that we want to examine but are not yet prepared to define."

This inclusiveness is a far cry from the models of Jewish literature developed in Israel, which are considerably more precise and limiting in their definitions of Jewish-American literature. A few examples from Israeli scholars will suffice. Taking up Kurzweil's metaphysical and religious approach to the definition of Israeli and Jewish literature, Harold Fisch has devoted much of his research to identifying Jewish archetypes as they emerge from historical experience. As a result, he can deny Philip Roth a place in the canon of Jewish literature because he replaces the Jewish father with a Jewish mother that Fisch claims is not authentically Jewish at all, but rather the product of "western Emancipated

Jewry." According to Fisch, the traditional Jewish mother from the Bible and down the centuries is the one "who heroically severs the umbilical cord," and he cites Sarah, Rebecca, and Hannah as examples. Abraham Cahan, on the other hand, belongs in the tradition, for while his David Levinsky wanders far from the Jewish patriarchal home, he nevertheless remains true to the "kindred points of heaven and home." The domination of the mother, Fisch claims, is at bottom a gentile disease. In his search for what he terms authentic Jewish patterns, he takes Kurzweil's lead and applies it to Jewish literature in languages other than Hebrew. Hence, his decidedly more exclusive canon.

Like Ratosh, but descriptive and scientific rather than prescriptive and ideological, Itamar Even-Zohar claims that the only unequivocal criterion for determining what is the national literature, that is Israeli Hebrew literature, is territorial. Hebrew literature in pre-Israeli periods is multiterritorial and a "multiple false polysystem" because it existed in a literary symbiosis with other Jewish literatures such as Yiddish, where the other literature usually functioned as the noncanonized system. This is because no one language in the multilingual Jewish community was sufficient to express all aspects of the speakers' lives. In a multilingual situation "where Hebrew functioned only for a part of the linguistic necessities of the Jewish community," Even-Zohar argues it is possible to speak of "Jewish literature" which is the outgrowth of linguistic symbiosis. Thus, writers like Shalom Aleikhem are members of a multilingual Jewish literature, but *not* Saul Bellow or even Isaac Bashevis Singer in whose works this linguistic symbiosis is no longer evident. In short, there can be no such thing as Jewish-American literature unless there is multilingual symbiosis: "Only a nationalistic Jewish approach, or a racist anti-semitic one, or ignorance . . . would adopt the term 'Jewish literature' on the basis of the origin of writers. It is not enough that a writer be a Jew or even use a 'Jewish' language to entitle us to speak of a Jewish literature." Even-Zohar would see the Kurzweil-Fisch metaphysical approach as essentially imperialistic and imprecise. He would undoubtedly relegate Shechner's to the province of the ignorant and even racist.

Yet another significant model from Israeli scholarship that has a bearing on defining Jewish-American literature is that of Benjamin Harshav (Hrushovski), whose view is more synthetic, in that it is not as exclusively territorial as that of Even-Zohar, nor as exclusively religious and metaphysical as that of Harold Fisch. Harshav's original work in the general area of poetics and semiotics has led him to an attempt to define a Jewish semiotics, both thematically and structurally. The roots of this, with regard to modern Jewish literature, he locates in the semiotics of Yiddish communication which he claims was internalized in "Jewish" behavior and is evident in a writer like Saul Bellow. The core of such a Jewish semiotics is in a "profusion of questions and associative composition." In his search for what is most innovative in Jewish literature, Harshav creates a model that is international, multilingual, and cultural. But it is still far more exclusive than the broad models suggested by Jewish-American literary critics.

Harshav's contribution to the ongoing debate about Jewish-American literature, while it is similar to the work of scholars already discussed who draw smaller and more provocative circles around the canon drawn by American critics, is also markedly different from their strict setting of boundaries. Harshav is in the unique position of actually adding works to that tradition through drawing attention to neglected Jewish-American writers who should be canonized, namely American poets who wrote in Yiddish. In his landmark bilingual anthology, *American Yiddish Poetry,* Harshav introduces the American reader to an aspect of what he argues is his own diverse cultural heritage. Among the poems written by poets unknown to an American audience such as A. Leyeles, Jacob Glatshteyn, Moshe-Leib Halpern, Joseph Teller, and H. Leyvik are titles which indicate their resolutely American subjects: "New York," "Manhattan Bridge," "Subway," "Madison Square," "On Broadway," "In Central Park," "New York in a Jewish Mood," "To America," and "Meditation at Stuyvesant Church." Harshav writes: "From an American perspective, Yiddish poetry must be seen as an unjustly neglected branch of American literature, a kaleidoscope of American experience and art entombed in yellowing, crumbling books, in the muteness of its own dead language. . . . They were our cousins, a branch of the same evolutionary tree that came to a dead end, a bough that bloomed and withered away by a quirky twist of history."

To cite one example of the Yiddish poetry that Harshav identifies as American literature, J. L. Teller's "New York in a Jewish Mood," written after the Second World War, sets the American myth of a New Canaan seen as both a refuge and a utopian dream against the origin of that metaphor in Jewish history, the children of the desert gazing at the land of Canaan but being denied entry. Teller reinterprets America in the context of both ancient and recent Jewish history, seeing America as simultaneously the modern hope which fulfills the myth of a promised land and as a pagan betrayer of the Jewish people, a nation whose locked doors precluded escape from the Holocaust and made that modern hope empty. New York is conflated with the European city, emptied of Jews, just as the Christian/American New Canaan is conflated with the Jewish historical one. Here, the poet's view of his America is clearly haunted by his Jewish identification with the victims of Nazism.

In summary, Israeli scholars with divergent backgrounds, such as Even-Zohar, Fisch, and Harshav, have offered diverse theories for defining Jewish-American literature; each theory, of course, generates a different canon, canons that can be distinguished from those prevalent among American critics.

Despite this diversity of definitions of Jewish-American literature among both American and Israeli scholars, it is possible to trace a larger pattern. The American critics have tended toward greater vagueness, mystery, and inclusiveness in their concepts, perhaps because they are speaking out of a Jewish culture that is greatly attenuated. Thus, their claims for Jewish-American literature are often very broad, such as the religious identity of the author, some mysterious self-explanatory genre based on consensus, or some thematic concern that is consciously moralistic, often stressing victimization as a Jewish theme. Israeli critics, speaking out of a culture that is in its early stages of formation, tend to focus on conscious acts of collective identity that measure themselves against familiar traditions, that are always aware of the alternative route, of what Philip Roth has called a "counterlife." Each literary history and canon is a reflection of the prevailing story of that branch of Jewish history, whether that narrative is moving toward assimilation into another culture or conscious separation from that alien culture in the work of nation-building.

Let me explore this notion of the counterlife as a framework for regarding Jewish-American literature. I will proceed not in order to provide an answer to the problems facing contemporary critics of Jewish-American literature, but to suggest the kinds of intrinsic concerns, the range of literary texts, and the sense of national involvement that characterize the state of contemporary Israeli scholarship in American literature. Moving from a more general consideration to a specific instance of the phenomenon of the counterlife, the instance of Philip Roth, this analysis should provide, in addition to a specimen of the specific density of contemporary Israeli criticism, an example of the manner in which Israeli concerns provide a basis and framework for other nations' or cultures' explorations of the relations between the national and the ethnic, between cultural identity and subcultural diversity.

It seems to me that self-conscious Jewish writers, when they write in non-Jewish languages, often feel the need to define for themselves an alternative literary tradition, one apart from that of the language in which they are writing. The literary symbiosis referred to by Even-Zohar with regard to multilingual situations is equally true for multicultural situations, where no one culture is sufficient for the needs of writers to express their vision. And there is often a recognition of what Robert Frost referred to as "the road not taken," the past choices which have determined in some irrevocable manner the course of the present. The choice to portray or suggest a counterlife, then, results from a triple desire: the need to recognize a past which has been submerged or denied by the imperatives of assimilation, the need for a literary and psychological enrichment which replicates the heterogeneity of actual cultural life, and the need to acknowledge that sense of loss which accompanies the knowledge that what one is has been purchased at the cost of rejecting what one is no longer.

When American writers actually have some knowledge of an alternative Jewish literary tradition, in Hebrew or in Yiddish, they locate their own works between the traditions. This can express itself in allusions to the other tradition, not only by linguistic borrowings through incorporation of phrases from the other language, but also by allusions to the other tradition or borrowing models and types from the other canon. Just as Yiddish poets in America also located themselves in the line of Whitman and Emerson, so a writer like Henry Roth, composing in the English language, draws on quotations from Jewish sources, intersperses Yiddish words, and turns his characters into types within two cultural frames of reference. In the last chapter of *Call It Sleep,* for example, the mob of Jews in the street is cast as pogrom victims, ancient Hebrews, and "the huddled masses" of immigrants to America. Moreover, the immediate environment is transformed into a mythic cityscape that intertwines Jewish and Christian traditions, with the redemptive theme presented as both the Passover and Easter stories simultaneously. Thus are the two strands, Roth's American life and his Jewish/Yiddish counterlife, spun into one imaginative thread.

In the writings of Saul Bellow, to cite another example, the alternative tradition is evident in the intellectual repertoire of his central protagonists, who repeatedly evoke European figures as predecessors, muses, and mentors. Just as Augie March is solidly in the tradition of Huckleberry Finn, Herzog and Sammler are children of Montaigne and Dostoevsky, of continental European thought and letters. The awkward Jew,

Asa Leventhal, confronts his counterlife in the person of the white Anglo-Saxon Protestant Allbee, while the assimilated Tommy Wilhelm confronts his in Dr. Tamkin, that comically exaggerated portrait of the European humanist.

In some cases it is the language itself of the other tradition that haunts the English prose, so that in the stories of Delmore Schwartz, for example, the English reads like a translation from the Yiddish, and reveals the text's linguistic counterlife. In Cynthia Ozick's "Envy, Or Yiddish in America," to name yet another variation, the imminent extinction of Yiddish language and culture is the very subject of the story, as the Yiddish writer is left wholly dependent on translation itself to assure some precarious survival.

In each of the above works, what marks the text as an example of Jewish literature is its emphasis on an explicit or implicit counterlife, on a divided identification with more than one culture. Jewish identity itself is a matter of eternal dispute and inner divisions, of nationalism and religion, of language and morality, of contradictions that the Jewish state has not resolved and has perhaps even exacerbated. Jewish literature reflects that double vision and allegiance. It is possible to argue, of course, that *all* American literature is ethnic literature of one type or another, identifying with the project of the new American culture, but also measuring that against another cultural tradition from which that group originates, against the road not taken. Hawthorne's novels could be read as ethnic literature measuring the American experiment against the home country, and in Frost's terms, foregoing one road irrevocably and taking the one "less traveled by." But Jewish-American literature is about the attempt to go down one road while simultaneously walking along the other in the imagination, to experience the genuine counterlife.

An especially intriguing case of Jewish literature as a corpus exploring what he calls a counterlife is to be found in the work of Philip Roth, whose fiction is followed closely in Israel. Because he is not well versed in Hebrew or Yiddish language and literature, Roth re-creates, in fictional texts, an alternative tradition centered on Jewish literary figures with whom he identifies. In this respect he is similar to writers in other groups, such as Virginia Woolf in *A Room of One's Own* or Alice Walker in *In Search of Our Mothers' Gardens,* who have felt the need to locate their work in an alternative tradition, one that has not often been documented and has therefore needed to be imagined and reconstructed fictively. Beginning with his story "Eli the Fanatic," in which an American suburban Jew dons the black caftan of a Holocaust survivor, Roth has consistently exposed the discomfort of the complacent Jewish-American writer who feels compelled to identify with his people's history of persecution, but who cannot honestly appropriate it as his subject matter.

Philip Roth has played out the fantasy of the road not taken to a degree unrivalled by any other Jewish-American writer. One strategy for his achieving this is to cancel out recent Jewish history by taking figures like Kafka and Anne Frank down the road not taken by them, but familiar to Roth, namely immigration to America. By rescuing Kafka and placing him on his own turf in New Jersey in "I Always Wanted You to Admire My Fasting; or Looking at Kafka," Roth can seemingly deny the awesome scale of European history that dwarfs Jewish-American experience and thus his own comic renderings of family dramas and adolescent problems, while simultaneously emphasizing that history and underscoring the moral and artistic quandary of the comic Jewish writer in America. In this, and in other works, Roth has clearly identified Kafka as a literary father, as the center of that alternative tradition in which he locates his works. In an even more ironic twist in this alternative tradition strategy, Roth has identified a surviving Anne Frank as his literary contemporary. In Nathan Zuckerman's fantasy in *The Ghost Writer,* Anne Frank remains incognito, even at the price of preventing a reunion with her father, because she is convinced that knowledge of her survival would diminish the power of her art. Accused as a betrayer of the Jewish people by his readers just like his author-creator Philip Roth, Nathan fantasizes marrying Anne Frank, the Jewish saint, as the ultimate validation of his career and his acquittal by the Jewish community. Instead he joins Anne Frank, the artist, in the ranks of those writers who have sacrificed familial bonds for the sake of their art. In the case of Kafka and Anne Frank, Roth explores the counterlife by bringing these icons in Jewish culture and history to *his* path, by reinventing them fictively and thus identifying himself with them, while simultaneously treating such fantasies on the part of his protagonists with irony, moralism, and wit.

In the epilogue to *Zuckerman Bound,* "The Prague Orgy," Roth does the opposite; his artist protagonist takes the road to Prague in order to retrieve the imperiled manuscripts of a Yiddish writer who was shot by a member of the Gestapo. Here the Jewish-American writer protagonist takes on the mission of rescuing one of his literary fathers and in so doing, reconstructing a lost literary tradition. This epilogue becomes an allegory for the strategy of retrieval of the alternate canon and of the literary symbiosis characteristic of Jewish-American writing. The epilogue is haunted by three literary fathers—Kafka, Roth's literary alter ego whose uncertain identification with his own Jewishness and comic treatment of alienation is most compatible with Roth's sensibility; Henry James, Roth's American predecessor, whose self-consciousness about the place of the artist in society and preoccupation with the interpretation and misinterpretation of fictional texts influenced Roth's exploration of the same motif ("The Prague Orgy" is a Jewish variation on *The Aspern Papers*); and Sisovsky, the *fictional* lost Yiddish author whose absence haunts the post-Holocaust Jewish writer. The epilogue draws on Roth's recurring theme of trading places, as Sisovsky's son remains in America while Zuckerman goes off to Prague to rescue the papers. In doing so, he must finally skirt real danger when he is arrested as a Zionist agent, and the shoebox full of manuscripts is confiscated. Momentarily realizing what it could mean to have political forces shape and jeopardize his life, Zuckerman flees from the road not taken for the safety of the Jewish homeland, which for him is the "construction of narratives out of the exertions of survival." Thus Roth takes the quest for an alternative and lost literary tradition to its limits in the emblem of the Jewish-American writer returning the fictive documents of a fictive writer because the risk entailed in the act of retrieval is martyrdom.

In a more recent book, *The Counterlife,* Roth translates this motif of the road not taken and the alternate tradition into a postmodern play of sophisticated ontological games, as writer, text, and characters infiltrate each others' spaces. In the novel he also boldly situates Israel as the counterlife for American Jewry, thus reversing the Israeli interest in America as *its* counterlife. Perhaps what makes Roth so intriguing to Israeli readers is the way that he has presented them with a mirror image of their own preoccupations, as he seeks his own identity by measuring it against an imaginary counterlife in Israel, just as Israelis are in the process of carving out a new collective identity measured against a variety of former counterlives in the Diaspora and the counterlife that remains possible for them, if only imaginatively, in an assimilationist America. And in the same vein, Israelis are attracted to those American writers whose works embody the struggle of a new nation to define itself, either in the celebratory and democratic spirit of Whitman and Emerson, or in the darker tones of the fall from utopian grace in the works of Hawthorne and Faulkner.

For as Israel celebrates its fortieth anniversary, two generations from the birth of the nation, it regards its future with hope and trepidation.

Israel and the United States are both projects, nations that began with a vision and an ideology, that see themselves as the fulfillment of a destiny. Forty years after independence, Thomas Jefferson feared for the future of the republic: "I envy not the present generation the glory of throwing away the fruits of their father's sacrifices of life and fortune, and of rendering desperate the experiment which was to decide ultimately whether man is capable of self-government." Israelis read such a passage today without the century and a half of hindsight enjoyed by American readers. Instead, they can read it as contemporaries of Jefferson, identifying with the fears and hoping that in yet another one hundred and fifty years, Israelis will also read it as passionate concern but false prophecy.

ʑ▪

A Place for All
Old and New Myths in the Italian
Appreciation of American Literature

MICHELE BOTTALICO

In the last several decades the activity of Italian Americanists has been intense. The great quantity of serious and important work that has been published on American literature in Italy has given rise to a well-established and important tradition of literary criticism. In Italy it is hardly possible to find an area of American studies that has yet to be explored, and the number of national and international conferences and symposia on American topics, the multitude of advanced seminars, has been almost countless. There is no doubt that the interest in American literature, which has never been separate from a wider concern with the whole American experience, is very deep. Yet despite this intense interest, it is safe to say that the relationship between Italian intellectuals and America has been one of both love and hate, attraction and repulsion.

From both a political and a sociological point of view, the United States is often criticized for its occasionally ethnocentric attitude, for its position as the mother lode of postmidcentury modern imperialism, and for its hospitality to such inhospitable politics as characterized the Reagan administration. In addition, it often seems to Italian intellectuals that the more we import and absorb American cultural models, the more we should be scared of them, since, consciously or unconsciously, through our adoption of them we risk losing our own cultural identity. American culture threatens the archetypes of our imagination, archetypes that are powerfully rooted in our own and Western classical mythology. In certain respects we are afraid of the leveling effect that the influence of high technology, so much of which originates in America, may have on the

Italian imaginative life and on the creative use of language by Italian writers.

This fear is cogent because as scholars and critics and writers we are so attracted to the cultural vitality of America, where any sort of experimentation finds fertile ground. America is the country where, for instance, the principles of modernism that were elaborated at the beginning of this century in Europe found a practical and tangible application, especially in the fine arts and architecture: the skyscraper is the most evident symbol of this process of practical implementation. Other aspects and elements of American life stimulate our interest: the great anthropological variety of the United States, with its many ethnic groups struggling to affirm their own identities, even in the field of literary production; the incessant renewal of its culture, as tradition is constantly sacrificed to the needs of modernity; the feeling of physical and psychological freedom suggested by its vast space and the mobility of both its society and its inhabitants. These elements contrast, in fact, with the somewhat homogeneous and less dynamic quality of Italian culture, a culture most often experienced as a prisoner of its past, cautiously tied to that past rather than projected toward its future. Moreover, it hardly needs saying that every Italian intellectual feels an urgency to confront this transatlantic nation that stands for a new Greece, for from its culture a renewal of Western mythology has sprung forth.

The mixture of love and hate dates from at least the time of Cesare Pavese, the poet and novelist who was a founding figure for American literary studies in Italy. For Pavese, America was like a large screen on which we could see our own Italian future performed. It had a prophetic valence. The difference between the two countries has lessened since Pavese's day as the prophecy has to large measure come true: our way of living has become Americanized and technology is now proceeding apace in Italy, too. In addition, as the outskirts of our cities are swarming with African peddlers and illegal emigrants from Sri Lanka and the Philippines, we are beginning to experience the unpleasant intolerance of local inhabitants toward outsiders, asymmetrically re-creating in the process the prejudice that Italian immigrants to the United States faced at the beginning of this century. In many ways, then, American reality is no longer very much different from our own: more and more, it represents a slice of our life enlarged through a magnifying lens. To know America means to know ourselves better and to understand more fully the multiform tensions and anxieties that characterize modern Western society.

Thus, our relation with American culture is a dynamic one, never static, never the same; it is complex and varied, sometimes as contradictory as the American reality that captivates us with its very mutability. For America frequently appears to us first as a democratic country, then as a traditionalist one; first progressive and then conservative; violent and then peaceable. What complicates this relationship still further is our constant attempt to separate the myth of America from its reality. In fact, various kinds of myths concerning the United States interfere with attempts to find an objective approach to American culture. Historically some of them have been generated by American political propaganda, especially through the work of that generation of filmmakers who frequently indulged in the diffusion of the image of a tolerant and optimistic America. Other myths have been created by Italians, who often need to find in the experience of this young country what is missing in our own older society, to fulfill "ideally" some of the momentary demands of our social, political, and cultural life.

If we closely examine the situation of American literary studies in Italy, we see that the attempt to supersede the myth/reality dichotomy seems to be one of the motivating forces behind the gradual evolution of such studies, and of their present vitality.

In Italy, the most powerful myth of America was born in the 1930s, in that decade of deep political as well as literary crisis. The New Deal era was seen by our young Americanists as defining the United States as the defender of democracy and the humanities. As Italian intellectuals faced the exigencies of the Fascist dictatorship, some of them felt the need to deliver Italy from its cultural isolation and provincialism, to reopen it to the beneficial influences available in the wider world. Even more important, they felt an urgent need to overcome their own bewilderment, to engage in a difficult search for a new role that could break the limits so far imposed on the European intellectual. The prevailing philosophy, that of Benedetto Croce, had in fact created an insuperable barrier between society and its intellectuals. Thus it happened that the literary production of the American realists of the 1930s—Steinbeck, Caldwell, Saroyan, Anderson, James Cain, Dos Passos, and Sinclair Lewis—attracted the attention of a few intellectuals, most notably Cesare Pavese and Elio Vittorini, both of whom enthusiastically translated some of their novels. It seemed to them that these novels stressed the importance of a social commitment that was lacking in Italian writers. These realist novels were also seen as helpful to Italian writers in their search for a new language that, in opposition to hermetic poetry (the Italian movement was given the name *Ermetismo*) and to the forms of academic and aristocratic prose writing then prevailing in Italy, would have a new and powerful connection to social reality.

This exaggerated exaltation of what may have been some minor aspects of American literature was followed, in the post–World War II period, by a sort of momentary refusal of the realist authors who had previously been celebrated. Overestimation led to reaction; once the Fascist dictatorship was over in Italy, America lost much of that mythological quality which had made it the symbol of freedom and social progress.

That myth reasserted itself in different form in the late fifties. Then, the literature of the Beat Generation, and in the sixties the emergence of American cultural radicalism, gave new life to the myth of antifascist America. Once again, the attention of Italian scholars was attracted toward the literary production of America. In this respect, the popularity acquired by the Beat Generation, which represented the only voice of dissent raised against the McCarthyism and neomaterialism of the Eisenhower years, was particularly relevant. Kerouac, Burroughs, Ginsberg, and Corso became, for the Italian younger generation, spokesmen for their own Italian revolt against the materialism and conformism that was blossoming in Italy during the sixties, at the time of our economic boom. Consequently, many scholars devoted their attention to this cultural phenomenon, to either exalt or demystify its value. After the initial enthusiasm, however, when the supporters of the Beats realized that the Beat revolt did not represent the voice of a majority of Americans but only the protest of a small group of intellectuals, their interest waned, and they abandoned this field of study. By the mid-1970s the failures of the American protest movements and the New Left led to the perception by some Italian scholars that once again Italians had been traduced into an excessive exaltation of the revolutionary aspects of American culture. Recognizing that in many cases their approach to American literature had been too emotional, they fostered more balanced and mediated forms of literary evaluation.

Still, the analysis of American literature in a more objective way had already begun in the fifties, when scholars and critics began to put aside many of their prejudices about its purported "naif" quality as opposed to more "sophisticated" European literatures, and started to avoid the extreme mythicization of the "planet" America. This process of approaching American literature with greater scientific rigor than had been done in the past was greatly assisted by the expanding emphasis on teaching American literature in Italian universities. A new generation of professional critics—Agostino Lombardo, Biancamaria Tedeschini Lalli, Alfredo Rizzardi, Claudio Gorlier, and Marisa Bulgheroni among them—analyzed the literary works of authors that had never been studied before and concentrated their attention on the American classics. The work of these critics provided new dimensions to the American myth, for they discovered that the reality of American culture was much more complex—and refined—than had previously been brought to light.

Because so many different impulses and variegated interests led Italians to the field of American studies, it is rather difficult to characterize the canon shaped by Italian critics without falling prey to overgeneralization. The popularity of one or another author is often owing to many sources. In recent years, for example, a deep concern with reconstructing the experience of women writers has led to great interest in Sylvia Plath; still, some critics have investigated not primarily her feminism but the mythopoeic quality of her literary production. At times the critical fortunes of a writer may depend on the particular attention of an individual scholar who has discovered or championed the writer. One such case is the novelist Henry Roth, whose one book, *Call It Sleep*, was masterfully translated and carefully studied by Mario Materassi: recently reissued, it has given rise to considerable critical interest in the Jewish novelist of the 1930s.

At any rate, in the past ten to fifteen years a broader and more balanced interest in the American "reality" has impelled many Italian scholars to reexamine those features which best define the specific identity of American literature. Their studies have often focused on Puritanism as a major shaping element of American culture and imagination; they have laid great emphasis as well on the social crisis of capitalism at the end of the nineteenth century and the way that crisis was reflected in the production of the naturalist writers. Nineteenth- and twentieth-century fiction and poetry have received the greatest attention; drama, with the significant exception of the most recent avant-garde productions, has been rather neglected owing to the belief that it is not a distinctively American genre and has thus always lagged behind its sister arts.

Another feature of the research conducted during the past two decades has been a deep concern with ethnic literature, with a special emphasis on Afro-American works. These are sometimes considered the best examples of the literature of commitment in the American tradition. Often a Marxian approach has been used to examine and evaluate these cultural phenomena. It is quite possible that the heavy burden of Fascism, a too-dark spot on our recent history, still lies heavy on the consciences of some Italian intellectuals, who are therefore prone to confer great importance only on the explicit political values manifested in a work of art. But Marxian approaches are not the only ones that have proved fertile: recently, there has also been great interest in the wider problems of ethnopoetics and the aesthetic achievements of ethnic writers. The field has gradually enlarged to include the culture of native Americans, which is examined not only from a political or ethnographic point of view but also from a specific literary angle; Navarre Scott Momaday, who was awarded the Italian "Mondello" literary prize in 1979, James Welch, and Leslie Marmon Silko are the writers who have most attracted the attention of Italian critics. There has also been an increasing interest in the literature of Spanish Americans—Puerto Ricans and Chicanos; academics display this interest cautiously unless the works under consideration are related to mainstream literature.

The most interesting aspect of recent studies, however, is the tendency to take for granted the national identity of American literature, and to examine instead the interaction between American and European cultural phenomena. Scholars range widely in their interests: from the fantastic to the initiation novel as literary genres; from American experimentalism of the 1920s and 1930s (which influenced Italian literature) to postmodernism (and the Italian influence on contemporary American fiction); and from Jungian and Freudian influences on American culture to comparative studies of nineteenth-century Italian and American authors. Once the profile of the American myth had been outlined with a scientific rigor, thus partly destroying the myth itself, it became necessary to reanalyze American cultural expressions so that Italians might develop a better understanding of the complex reality they reflect. In recent academic teaching, then, as well as in the publications of many Italian Americanists, the literary aspects of a given work or period are related not only to history, sociology, and anthropology but also to fine arts, architecture, cinema, music, and other creative expressions of human culture.

Finally, there is a relatively new trend in American studies, and that is the investigation of the area we may broadly define as the cultural relations between Italy and the United States. Since immigration to America has virtually stopped since Italy has become more self-reliant and more aware of its new role in the modern world, Italians have recently turned to examining what our compatriots have contributed to America, apart from their labor and the series of distorted stereotypes of them that have flourished in the American environment. There is great interest in Italian-American writers; a conference on that subject was held in Catania in 1983. In addition, having been nurtured so long by the myth of America, having made so many efforts to analyze that myth, it is fitting that Italians are now eager to see things from the opposite angle: to what extent have Americans had a myth of Italy, how have they perceived Italy, how have they conceived of Italian reality? There are intriguing studies in this field concerning prominent authors such as Hawthorne, James, and Pound, all of whom have lived in, or traveled extensively through, Italy. But there are also fashionable new books and articles on lesser-known American travelers to Italy; these pay specific attention to the reactions of those who visited the Italian destinations of the grand tours of the nineteenth century: Rome, Tuscany, Veneto, and Campania. This crosscultural focus is a means to a better understanding of traits of our own culture and also reveals our continuing disposition to confront America, although now marked by a new Italian maturity and self-reliance.

These new interdisciplinary and comparative approaches have opened fresh ground for the Italian criticism of American culture; they have rejuvenated Italian Americanists. Under the umbrella of the national Association for American Studies, which at present comprises 260 members, a broader confrontation with ideas and fellow scholars from differing disciplines has been encouraged: the Association has organized nine conferences aimed at moving American studies beyond purely literary or historical concerns. Although the historical-sociological orientation discussed previously as characterizing most earlier investigations still persists, contemporary scholars and critics make use of analytic methods which derive from linguistics, semiotics, structuralism, psychoanalysis, and deconstruction. No longer is there the former diffident attitude toward methodological innovation. While fertile Marxian and feminist approaches deserve special mention, most recent contributions by Italian scholars are characterized by an attempt to soften the rigid categories of Marxian criticism and to avoid the excesses of an overly fashionable feminist interpretation. While breadth and innovation are valued, so are a closer attention to textual analysis and aesthetic problems and to a less marked ideological involvement.

These trends are hardly specific to American studies, however. It is particularly difficult to come to grips with the identity of the Americanists who work in Italian universities, for few of them are defined as Americanists. Some may teach American literature, but others, even when they officially offer courses in American literature, are primarily students of British literature. There is also a large concern with African, Australian, and English Canadian literary productions, so that one may venture to say that a fragmentation of interests has occurred among Italian Americanists owing to the wide range of cultural curiosity.

This fragmentation also derives from more practical and contingent circumstances. For instance, the study of literary texts written in English is spread among three interrelated subjects, subjects almost considered interchangeable when making job assignments in universities: English language and literature, North American (or Anglo-American) literature, and literature of the English-speaking countries. The mobility between these three cultural areas, which is occasionally allowed to teachers within the intricate patterns of academic structure, does not favor specialization in the field of American studies. On the contrary, it causes a sort of disorientation among younger scholars, as they try to determine which path is most useful or convenient to follow.

More important yet, although students lean toward American culture more than British—hundreds of them every year choose to write graduation theses in American rather than British studies—for historical reasons the teaching of British literature and language greatly predominates in Italy. This means that there are more jobs in British literature than there are in American literature. The implications of this are profound. Subcultural studies in British literature—medieval literature, Gaelic literature, contemporary literature—are proliferating, while American literature has yet to be subdivided into any geographical, historical, or cultural areas of specialization. While only a limited number of universities offer compulsory courses in American literature, even though a great many students choose American literature for optional examinations, British literature is required everywhere. The number of compulsory examinations in British literature ranges from one to four, depending on the sort of qualification the curriculum is intended to confer.

As a consequence of these institutional disproportions, there is pressure on young Americanists to shift from American to English studies, since this may well lead to not only easier, but also more rapid, career advancement. While there are twenty-two chairs in American literature, there are eighty chairs in English language and literature. Even though there are numerous other teaching positions in American literature, a positive achievement, there is a widespread sense that we have reached a sort of dead point. Although the number of scholars who embarked on American studies is very high, especially since with the 1960s, the possibilities for them to obtain adequate positions in universities have been diminishing and will be practically nonexistent for the next fifty years.

What happens in the universities is particularly important, since American literature is not taught in the high schools. University studies counterbalance the often distorted or reductive image of American culture that is diffused by the culture industry and by the Italian media. Since the postwar years our collective imagination has essentially been captured by American cinema, music, and television: these have had far greater impact than literature. Owing to the increasing reach of American capitalism throughout not only Europe but also the world, American cultural products have flooded the Italian market; they have largely shaped our icons of the United States, in the process encouraging dangerous fashions and purveying all sorts of stereotypes. The work of university teachers helps to moderate the enthusiasms of young students for the most commercialized aspects of the American myth. It promotes an objective approach to American literature and broadens the students' previous knowledge by moving in two directions, demanding the careful evaluation of significant contemporary trends and authors long before they are discovered by the culture industry, and encouraging the study of American classics that would otherwise be ignored.

Despite their general interest in American matters, in fact current Italian students entering the university seem surprisingly unaware of the essential currents of American culture and of the texts of the American literary tradition. Until twenty years ago a great number of them would have read, in childhood, the abridged versions of *Moby-Dick, The Last of the Mohicans,* or several of Twain's novels. This reading has been replaced by American cartoons or by a youth literature that is produced in Italy. For many reasons, a general lack of interest in the classics and "media addiction" among them, students' knowledge today, prior to enrolling in an American literature course, is likely to be limited either to the most widely advertised cultural phenomena or to those writers— Kerouac and Bukowski are conspicuous examples—who have become the stereotypical symbols of the revolutionary voice of America. Science fiction is quite popular among students, largely when it follows one or another film which fulfills the unconscious longing for change that is typical of young people, offering a utopian dream of a reality different from the one in which they are living.

The shaping powers of the culture industry preclude university scholars from determining the reading canon of the nation. Publishers, book reviewers, and the media in general have more impact than academics. Unless they meet a specific demand of the market, Italian Americanists' suggestions about which old and new texts are relevant and should be translated are largely ignored. Thus it happens that several major figures of the eighteenth century, and most contemporary poets, are missing from the current catalogues, for both poetry and works written prior to the flourishing of the great American classics are little read in Italy. As everyone knows, in a battle between cultural and economic interests it is always the latter that win the day. Publishers need to sell books, and thus they have to take advantage of the particular fashions and interests prevailing at a given moment; they answer the needs of their audience.

Publishers' choices are often influenced by the publicity gained by best-sellers in the United States. The echoes of this popularity circulate through the Italian press and prepare the Italian audience to receive cultural products that have already been tested on the American market. These books are immediately translated into Italian by professional translators who work remarkably swiftly. Arthur Hailey, Wilbur Smith, and Harold Robbins, for example, have easily found many fans among Italian readers. The notoriety of Hailey in particular has been augmented by the film productions of his novels; as might be expected, the influence of cinema and television is highly relevant to the diffusion of literary works. Cinema determined the popularity of Doctorow's *Ragtime* and West's *The Day of the Locust* and was responsible for introducing Isaac Bashevis Singer to a wide audience by means of the cinematographic version of *The Magician of Lublin*. Curiously enough, all of Woody Allen's books and film scripts have been translated and sell very well, even though Jewish humor is not fully understood by the general Italian public. On the other hand, most novels by Isaac Asimov, Stephen King, and Ursula K. LeGuin have large market appeal, not only because they are tied to the success of cinematographic versions of their work but also because they fill a gap existing in Italian literary production, where science fiction is notably absent.

Publishers are always ready to announce the publication of the most recent novels—or newly discovered manuscripts—of those writers whose fame is already consolidated in Italy. Works by writers such as Saul Bellow, Norman Mailer, John Updike, Truman Capote, Philip Roth, Bernard Malamud, and the ever-present Hemingway and Fitzgerald are immediately published, sometimes even before the original texts have appeared in the United States. These books may not always become best-sellers, but they find an assured readership. Fitzgerald's *Notebooks*, to cite an interesting example, sold quite well when it was published several years ago.

But publishers alone do not determine which American writers are prevalent in Italy. Old and new myths conjoin in shaping the literary tastes of ordinary readers. The myth of America as a young country where young people are the protagonists of life endures, associated as it is with the idea of vitality, with liberation from ideological and moral traditions, with a freshness and spontaneity of style. This myth has implicitly fostered the continuing popularity of the Lost Generation and the Beat poets and novelists; it has led to popular acceptance of the so-called minimalist and postminimalist writers as well. Thus, Fitzgerald and Hemingway are by far the most well-known authors; many people identify American literature with them. Kerouac's *On the Road*, along with Ginsberg's poems, are still widely read. In recent years Raymond Carver, and thereafter David Leavitt, Jay McInerney, Bret Easton Ellis, Lorrie Moore and Susan Minot (most of whom are under thirty) have successfully won over a legion of readers waiting for "new waves" to come from across the ocean. The Italian audience, as Leavitt candidly affirmed in an interview with the critic Fernanda Pivano when he said that his American success was propagated out of his earlier successful reception in Italy, is remarkably ready to confer the utmost importance on "novelties" imported from America. So adulatory is this favorable disposition toward the new talents of America that one Italian reviewer was led to define it as "the applauding attitude of a province of the Empire."

In addition to those writers whose readership is attracted to them by the myth of American youth, the writers of the 1930s and 1940s who gave rise to the long-standing myth of a democratic America are still popular among older readers. Novels by Steinbeck, Dos Passos, Erskine Caldwell, and Sherwood Anderson, at one time censored by the Fascist regime, are now easily found on the shelves of any bookseller. Edgar Lee Masters's *Spoon River Anthology* is widely appreciated, even by young people, as is witnessed by the two new translations which have recently appeared on the market, one of them by the poet Antonio Porta.

An abiding interest in the nineteenth- and twentieth-century classics has never been found wanting, particularly among the more sophisticated readers. All the major works of Edgar Allan Poe, Hawthorne, Melville, Thoreau, Emily Dickinson, Henry James, Faulkner, and Gertrude Stein are readily available. The most popular of these texts, above all *The Scarlet Letter, Moby-Dick,* and Poe's tales, have been translated several times. Others need to be retranslated into a more up-to-date language, or, like Hawthorne's *Twice-Told Tales,* should appear in a more accurate and unabridged edition. (It should be noted that in fact complete collections of tales are rarely published; Italians are not keen on short stories, as the lack of works in this genre by Italian writers attests.)

Generally speaking, the first translations of the works of the authors mentioned above were made by prominent writers and scholars like Cesare Pavese, Elio Vittorini, Carlo Izzo, and Gabriele Baldini; these are periodically reissued. Such reissues can shed much light on the problematics of translation. The case of Pavese's translation of *Moby-Dick* (1932) is an important case in point. Recently reissued, there has been a debate about its quality. Owing to Pavese's great capacity to render fully the power of the language and symbolic structure of the Melvillean text, his translation is still considered to be the best ever published in Italy. And yet its philological rigor may be questioned; Pavese himself once stated in a letter that he considered translation as "a re-creation of a work of art, exposed to the dangers of any creation and, above all, aware of the audience to which it is addressed."

Italianists frequently study both Pavese's and Vittorini's translations to shed light on the poetics and ideological choices of the two novelists and to help critics understand peculiarities of their style that can be traced back to the American works they translated, and which may have been models for their writing in Italian. It is worth noting that up to and through the 1960s the influence of American literature on Italian imaginative writing was widely felt. Italian writers, it is true, were more drawn toward imitating American realism than American symbolism, because they saw the latter as too closely tied to a Protestant heritage alien to their culture. Pavese and Vittorini, as well as Italo Calvino and Alberto Moravia (both of whom often stated that their early work was influenced by Poe's and Hemingway's prose), had a firsthand knowledge of American books, either because they spent time translating them, or because they spent time teaching in the United States. On the contrary, the narrative language of the neorealist writers was shaped secondhand, by the massive bulk of indiscriminate translation that appeared in the postwar period: they imitated American models they had read only in translation.

Translation has been extremely important to the development of Italian literary culture. The language of Italian fiction has been influenced by translation, most notably in the early decades of this century. Since Italy never had a long and consolidated tradition of writing prose fiction, the only outstanding eighteenth-century novel being Manzoni's *I promessi sposi*, most writers absorbed French, English, and, later, American models that were accessible because they had been translated into Italian.

Thus, it is not surprising to find that the major conduit into the Italian market for American literature has been through translation. Owing to the linguistic provincialism of the Mediterranean people, in Italy the habit of reading foreign books in the original is reserved for specialists. Still, important as translation is, it is neither economically rewarding nor valued highly by those in academic life. It is mostly left to the hands of professional translators who, generally speaking, have reached a high level of competence. The exceptions to this are university scholars who devote some of their time to the translation of major traditional and modern classics and particularly poetry, which is seen to be a challenging activity. Creative writers are also drawn to this difficult task, since those series of publications which are advertised as "poets translate poets" or "novelists translate novelists" are usually very successful.

Through translation, through widespread publication, American literature is made available to a large and appreciative Italian audience; it is not limited to a scholarly audience. And, despite economic constraints and institutional handicaps, academic study and research in American studies have great vitality. In the near future, many scholars maintain, the principal task facing Italian Americanists is to steer clear of that mythical vision of the United States which still prevents us from coming to a full understanding of America. Yet herein arises an important question. In literary terms, is the myth of America that characterizes so much of our approach to and appreciation of American literature, so negative and dangerous after all? Does it not revitalize our knowledge of America and prevent it from becoming outworn? Myth is, after all, always a guide toward and stimulus for the search for new and unexpected interpretations. Perhaps we should not be so quick to give up our American myths, for the death of those myths might provoke paralysis and the end of that creative tension which leads to understanding anew the most hidden aspects of American cultural experience.

🙛

Cultural Colonization?
American Literary Studies in Japan

KEIKO BEPPU

One of the cultural clichés of American film and journalism is the New York cab driver whose city-smart straight talk delivers the real goods on what is actually going on in America. The image of this streetwise interpreter of big city life is so powerful that one forgets that not all taxi drivers were born in Brooklyn, and that taxis are a fact of life in cities all over the world, not just in New York. Let me begin this examination of American literary studies in Japan by borrowing this cultural cliché and at the same time inverting it. A Japanese taxi driver can reveal much about contemporary life and attitudes in Japan, including how Japanese people think about American culture.

Upon returning recently to Japan from a conference abroad, I hailed a cab at the airport and asked the driver to take me to my home. The cab driver was a man of middle age who, as we talked and he learned that I teach English at a college, proudly informed me that he had taught himself English, since his job required a minimal proficiency in this modern lingua franca. When he found out that I was returning from a conference on American literature he revealed that he read American fiction in translation, prolifically though at random. He was especially attracted to Hemingway, Faulkner, Malamud, Roth, Bellow, and a host of other contemporary novelists.

I feel confident in drawing two conclusions from this happenstance conversation on the road between the Osaka airport and my home. One of these is obvious; the other would be obvious to a Japanese observer, but would likely be invisible to any other person who overheard our dialogue. The first conclusion is that the taxi driver served as eloquent testimony to the fact that American novels are translated and widely read in Japan, not only in academe but outside it. Surely my taxi driver would not be replicated every time one hailed a cab in Japan. Still, he existed, and others like him exist as well. One cannot easily imagine a similar situation occurring in the United States: could an American professor of Japanese literature carry on a conversation with a cabbie about Japanese authors as they drove from O'Hare Airport through the streets of Chicago?

The second conclusion derives from the phenomenal transformation undergone by the Japanese during the past half-century. Japanese people of the generation of my middle-aged cab driver have experienced a radical displacement of the traditional virtues and values which characterized prewar Japan, with its highly hierarchical and male-dominated society. In prewar Japan, and even fifteen years ago, it would have been unthinkable for a woman of my upbringing to dare talk to a cab driver—or even to get into a taxi all by herself! Yet here I was, in the closing years of the twentieth century, a Japanese woman in a profession not many years past reserved entirely for men, exchanging opinions on American literature with a Japanese man in the most casual manner.

Japan has had two major encounters with the United States, and the second, which dates from the American occupation of Japan following the Second World War, was more profound and far-reaching than the first, which took place when Japan's ports were opened to the Western world. In the earlier encounter, occasioned by the visit of Commodore Perry and his naval squadron in 1853, the impact of the United States was confined to influences on an elite composed of statesmen and educators. These leaders of nineteenth-century Japan looked to America as the model of democratic government and egalitarian society, an alternative to the long sleep of feudalism and closed culture which at the time characterized Japan. They read Whitman and Emerson for their political and philosophical ideas; their image of America was of "The Sacred Land of Liberty," as Shunsake Kuamei points out in his excellent discussion of the period in a book of that name.

But after the second encounter, in the period following the Second World War, the images of America were both more widely consumed and less consciously political. There was, for instance, the image of democracy on the domestic level, the image of the happy home which was purveyed by Hollywood comedies and by cartoons, *Blondie* in particular. The inflow of things American during the 1940s and 1950s, whether a bar of chocolate distributed among school children at lunchtime, jazz, Hollywood movies, or a cheap paperback copy of Norman

Mailer's *The Naked and the Dead,* left fatal and indelible marks on Japanese youth. Exposed to cartoons, to jazz, to GIs' slang, they grew up with the onslaught of cultural colonization, which revolutionized the traditional old Japan, geared as it was to hierarchy and patriarchy.

Such cultural transformation can be seen in miniature within the structure of our higher education, which expanded greatly as it opened opportunities to more Japanese youth, men and women, and as it stressed English as the foreign language of choice. The new constitution of 1947 decreed that women would have equal opportunity with men for higher education. National universities opened their gates to women. Foreign language study concentrated on American English rather than German or French. English was the first and only foreign language required in compulsory education, from the seventh to ninth grades, as well as being a required subject through high school and the first two years of university. This, of course, has created a great demand for teachers of English. Some sense of the large size of the educational establishment is seen in the number of colleges and universities in Japan: as of 1986 there are thirty-seven national and ninety-five public universities; as many as 342 private universities and colleges; and 561 junior colleges throughout the country. Most of these institutions have English departments or at least a faculty of teachers who offer freshman English courses. As a rule, these professors of English-American literature and teachers of English belong either to The English Literary Society of Japan, established in 1928, or to The American Literature Society of Japan, or both. The American Literature Society, founded in 1961 as a national organization, currently has fifteen hundred members.

Despite the radical influence of the United States immediately after the war, which I have indicated might appropriately be called a period of cultural colonization, the social structures and conservative life-style of a traditional society such as Japan die hard. Traditionalism and an almost hereditary system affect the structure of academe, which is Tokyo-centered. Tokyo's prominence is not only the result of its centrality in international relations and in publishing, but also the consequence of Japan's intensively status-conscious and hierarchical educational system. What is studied in the curriculum is usually determined, or used to be, by the professors of leading national universities, especially *The* Tokyo University, which dominated academe for a long period of time. Such professors often have control over the publication of scholarship; without proper "connections" it is extremely difficult, even impossible, for an "outsider" to publish at all.

As an index one can observe the case of Faulkner studies in Japan. The twenty-five-volume translation of the novelist's works began in 1967 and was completed in 1981. These translations, and the entire Faulkner industry, are dominated by one Tokyo-based scholar, Kenzaburo Oha-shi, who enlists as his cohorts either his "disciples" or other Tokyo-based scholars. The example of Faulkner is not happenstance, and will therefore recur throughout these pages. Of all twentieth-century writers Faulkner is the favorite of Japanese scholars. Even my taxi driver was attracted to Faulkner: he raved about *Light in August* and in particular about its heroine, Lena Grove, the more so since she corresponded to the stereotypical image of women favored by men. General readers and scholars alike are attracted to Faulkner because his involvement with traditionalism and his concern with the genealogy of Southern families mirror and reflect many of the central concerns Japanese readers have with their society and world, real and imaginary.

What is true for Faulkner is also true in a larger sense: the canons created by academics and by readers in Japanese society have never been mutually exclusive: what one group favors is, more or less, what the other group favors as well. Interest in contemporary and twentieth-century writers has been and is much greater than that shown in nineteenth-century and earlier American writers. Fiction is both more widely read and more thoroughly studied than poetry.

Faulkner, as has been mentioned, is the single writer who has been most read, studied, and written about. Although he is widely accepted as a modernist deeply engaged in formalist experimentation, the Japanese interest in Faulkner is largely attributable to his thematic and moral concerns. Japanese culture is extremely receptive to literature that explores traditional themes and the place of tradition itself, both in the lives of individuals and in the definition of a culture. Writing which is aesthetically self-conscious, on the other hand, finds a less hospitable readership, unless that aestheticism is linked either to high moral seriousness, or to specific concerns of the social milieu of the reader. Thus, it is more for what he writes about, rather than how he writes, that Faulkner is honored in Japan.

Generally speaking, Japanese scholars and readers find most congenial those American writers who present problems of family tragedies, filial conflicts, and relationships between parents and children, or those who explore other moral and social issues; and less congenial those who solely depend on the verbal and stylistic execution of their artistic principles. It is his concern with family and social issues that has made Faulkner an all-time favorite among scholars and readers; indeed, he was first introduced to Japan by the novelist Takehiko Fukunaga in 1947, which is much earlier than he was introduced to most general readers in his own country. Japanese readers, for example, easily understand and identify with Thomas Sutpen's rage over his failure to sire a male heir and his obsession with begetting a boy by the servant girl in his advanced age, for his concerns are seen by Japanese readers as their own.

Likewise, the Japanese interest in familial and moral concerns explains why among contemporary American authors Jewish-American writers receive substantial criticism, and their works are eagerly translated. Representative works of Bellow, Malamud, Salinger, and Roth have either been translated and published simultaneously with their original publication, or at least within a few years of publication in the United States. Jewish culture, characterized by a patriarchal society since the time of the Old Testament, investigates values identical with fundamentally Confucian Japanese values and ways of life: respect for one's elders, a sense of social obligation, the commitment to saving face (honor). These are the values and emotions that undergird Japanese society, which remains quite immune to social change on the psychological level, at the same time as the nation undergoes radical changes brought about by technological innovation, scientific exploration, and massively successful business ventures. Midway between these remarkable technological changes and the resistance to change in individual psychology lies the transformation of Japanese culture, and in particular its absorption of American culture. The cultural penetration of the United States into our traditional society progresses steadily, but much more slowly than the rate registered during the immediate postwar period. The productivity in American literary studies is a good indication of such a phenomenon.

To be sure, there are notable exceptions to the general rule of reception favoring twentieth-century authors. Such nineteenth-century writers as Hawthorne, Melville, Poe, Whitman, Dickinson, Twain, and James—all canonized in the United States—are widely studied, read, and translated in Japan. Their critical importance remains constant and secure with our scholars, as exemplified by the books and articles produced each year, as well as by extensive translation. Available in Japanese are *The Complete Works of Herman Melville* in twelve volumes and *The Works of Henry James* in eight volumes. Several versions of Hawthorne's *The Scarlet Letter* and his tales are available, as are Twain's *The Adventures of Tom Sawyer, The Adventures of Huckleberry Finn*, and *The Gilded Age*. Most of Dickinson's poetry has been translated; Whitman was first introduced and translated as early as 1919. The great exception to the Japanese preference for the thematic and moral over the purely aesthetic is Edgar Allen Poe. Poe has always been popular in Japan, probably by way of French influences. And he remains popular, as two recently published, significant studies testify: Toshihiko Ogata's *Edgar Allan Poe: The Poet* and Shoko Ito's *The Literature of Edgar Allan Poe*.

The particular shape of the canon of American literature in Japan can be seen graphically in the literary societies dedicated to individual writers, given in the order of their establishment: the Black Studies Society (1954), Whitman Society (1964), Thoreau Society (1965), Steinbeck Society (1977), Faulkner Society (1978), Pound Society (1979), Dickinson Society (1980), T. S. Eliot Society (1980), Hawthorne Society (1981), and the Melville Study Group (1982). These literary societies are a reliable index to the Japanese academic reception of American literature. Noteworthy is the early founding of the first literary society: the Black Studies Society was founded a decade before most American academics paid any attention to black writers. The Japanese interest in black writers derived from two major factors. One was the sense that America's treatment of black people revealed important ways in which American democracy did not fulfill all its promises. The other was the continuing Japanese concern with cultural definition and the problems of heterogeneity and homogeneity. One might note, however, that although the Black Studies Group is the oldest literary organization, even predating the establishment of the American Literature Society, only recently have its activities had a substantial impact in the world of published scholarship. Recent publications—the two latest are *The World of Black Women Writers* and *Black American Literature and Folklore*—testify to the enduring interest in black American literature, to the inclusion within the canon of writers regarded as marginal in the United States, and to the only recently diminished influence of Tokyo as the arbiter of literary studies. For the Black Studies circle, although ancient by contrast with other literary societies, is exclusively Kansai-based; as such, it has until recently been outside the locus of publication prescribed by Tokyo scholars. Both the recent publications in black literature and the diminishing control by Tokyo of literary studies have widened, and will continue to widen, the horizon of Japanese scholarship on American literature.

The virtue and strength of these literary societies is what I would like to call "the industrialization of literary studies." The exchange of opinions and information among fellow scholars makes it feasible to conduct research as a group—research which often results in publication. This collective or what might be called industrial approach to literary studies is becoming more of a common practice among Japanese scholars, perhaps in part because it allows us to cope with our disadvantageous work conditions, which offer neither adequate time for research nor a system of sabbaticals to subsidize academic scholarship. In a sense, Japanese literary scholarship has developed analogously to the Japanese management style which in recent years has become so successful and influential worldwide. Japanese management, so it goes, allows all involved in the process of production to have a role in making decisions as to how production/management processes can be made more efficient and satisfactory. In addition one might point out that the Japanese are possibly psychologically attuned to collective work. Collaboration means a shift from "monologue" and working in isolation to "dialogue" and affording allowances for the relativity of ideas and views. What is regarded as a uniquely Japanese style of management and of scholarship is, however, a comparatively new phenomenon. Japanese academe has perhaps learned from the open democratic system propounded by twentieth-century America that it does not pay to monopolize.

In the past few years, significant works of scholarship have been accomplished in collaboration by members of the various literary societies. The Melville Study Group was instrumental in the publication of *The Whale and the Texts*, edited by Kenzaburo Ohashi (1983), which includes articles by foreign contributors (Charles Olson, Carolyn Karcher, Barbara Johnson, and others) as well as leading Melvillians in Japan. *Essays on Ezra Pound* was prepared in commemoration of the hundredth anniversary of the poet's birth in 1986. A similar project by the Emily Dickinson Society—*After a Hundred Years: Essays on Emily Dickinson*—was published in 1988. Still another accomplishment in this category is *Faulkner: After the Nobel Prize*, coedited by Michel Gresset and Kenzaburo Ohashi in 1987. Significantly, the last two works mentioned are written in English. American literary studies in Japan have long been confined to domestic consumption, as it were, for fellow scholars and mostly for students. Hence books on American literature have invariably been written in Japanese, and translation has been the most fundamental form for introducing and interpreting foreign literature. In all four collections the contributors are mixed groups of foreign and Japanese experts on the respective writers. These collections illustrate well recent trends in Japanese scholarship on American literature, of which the industrial approach to literary studies is one, and another is the multinational perspective—the awareness of foreign readers—on American literary studies.

Besides the activities of literary societies, national conventions of English and American literary societies and special topics seminars are conducive to the industrialization of literary studies. Literary meetings include, along with the reading of papers, various symposia on issues of shared and current interest. As a result of these symposia, books are likely to be published. Examples of the outcome of such collaborative activity by participants at national conventions, who thereafter work together in groups of three to twenty people to investigate a topic from different perspectives, are *Whitman and Dickinson: Cultural Symbols in Their Writings* and *What Manner of Woman: Images of Women in American Literature.*

Seminars held under the auspices of the Fulbright Commission and Japan Foundation, both the Kyoto American Studies Summer Seminar (unfortunately discontinued in 1987) and the Sapporo Cool Seminar, have been a great attraction to Japanese professors of American literature. They have also been likely to result, though not always, in the production of books. For example, *American Writers and New York* is a collection of essays on the relationship between the megalopolis and the American literary imagination from nineteenth-century through contemporary writings, while *American Writers and the Gilded Age* consists of essays that evolved out of a summer seminar held a few years ago. In each case an American scholar is a guest contributor: Irving Howe and Alan Trachtenberg were lecturers at the seminars, and their presence—both to lead the seminars and in the volumes—highlights the increasingly international context of American literary scholarship in Japan.

This kind of collective research, which takes place within the framework of a mutually agreed-upon topic, has become increasingly acceptable in Japanese academe. If we extend the metaphor of the industrialization of literary studies introduced earlier, these volumes can be regarded as loose imitations of assembly-line production. They have all the benefits of such production without the undesirable problems inherent in industrial mass production: each researcher profits from his or her collaboration with other participants, and each is stimulated intellectually by the mutual interaction, while at the same time the scholarship that results has the sort of solidity and quality which guarantee a successful reception in the professional marketplace.

So far we have observed several important changes that are taking place in American literary studies in Japan. Tokyo is no longer as central to, or as dominant over, academe. Related to this development is the increasing number of collaborative projects which have been initiated and have come to fruition in the past decade. There may be a parallel between this widening of the scholarly community and "the opening up of the canon," as Leslie Fiedler puts it, which is occurring in Japan as it is in America. Homologous with these three changes, and to this writer yet more noteworthy, is the fact that these changes signal changed gender relations: the male domination of universities and of scholarly life and the centrality of Tokyo's male establishment are in decline. As my opening anecdote of the conversation with the taxi driver indicated, there have been profound changes in the roles available to women. These have been as noticeable in academe as elsewhere in Japanese society. Opening up the canon has brought increased attention to women and other marginal American writers, and indirectly to women scholars and critics. Participation of women scholars in American literary studies is no longer ignored in Japan. More women professors are writing and publishing, collectively and singly.

In almost all the books mentioned so far in this essay—and the books were not selected deliberately for that purpose—there are a number of women contributors. Of the eighteen contributors to *Faulkner: After the Nobel Prize,* four are women, all young and promising scholars. *Essays on Ezra Pound* includes five women among its twelve contributors. The majority of the contributors to the forthcoming volume on Emily Dickinson are women—eleven of seventeen. The inclusion of women contributors in these collections indicates that Japanese women are now assuming new roles in scholarship. They are evidence of the phenomenal thawing of the rigid traditionalism and patriarchy which permeate every aspect of life in Japanese society. It is true that the ratio of published women contributors to women academics is remarkably small, but that ratio is misleading in two ways. First, it belies the importance of women publishing at all; second, the small percentage only ratifies the enormous impact of Japanese women on the *teaching* of American literature in Japan.

As was mentioned earlier, the equal opportunity for higher education for women decreed by the new Japanese constitution (1947) had a great impact on Japanese colleges and universities, for it generated a great number of professional women, especially in the humanities. Enrollments in 561 junior colleges in Japan are mostly women. With the popularity of America and American literature after the end of the world war, enrollments in English departments at colleges and universities throughout Japan, both national and private, are overwhelmingly women. These women students in turn become teachers of English or professors of American literature. Because American literature as a discipline is relatively new in Japan, as it is in most other countries, it enjoys a greater freedom from the hierarchical structure of the academy. In this it is unlike philosophy, law, history, psychology, the other social sciences, and the natural sciences. (Yet even this is now subject to change; as there is an increased enrollment of women students in economics, commerce, business administration, and natural sciences, so traditional definitions of these disciplines are undergoing change.) Since American literature is a discourse marginal to power, it has happily meant a greater opportunity for women scholars, while men paid more attention to other concerns. Indeed, as the adage goes, it is women and stockings that gained power after the war while everything else was deflated. This famous saying, often used as a slur against women who go into a career, has now literally become true.

The aftermath of the feminist movement of the sixties and seventies in the United States, and by proxy in Japan, has yielded a positive reassessment of American women writers. The object of literary exploration until the present decade had been severely limited to only a few so-called major women writers, like Willa Cather and Edith Wharton. Among the fifteen American writers selected for the Tohjusha men of letters series only one woman writer is included, *Willa Cather: A Devotee to Beauty,* by Hiroko Sato. Miyoko Sasaki's *The World of Edith Wharton: Its Frisson and Raison* and a monograph on Cather are the only other book-length studies which appeared before the present decade. The measure of the change taking place in Japanese perception, and in the Japanese canon, is the fact that today each new book published on American literature includes chapters or sections on women writers or the treatment of gender.

This interest in "literary women" and "heroinism" (both terms of Ellen Moers's coinage) has prompted women scholars to question the validity of the accepted canon, one authorized by male critics. In the eighties Japanese women scholars have published prolifically on women writers. Especially significant in this regard has been reader-response theory, for it not only validates a Japanese response to American literature but also a woman's response to this formerly male-dominated area of study. Two biographies have appeared, both of which raise issues of gender: *Sylvia Plath: The Woman Poet-Martyr* and *Emily Dickinson: The*

Martyr of Love and Poetry. Similarly, books on Flannery O'Connor and Joyce Carol Oates were recently published.

Women have also taken up the industrial approach to literary studies: various groups of women have collaborated on work which investigates writing by and about women and have published the collections cited below. It is difficult for the non-Japanese reader to understand how unimaginable such publications would have been even fifteen years ago. Until recently, almost no publishers took women seriously, as authors, critics, or subjects. The male-dominated world of academe has seldom shown any interest in what the female sex has to say about the experiences of women and has often misrepresented what women writers say about men. In fact, for the traditional Japanese (male) critic, the highest compliment that could be paid to a woman writer has been, "She writes like a man." (Indeed, you are what you read.) Given this hostile climate, the appearance of gender-based studies by women critics has been revolutionary. For example, *Contemporary American Women Writers* discusses the female experience and consciousness of nine writers: Ellen Glasgow, Mary McCarthy, Zora Neale Hurston, Anaïs Nin, Eudora Welty, Susan Sontag, Joan Didion, Joyce Carol Oates, and Alice Walker. *What Manner of Woman: Images of Women in American Literature* is a historical survey of images of women portrayed in the works of both men and women writers from the eighteenth century through the present time. *The Images of Women in Contemporary American Literature* examines fictional women of ten contemporary authors: Anne Sexton, Ann Beattie, Toni Morrison, Margaret Atwood, and Cynthia Ozick are the five women writers selected for consideration.

The work by Japanese women in the area of American literary studies is remarkable enough. The list of books given above is a good index to the diversity of concern of Japanese scholars with American literature, showing an intimate correspondence between the interest in feminism and the scholarly activities of Japanese women critics. This may give an impression of the cultural revolution taking place in, and by means of, literary studies.

Yet a major question remains: Will this feminist turn endure, or is it merely a transitory phenomenon? I am less than sanguine about the impact of feminist studies which, while enduring, may not yet have the impact foreign observers might expect. Japanese society, with its long-established mores, seems quite immune to being undermined by radical change. When Henry James in *The Bostonians* has Mrs. Luna, Olive Chancellor's odious sister, prefer to be trampled by men rather than by her own sex if she is to succumb to anyone, I think James speaks with a vision applicable to Japanese society. Even so, I would like to believe that there will be no reversal or slackening of momentum. The images of women in contemporary American writing are definitely different from those found in nineteenth-century American literature; they seem freer from restrictive social norms. If literature provides either a mirror image of or a constituting archetype for the contemporary life we live, then feminism and feminist criticism have done major work. In Japan, feminism has already procured for women equal rights and opportunities for publishing and performing professional activities; we can now leave the rest to the law of natural selection to which any scholarship is subject. After all, it is the quality of work accomplished that matters, not the gender of the critic. So there is always room for hope.

To be sure, there are other concerns that loom importantly in American literary studies in Japan today. One concern is the question of new literary theory. Obviously, Japanese scholarship on American literature is sensitive to new literary theory, as it is to the imminent sociopolitical factors examined in the foregoing discussion. Since one's training and education shape one's critical methodology, scholars of the rising generation are necessarily more adept at implementing new literary theories such as poststructuralism, deconstructionism, and reader-response theory to their criticism of American writers. Just the same, the introduction and explication of literary theory is one thing—books on de Man, Lacan, Derrida, Iser, or Todorov are available in translation—while the application of these critical tools is quite another story. It suffices to mention here, with brief comments, a few important achievements that show the influence of new literary theory on Japanese critics.

Despite its title, Toshio Yagi's *Deconstructing the Whale* only partially succeeds in applying Derridean perspectives to *Moby-Dick*. More extensive and more satisfying is Sanae Tokizane's *Faulkner and/or Writing: On "Absalom, Absalom!"* This young woman scholar, writing in English, published the first book-length study I know of to employ a deconstructive approach to Faulkner's novel. Yet even here the approach seems less original than derived from the American critic Barbara Johnson's *The Critical Difference* (1981). There are fine articles on James and Poe by deconstructive critics, yet—and this is perhaps a failing not of these Japanese critics but of deconstruction itself—the theory assumes its own autonomy and leaves the authors, though not the act of writing, out of the realm of critical concern. Japanese scholars, and obviously I among them, have not, on the whole, become acclimated to such approaches.

The general reaction to literary criticism of this sort may be summarized by the often heard response: "Clever, showing great expertise! But where is the work?" Is this, too, a sign of the deep-rooted traditionalism of Japanese academics, most of whom are happy in the stable world of humanistic literary criticism?

More worthy of note, concerning the impact of literary theory, is the influence of reader-response theory on American literary studies in Japan. Japanese scholars of foreign literature suffer from the Eurocentrism of the discourse. The cause and effect relationship between reader-response theory and the interest in feminism has already been referred to. Just as it has justified the responses of women, as they read and then write about American literature, so reader-response theory validates a Japanese view of American writers. Reader-response theory has helped Japanese readers and scholars to gain self-confidence in their reading and writing about American literature. It has emancipated us from the Eurocentric orientation of the discipline. We have become self-conscious of our national identity, emphasizing it rather than concealing or impersonalizing it; we have thereby come to believe that we can make original contributions to American literary scholarship. The penchant toward comparative literary studies has been on the increase since the seventies. For example, in *Faulkner: After the Nobel Prize* "a Japanese view" is underlined along with "a French view."

Reader-response theory has also stimulated comparative approaches to American literary studies, as Japanese critics respond to their own interest in the complex relations between Japanese and American writing. The influence of Japanese poetry, *haiku* in particular, upon the modernist movement in poetry has been extensively examined. There is a chapter comparing and contrasting Emily Dickinson and Japanese poets in *Emily Dickinson: Strategies for Immortality,* and a book which examines her work in its relation to Japanese religion. Similarly, *American Poetry and Japanese Culture* is a comparative literary study investigating the Japanese influence on Whitman, Amy Lowell, Pound, Rexroth, Ginsberg, Snyder, and Wright.

American fiction, far more popular in Japan than American poetry, has also proved fruitful in comparative studies. Poe, Melville, and Hawthorne have been studied from this perspective. Henry James has often been compared to Natsume Soseki or Yasunari Kawabata, the Nobel Prize winner, for the subtlety of human relationships depicted in their works. Ohashi's *The Head and the Heart: American and Japanese Writers in the Modern Age* marks a turn in this cross-cultural direction by Japan's most prominent Faulknerian, who argues that estrangement of the heart from the head is a unique modern malaise which affects the creative imagination of both American and Japanese novelists, because the two cultures share both the "bliss and bale" of being highly industrialized societies in the technological age. Cultural and literary exchanges between the United States and Japan are also the focus of discussion in a chapter of *An Invitation to American Literature* (1985), one of the latest literary histories of the United States.

Japanese interest in this area of comparative literary studies should be further augmented in the future. The special number of *The Trends,* a journal published by the United States Information Service, celebrating that publication's fifteenth anniversary in April 1986, featured two important articles on cultural cross-pollination. Donald Richie's "Japanese Cultural Influences in American Life and Art" and Hisao Kanaseki's "Arts and Letters in America and Japan" clarify the bipolar nature of cultural exchanges between the two countries. The one-sided impact on Japanese culture and life of the United States during the postwar period is now being counterbalanced, for cultural traffic between the United States and Japan has become a two-way street. As Japan becomes ever more important in the world economic scene, its culture and literature will gain new significance. Already Japanese management techniques, Japanese products, and Japanese food have had the kind of impact on American culture that was formerly reserved for the American influence on Japan. My essay began by noting how fatal and far-reaching that American influence was in the postwar period; it ends by noting that the influence is now becoming reciprocal.

Earlier I recounted my experience with a taxi driver in Osaka. His familiarity with Faulkner, Bellow, and Malamud is an index of the spectacular interest in American literature in Japan. That interest is partly academic: the coverage afforded to Japanese contributions in *American Literary Scholarship: An Annual* has increased fivefold between 1974 and 1985. Books on American writers and poets continue to be written and published in great number: Faulkner is the most commented upon, followed by Hawthorne, Melville, James, and Dickinson, while contemporary American writers receive substantial critical attention. Recent interest in women writers in America and in Japan has boosted the production of scholarship in this particular area of American literary studies.

But the interest in American writing is not only academic. The wide-ranging and diverse academic concern with American literature reflects the interest of general readers, like my taxi driver. The translation of American writers makes up eighty percent of all the translation done in Japan each year: the average rate of publication is twenty titles a month. Certainly, the majority (80 percent) of these translations consists of what is generally termed popular culture: science fiction, detective stories, and other popular novels. Translation is a lucrative business. At the same time, there are academics engaged in the translation of serious literature—not only of James, Faulkner, and Melville, but also of postmodern writers such as Barth, Pynchon, and Barthelme. Translation of books by these authors is *not* a paying job; still, when published, such books find readers outside the academy, as is seen in the case of the taxi driver I encountered.

American literature has found and continues to find an ever larger place in Japan, both among the Japanese reading public and in the sphere of universities, scholarship, and research. Its reception is an index of the extraordinary impact of American life, culture, and political ideals upon the traditional fabric of Japanese life and society. Likewise, its study points to the loosening of some of the tightly woven threads in that fabric: the recent emergence of women scholars and gender studies suggests that Japanese patriarchy is not exactly what it once was. The diminishing dominance of Tokyo in American literary studies may also indicate that small changes in the rigid Japanese hierarchy have occurred. It is possible that the study of American literature has been not only an index of those changes, but even a contributing factor to the transformation taking place in Japan today.

No Country Is an Island
Some Aspects of American Literature in Mexico

FEDERICO PATÁN

Let me begin with a widely and well-known quotation: "No man is an *Island,* intire of it selfe." John Donne, of course. But I came to him first through Ernest Hemingway, thanks to the epigraph to *For Whom the Bell Tolls* (1941)—an American author expanding my knowledge of English literature. Is this not one of the purposes of culture, to widen the boundaries of what we know? And today, in Mexico, we go back to Donne and Hemingway, to take advantage of something quite easy to deduct from all this: no culture can survive in isolation or, adapting Donne, no *country* is an island, intire of it selfe.

When we look at literature, at any literature in almost any century we may choose, the presence of foreign voices is there, working to create something new out of the old and, especially nowadays, something new out of the new. These foreign voices come to us as a direct influence, for often native writers become acquainted with writers from other countries by reading them in the original. Sometimes these foreign voices come to us by a more roundabout way, through more or less valid translations. Or, even more roundabout, there is the route of generalized influence: a few creators transform literature to such a degree that they change the approach and manner of writing for all those who come after them. No small amount of fiction writers today are second-rank and secondhand Prousts, Joyces, and Faulkners, often without really knowing it. Or, to cite more recent examples, there is a great current tendency to imitate Borges, Cortázar, and García Márquez. Occasionally such inheritors, such imitators, are even good.

Mexico was never an island. If, as a natural consequence of the Spanish Conquest, our writers had a clearly peninsular manner of expression during the ensuing two centuries, little by little the touch, the tone, the feeling, the nuances of other and more distant voices came to infiltrate their styles. It was not only a matter of getting new tools for the labor of writing, but of becoming independent from the too obvious, and sometimes too stultifying, presence of the Spaniards. In this way a more recent influence is able to neutralize an older influence. Nevertheless, the older, displaced influence does not disappear but rather sinks deeply into the memory of the people. And from memories, from experience, from our natural way of being, we create something pertaining only to us: our particular view of the world as expressed in our literature. In other words, we are ourselves because, among other things, we have accepted others.

In the second half of the nineteenth century French literature overpowered all others as an influence on our writers. There is nothing surprising here: go to the Russians and you will find a similar phenomenon. Can one understand Turgueniev without the French? Certainly not. One discovers that the noblemen of *War and Peace* speak in French. It is a point of general agreement among our literary critics that it is easy to detect the presence of Hugo, Verlaine, and Baudelaire in Manuel Gutiérrez Nájera (1859–1895) who, according to Isaac Goldberg, "introduced melody into the structure of language . . . fulfilling, in our national literature a double role: as a precursor and as an innovator." Melody into the structure of language: the presence of Verlaine seems certain. One finds the sense of tenderness toward his characters exhibited by Alphonse Daudet appearing as well in Angel del Campo (1886–1908), as Federico Gamboa (1864–1939) pointed out. And, of course, Emile Zola is the paternal shadow that looms behind Gamboa himself.

It would be excessive to provide a longer list of French influences on Mexican writers: I want merely to demonstrate that French literature was for literate Mexicans an extremely important cultural element in the second half of the nineteenth century and in the first years of the twentieth. This does not mean, to be sure, that Mexican writing should be read as a sort of Latin American branch of French writing, as nothing but a French literary province. When scholars identify certain aspects of Dumas *père* in Justo Sierra's (1814–1861) and Vicente Riva Palacio's (1832–1896) historical novels, it is in the same sense that one sees the presence of Sir Walter Scott in the novels of James Fenimore Cooper. One feels the impact of certain narrative models rather than a specific way of using the facts of history.

This undeniable preference for French culture left behind a curious heritage. To cite one orthographic example: many Russian writers came to us thanks to indirect translation, that is to say through French versions of the texts. Even nowadays it is not too unusual to see a *Tchekhov,* a *Turgueneff* or a *Pouchkine*—the phonetic French transcription of those names—in the prose writing of some essayist, even though *Chejov, Turgueniev,* and *Pushkin* are the accepted forms in Spanish.

Around 1900 the United States was still a country working at consolidating its inner strength. Not until the end of the First World War can we speak of a solid and important American presence on the international scene. And not until that same period—the twenties—was its literature of any consequence to other nations. I shall examine below the importance of the literature of this period, especially that of Hemingway and Faulkner. But first a few words must be said about the presence and influence of American writers of the nineteenth century on the Mexican cultural scene at the end of that century and the beginning of our own.

Although before the 1920s some people knew of the work of American writers, it was largely on a personal basis. Baudelaire's knowledge of Poe is the example everyone mentions when discussing the impact of American writing on European literature. José Martí (1853–1895) is a Cuban analogue: he wrote on Emerson, Whitman, and Longfellow; but then we also recall that he was exiled in the United States. In the first phase of influence—the five years between 1898 and 1903—eight American writers are present in the pages of the very influential *Revista Moderna,* including Twain, Longfellow, Poe, Bryant, and Whitman. Each is represented by four or five poems, or one or two short stories. Compare this with the eighty-four French writers who were included, and the point made earlier about the dominance of French culture stands forth even more clearly. Indeed, not a few American poems were translated from the French!

If we look at American literature of the nineteenth century, one important name comes to the fore, not surprisingly the same name that we just saw linked with the great French symbolist Baudelaire: Edgar Allan Poe. Poe was well known to Mexican poets and fiction writers, and his way of dealing with composition, his sense of rhythm, and his peculiar creation of atmosphere are to be seen in aspects of Enrique González Martínez (1871–1952), Amado Nervo (1870–1919), and Efrén Rebolledo (1877–1929). But what about other names? Although the proper study of the influence of American letters on Mexican literature is something which still awaits the future as a fascinating field of research for scholars and critics, there is small risk in claiming that such important writers as Hawthorne and Melville were nevertheless unknown in Mexico until the second decade of this century. Much good literature, it seems, crossed the frontier between the United States and Mexico at a leisurely rate.

Mexican literature became really urbane in the 1950s. It is an attractive hypothesis to connect this urbanity with the increasingly amplified knowledge of American fiction by our writers of the period, but this was by no means the decisive element. What happened in the fifties has to do with the industrial growth of Mexico and other important internal factors. Yet, as it is impossible to separate this increased urbanity from the obvious and powerful presence of the richest nation of the time, the United States, directly across our northern border, the influence of American writing on Mexican writing of this period cannot be gainsaid. We must add, too, another point: from the forties on, the production of books increased enormously in Mexico, and this in turn led to a stepped-up pace of translation. In other words, there were a multitude of conditions which were in place for an "internationalization" of our literature. And this is just what took place.

The Lost Generation was a group of writers whose literary styles were important to us. The brisk and direct prose of Hemingway came to signify a new approach to narration not only in American fiction but also in the short stories of René Avilés Fabila (1940) and others. Still, William Faulkner is and has been, undoubtedly, the American writer who has had the most impact as a model. It is impossible to imagine that Carlos Fuentes' *Where the Air is Clear* (1958) could have achieved the shape it did without the sense of plot structure and language that are seen in Fuentes' Mississippi forebear, although the presence of John Dos Passos's fiction also played a shaping role on that novel. The same can be said of Fuentes' *The Death of Artemio Cruz* (1962). Juan Rulfo (1918–1986) was very assertive in rejecting any Faulknerian influence, claiming that he had not yet read him at the time he was writing *Pedro Páramo* (1955). But criticism differs. Meanwhile, among our young novelists Eugenio Aguirre (born 1944), Silvia Molina (1946), and Ethel Krauze (1954) all admit to a Faulknerian influence on their work.

The Beat Generation was another important discovery for Mexican writers. The Beats brought to our poets a sense of irreverence concerning the Establishment, a new vision of language as a fighting tool, even when—especially when—writing verse, and a sense that urban life is *the* theme of modern composition. Dario Galicia (1954) and José Vicente

Anaya (1947) are two young poets whose contact with Beat poetry was a stimulating experience. This combative use of colloquial language and deep interest in city life have developed an ironically nostalgic tinge in those writers who, ready to turn thirty years old or already having passed that threshold, find that the Establishment is just around the corner, waiting to seduce them: Arturo Trejo (1953), Arnulfo Rubio (1953), Raúl Bolaños (1954), and their contemporaries.

Just to give an idea of the American influence on young Mexican fiction writers, let us attend to what the writers themselves say about their models: "Recently, I have been digging a lot in Sciascia, Updike, and Milan Kundera . . ." (Agustín Ramos [1952]); "Well, I can mention some American writers: Henry Miller, but also Hemingway and Faulkner, whose influence goes deep in me" (Rafael Ramírez Heredia [1942]); "If you're going to give a brother to *Profile,* it has to be J. D. Salinger's *The Catcher in the Rye*" (José Agustín [1944]); "Influences? To be sure. Let me name, apart from Quevedo, who's tops, Camilo José Cela, Swift, Sade, and Henry Miller" (Federico Arana [1942]); and "Later on, already in high school, I began to read all sort of classics: García Márquez, Julio Cortázar, Hemingway. . . . I am a grandchild of Hemingway. . . . This is a sentimental metaphor. I say it in the sense of taking life as an adventure, an adventure worth talking about" (David Martín del Campo). Even though I have focused on those parts of interviews dealing with American literature, and have left out many European and Mexican writers also mentioned, the point I am trying to make is clear: there is a never-ending relationship between American and Mexican literature. The movement between the two countries is mainly from north to south.

Possible inference: American literature is an everyday presence in our libraries and bookstores. Well, yes . . . but. . . . Shall we ever come to live without a "but" butting in? In this case the condition is this: the books are on the exhibition shelves and tables all right, but buyers and takers are few. Once in a while a good writer hits the best-seller lists in the United States and, by association, is famous among us for just a few weeks. Norman Mailer is one such example. The usual state of things is quite predictable. Writers of high literature have a status similar to that of classic writers: the name is familiar; we can even faintly remember the title of one, or perhaps with luck two, books. But reading these authors? What for? Such is the situation with nonspecialized readers and bookstore customers, the everyday citizens coming and going from home to work in overcrowded buses, the sports newspaper under their arms.

So, exceptional writers are read by, and belong to, an elite of readers: other writers, students of literature, a small number of intellectuals interested in quality. The choices of these readers make up what might be called the commercial canon, since it is composed of works that are commercially saleable and therefore available. As for the official canon, propagated by the academic establishment, that is a different matter. Are the two canons similar in Mexico? Not by any means, although once in a while they touch hands because of a coincidence inspired by the best-selling "hit parade."

In Mexico one will find courses in American literature in only a few universities: Xalapa, Guadalajara, and Mexico City. In the case of the Autonomous University of Mexico, the largest in our country, the Department of Modern Languages is divided into four branches: English, French, German, and Italian literature. By English we mean exactly that: British writing; nothing from Canada, Australia, or the West Indies. Why? Because where could one find specialists to teach these things? Where find the money to support these courses? Where obtain the books to be read?

So what about American letters? Well, out of seven English courses, only one is on the literature of the United States. The teacher of that course must cover a spectacular amount and wealth of material in the fifty-two hours of class time spread over two terms. To Cooper, Poe, Hawthorne, Melville, Twain, Crane, Dreiser, Stein, Hemingway, Faulkner, Pound, Eliot, and O'Neill must be added still other names. It is indeed a sorrowful situation, mitigated only by the appearance now and then of a seminar intended to help deepen the understanding of an important figure, group, movement, or genre.

But students do get acquainted with big names, outstanding works, and even a few critics such as Edmund Wilson or Lionel Trilling. The theory goes that this exposure helps them to acquire a certain curiosity about American literature. To tell the truth, some do. Yet the number is small: the English branch of the Department of Modern Languages teaches no more than thirty to thirty-five students a year at the fourth level, which is where American literature is offered. This is a drop of water in an endless sea of inhabitants.

Fortunately, Mexican writers and scholars do read a good amount of foreign literature, and they use it in ways that change our culture's conception of writing and research. They keep in touch with the latest developments in American literature, and know about Frederick Barthelme, Reginald Gibbons, and Alice Walker. They can manage this by buying books in English, books translated into Spanish, magazines, and literary supplements.

Yet one can never ignore the importance of the endless sea of inhabitants referred to above. Millions of them enjoy a weekly reading of comic books, quite a few of which are of American origin, such as *Archie, Superman,* and *Batman.* A substantial number of people of the middle class amuse themselves by reading fiction, especially novels. It is among these readers that the American best-sellers rule without real opposition. These best-sellers can be obtained not only in libraries, but they can also be bought in supermarkets, coffee shops, restaurants, and diverse other places. Their kingdom is vast. The authors known to housewives, clerks, and salesmen are many; these people of the middle class have a speck of pride in saying, "Excuse me, but I do read books." By books they mean the works of Stephen King, Irving Wallace, Mario Puzo, Taylor Caldwell, and not so long ago, Frank Yerby, Lloyd C. Douglas, and the eternally alluring Margaret Mitchell and her *Gone with the Wind.*

We can see how powerful the enterprise of publishing American best-sellers in Mexico is by listing the latest additions to the already long catalogue of titles. In the first three months of 1988 these books appeared: *The Eagles Gather, Ceremony of the Innocent* (2nd ed.), and *Strong City* by Taylor Caldwell; *The Celestial Bed* (2nd ed.) and *The Almighty* by Irving Wallace; and *The War of the Roses* by Warren Adler. What a difference from the official canon, which saw only the publication of *Poems and Interviews* by William Carlos Williams (University of Puebla) and an anthology of American poets (University of Mexico). It does tell, does it not?

In considering American literature, one has to consider as well the major importance of movies and television shows, for often people go from *It,* the film, to *It,* the novel, from *Twilight Zone* to science fiction books. Is it possible that the regular Cosby fan watches the British Broadcasting Corporation's Shakespeare, and then later buys the Penguin or Arden edition of *Hamlet, Romeo and Juliet,* or *Twelfth Night?* Hardly. Each television show, each movie, each book attracts a specific audience. We live in culture today as we live in a condominium: in the same building, in different apartments, with different tastes in furniture.

As noted above, universities support the publication of classical or emergent classical authors. In general terms, we are on safe ground in claiming that the literature of the official or academic canon lives because of universities, because of government efforts, and because of individual Mexican writers. The commercial canon has little use for this sort of writing, except in those rare moments when it proves to be a solid monetary investment.

For example, some classical authors have achieved an eternal life in catalogues and libraries owing to a very simple circumstance: tradition has made them representative, and they serve as compulsory reading. If we turn to what is called literature for the young and look at the publication lists of different Mexican publishing houses, we shall surely find a collection of books for children and teenagers. It is not hard to predict which authors and titles will appear. A short sample drawn from current catalogues includes: Alcott's *Little Women* and *Little Men;* Irving's Alhambra legends; London's *The Call of the Wild;* Poe's tales and, perhaps surprising to United States scholars, *The Narrative of Arthur Gordon Pym;* Stowe's *Uncle Tom's Cabin;* Twain's *The Adventures of Tom Sawyer* and *The Adventures of Huckleberry Finn;* Wallace's *Ben-Hur.* Some time back, in the sixties, Argentine translations of Cooper's *The Last of the Mohicans* and *The Spy,* and Twain's *A Connecticut Yankee in King Arthur's Court* were on these lists; in the seventies Spanish editions of Hawthorne's tales, Melville's brief prose, and Steinbeck's *The Red Pony* appeared. Although this list is not exhaustive, it should surely show two things. First, it reveals a kind of classical canon of American literature as it has been shaped by Mexican publishers, teachers, and readers. Second, it reveals that this particular canon has been shaped by the need to educate the young and by the reading interests of the young.

Before leaving this consideration of the influence of publishing on the reception and study of American literature, we must consider four specific genres that have their roots in that literature and are popular in Mexico. The first is not a conventional literary genre, although it represents the presence of a foreign voice—Mexico is not an Island, intire of it selfe—which we began by considering. This is the genre of "how-to" books. In Mexico there is a wide market for books telling people how to be a better wife, lover, housewife, husband, friend, father, mother, and so forth, and a rich market as well for do-it-yourself books. Xaviera Hollander is a case unto herself.

Two other specialized genres deserve attention: science fiction and detective stories. Both represent an area where the commercial canon overlaps in places with the intellectual world. Most science fiction books come to us from Argentina or Spain. As these countries keep up with the latest authors, readers with a taste for this genre can enjoy Bellamy, but also Bradbury, Paul Anderson, Theodore Sturgeon, Philip Jose Farmer, and so forth. Yet the economic crisis that Mexico is suffering at present has turned Spanish and Argentinian books into objects of luxury, and science fiction fans are finding it harder and harder to get the works they crave.

In Mexico detective stories have a faithful and large reading public. The easiest authors to find in libraries are the British: Sir Arthur Conan Doyle, Agatha Christie, and Patricia Highsmith. But there is substantial representation of both the hard-boiled detective fiction of Dashiell Hammett, Raymond Chandler, and John D. MacDonald, and the logical unravelings of Rex Stout and Erle Stanley Gardner (as well as his pseudonym A. A. Fair). More recent writers such as Ross MacDonald and William Irish are also widely read.

The detective novel has had substantial impact on Mexican writing. We can pinpoint with almost complete certainty the beginnings of Mexican detective stories with the publication of Usigli's *Essay of a Crime* (1944). Almost immediately thereafter María Elvira Bermúdez wrote *Death Has Diversified Reasons* and *Stop, You Shadow!* In both she follows closely the school of Doyle, and particularly the example of Christie, a line also taken by recent writers such as Malú Huacuja and José Huerta. Some fifteen years ago Rafael Bernal and then Paco Ignacio Taibo II began to write hard-boiled detective stories, following the approach of Hammett and company. A sort of war between American and British factions kept the newspapers amused several years ago. Today the American tradition of the hard-boiled detective has a more definitive presence among Mexican writers than does the British tradition of Doyle and Christie. Along somewhat similar lines, Truman Capote's *In Cold Blood* influenced Vicente Leñero in some aspects of his reportorial prose in *Murder* (1985).

The final genre is that of the western. A very minor, poor, and simplified literature in Mexico, the western is less successful than science fiction or detective fiction. A series called "The Weekly Cow-Boy Book" was sold until very recently in supermarkets and similar places. It appeared in pulp editions. The translations were disastrous, and some of the titles were the product of ghostwriters using American-sounding pseudonyms.

Translation is usually the main route by which a foreign literature makes its way into another culture. Unfortunately, the most superficial examination of translation in Mexico shows that literature receives minimal attention. We do translate, but mainly technical books with, as might be expected, a captive market. This has been the case since the beginning of the Mexican nation. In the twentieth century, literary translation has been and is almost exclusively a matter of concern for our universities, because only they can publish books which need not have making a profit as their central purpose.

The University of Mexico is the most important contributor to the knowledge of foreign literature in Mexico. A short account of its efforts in American literature may be illustrative. Recently, it has published a selection of Ezra Pound's poems (translated by Rafael Vargas); *Seven American Female Poets* (Beth Miller); *The Waste Land* (Manuel Núñez Nava); a selection of Robert Lowell's poems (Carlos Monsiváis); an anthology of Elizabeth Bishop's poetry (Margo Glantz); a selection of Edgar Lee Masters's poems (Sandro Cohen); *An Anthology of Modern American Short Stories* (Federico Patán); and a survey of the imagists, translated by diverse hands.

The Mexican government, through the Ministry of Education, prints and distributes books at low prices and in editions of twenty-five thousand to thirty thousand copies, an exceptional number by any standard in Mexico. Two main sources of distribution are used across the country: newspaper stands and small libraries, called "modules." In the collection "Clásicos Americanos" (American Classics), what appears of the literature of the United States? Hawthorne's *The Scarlet Letter* (Josefina Gonzàlez de la Garza); Whitman's *Leaves of Grass* (Carlos Montemayor); Melville's *Billy Budd*, Crane's *The Red Badge of Courage*, and Twain's *The Man That Corrupted Hadleyburg* (all translated by Federico Patán); and collections of political writings, twentieth-century essays, and twentieth-century short stories. It is clear that this series sticks with works whose quality has been proved by the best of judges, time. Even the materials from the twentieth century never include the most recent authors. But then this is only to be expected, if we take into account the purpose of the series, which is to allow common readers to get in touch with what are universally recognized as the best works of American countries. How, with such a stringent purpose, would it be possible to guarantee that the novels, poems, or essays of the present moment are sure classics?

Thus the official structure of translation has left room for what I call "labors of love": the individual enterprise of translation. It is a tradition, and one not limited to Mexico, that writers interested in the work of a foreign contemporary do their best to make him or her as widely known as possible in their country. This process inverts the usual procedure of translation: it is not the publishing firm that looks for the fittest translator, but the writer with a knowledge—sometimes excellent, sometimes not—of another language who translates into Spanish the poems or fiction of an admired contemporary and then seeks a publisher. Poems and short stories predominate, because the logical outlets for these efforts are magazines, which have no way to include an entire novel, except when they sometimes adopt the nineteenth-century habit of publishing a chapter in each issue. Another reason for the predominance of shorter works is that translators who offer unsolicited translations, often of poets and fiction writers little known outside their native country, risk a vigorous "No!" from editors, and it is far easier to accept such rejection when one has in one's hands a few pages of translation rather than reams of paper.

Thus, the most recent literary works from the United States find entry into Mexico, as in many other countries, primarily through the efforts of individual writers. This is true not only for poetry, but for all fiction not on the best-seller list. Though the quality of these translations often varies widely, the translations more often than not fulfill their most urgent purposes: they widen the readership and knowledge of foreign works, they give voice to the most recent voices emerging abroad, and they tell about new models for giving expression to our picture of the world.

From 1953 to 1963 the *Revista de la Universidad de Mexico,* under the sure guidance of the poet Jaime García Terrés, published texts by Dickinson, Ferlinghetti, Ginsberg, Levertov, Cummings, and Thurber; it also published essays on Ezra Pound (by José Coronel Urtecho), William Saroyan (Huberto Batis), Henry Miller (Juan García Ponce), and William Faulkner (C. E. Zavaleta). Later, in the 1960s, Huberto Batis edited *Cuadernos del viento,* in consecutive issues presenting the works of Cummings, H. D., Eliot, Langston Hughes, Sinclair Lewis, Henry Miller, Erskine Caldwell, Dos Passos, Pound, Salinger, Saroyan, F. Scott Fitzgerald, and Edna St. Vincent Millay among others. A fine display, although it is perhaps not without importance to state that the significance of Caldwell and Lewis has not endured to the present day. They serve nowadays only as remote echoes of a writing displaced by more recent narrative approaches.

The list of writers most widely published during the past fifteen years overlaps, but also augments, the names cited above. Another list is unavoidable and, one hopes, valuable. It is worth citing the various translators of each writer, for in every case the translator is himself a poet or novelist, thus proving my earlier contention that important translation of recent works is almost always undertaken by people who are themselves writers. Recent years have seen extensive translation of Ezra Pound (Agustí Bartra, Alberto Blanco, Rafael Vargas), Allen Ginsberg (Blanco, Vicente Anaya, Pura López Colomé), Kenneth Patchen (Bartra, Blanco), E. E. Cummings (Bartra, Blanco, Colomé, Federico Urtaza, Jaime Moreno Villareal), Robert Lowell (Bartra, Blanco, José Emilio Pacheco), and T. S. Eliot (Bartra, Octavio Castro López, Alfonso René Gutiérrez). To celebrate Eliot's centenary, the Fondo de Cultura Económica published Pacheco's translation of Eliot's *Four Quartets*. In addition to the above, there are translations available of Langston Hughes, Elizabeth Bishop, Sylvia Plath, Gary Snyder, and many other poets. The central point I would like to make is this: Mexico pays a good amount of attention to modern American writers, but the readership of these writers is not very widespread. This leads to a paradoxical situation: although the works of these writers are visible, their existence in terms of consciousness is hidden.

It is time to sum up the different aspects of this overview of the place, role, and reception of American literature in Mexico. Although it is clear that many names, of American writers and Mexican scholars and translators, are missing, certain telling points emerge. First, certain well-established writers and movements are part of an official canon: they are accorded the status of "classics." These works serve as a hunting ground for Mexican writers and translators, but they do not circulate widely in the lives of common citizens. Second, as we have seen, there is a wide gap between this official canon and the commercial canon which is defined by what the common citizen reads, if and when he or she reads. In general, we may define three groups with different interests: university students, who study in their courses the immovable figures of literary history, the so-called classics; writers, who read and translate their contemporaries, interested more in what is new than in what has obtained classic status in the past; and everyday citizens, who when they read books at all, are interested in reading best-sellers or fiction which is easy to assimilate.

Summing up translation, we may say that literary translation is an almost nonexistent commercial activity in Mexico. What is translated is primarily done as a labor of love. Most of the foreign books we read are in translations published in Spanish editions, and with the economic situation of contemporary Mexico being what it is, that makes such editions quite expensive. When domestic publishers go for American literature, it is safe to bet that they will either give us a new version of a traditional text for which there is a sure market or offer us a best-seller. Making commercial publication of literary works even more risky is the fact that translation rights for modern writers are extremely expensive when figured in pesos, and even the down payment required prior to translation often proves an insurmountable handicap to Mexican publishers. No publisher, then, will risk money on what is almost definitely going to be a mediocre or weak-selling book. Thus, writers like John Barth, Charles Bukowski, Philip Lamantia, both the Barthelmes, Harold Norse, David Ray, and their contemporaries find a natural habitat only in noncommercial translations: in magazines, in the literary pages of one or another newspaper, or, if they are really lucky, in a volume published by a university press.

If I have said next to nothing about the politics of American literary study and reception, it is because American literature is of no political interest to our government. That means there are no objections to its presence in Mexico. After all, is it not a smallish affair, as all literature seems to be? Once in a while a scandal breaks around a book, as with Oscar Lewis's *The Children of Sanchez,* and someone is "beheaded" as a sort of scapegoat in order to restore peace and quiet and smiles to the faces of politicians once again. University studies tend to be isolated from direct political pressures: the dominant approach to American literature tends to be descriptive, open-minded, and supported by modern methods of analysis. A deep respect for literature is to be found in the university. At times one author or another, one group or another, presents a radical critique of the established political system and becomes a guru for young people. Yet, the government takes little note of this.

American literature, then, affects Mexican life in two ways, one obvious, the other less so. The obvious way is through best-sellers of all sorts, by which the everyday citizen is mildly infected with a knowledge of American culture. Less obvious is the direct knowledge of American writers by Mexican writers, who obtain such knowledge either through reading in English or through translations by yet other Mexican writers. This form of cultural transmission is an important element—although neither the only or even the most important element—in the continuing growth of Mexican letters and, by extension, Mexican culture.

We must always remember that literature is the regular dripping of water into a measureless sea; only after a time do we understand that it does eventually change the color of that sea.

Cutting Loose
American Literary Studies in The Netherlands

THEO D'HAEN

The Dutch have had a lively interest in the United States since the early days of its emergence as a nation. However, for a very long time, as was the case in most European countries up to the Second World War, interest ran almost exclusively along geographic, social, economic, and historical lines. Literature entered the picture only recently, especially from an academic point of view. Three studies illustrate the ways in which Dutch intellectuals saw the United States as an example, either positive or negative, of emergent modern practices and values.

In 1899 the Dutch academic R. P. J. Tutein Nolthenius made an extended trip to the United States. Upon his return he wrote *New World: Impressions and Notes Made during a Trip through the United States of America.*[1] All through his book Nolthenius extols the virtues of America, for what he finds to admire in the United States is what he would also like to admire in the Netherlands, "a *human race,* superior to all other races because of its youthful vigor" (361).

Whereas for Nolthenius America served as a positive example, the Dutch author and critic Menno ter Braak, in his 1928 essay "Why I reject America," uses the idea of a particular America to castigate those aspects of contemporary civilization he wishes to reject in Europe, in particular Holland: massification, the influence of the media, a certain frenzied busyness. As such, he voices feelings quite common to European intellectuals during the interbellum.[2]

A similar attitude emerges from the essays of the historian Johan Huizinga. A recent commentator sees Huizinga as a spokesman for an attitude of "conservative apologia," an attitude that culminates in Huizinga's writings from the late thirties and early forties, "when America served him only as evidence in his more general complaint against contemporary history's loss of form."[3]

The earliest signs of any sustained academic interest in American literature are to be found with Huizinga. In his *Man and Masses in America: Four Essays in the History of Modern Civilization* (1918), Huizinga discussed American literature in some detail, finding in it values strangely disconsonant with his overall rejection of American culture.[4] "The essence of the spirit of America," Huizinga announces, lies in a "tremendous zest for life and for the present and future world" (190). It is a spirit of "healthy-mindedness" whose purest literary embodiment he finds in the works of Ralph Waldo Emerson and Walt Whitman. With regard to the typically *Dutch* character of American literary studies, though, it is well to point out that Huizinga adds a third name to his list of select Americans, that of the now forgotten Ralph Waldo Trine! Huizinga calls "Emerson, Whitman, Trine . . . the few, the best" (196), and even quotes from Trine's *In the Fire of the Heart* in order to ask these rhetorical questions:

> Do you feel how close this is to Whitman?—Slowly now can we discern what is the essence of American individualism in its more elevated meaning, a composite of optimism, rousing one's own personality to higher action, cherishing mental and physical health, and admiring noble and vigorous action? (196)

It is no coincidence that Huizinga singles out this "moralist and ethical philosopher" (150) for inclusion in the American spiritual triumvirate. Dutch society, well into the twentieth century, has shown a remarkable penchant for reasoning along moral or ethical lines, and Huizinga to a large extent applies a yardstick in common use in his own Dutch cultural background.

In the final analysis, Huizinga appreciates Whitman as the spokesman and embodiment of the American mind and, albeit only implicitly, as a remedy for what he feels is lacking in his own European culture. After all, his was the Europe of the aftermath of World War I, and of Oswald Spengler's *Untergang des Abendlandes*. That is why Huizinga renders his final judgment on Whitman in terms such as: "Whitman devoured life. His attitude towards life cannot be better expressed than as the very opposite of 'spleen'" (215), and "He was always concerned with the effect of his poetry, with its impact on the life of his people and of humanity; in this too he is typically American. No one was further removed from 'l'art pour l'art'" (217). Though more sophisticated, Huizinga, like Nolthenius and ter Braak, uses America and American literature to diagnose the evils and weaknesses of his own culture.

The early Dutch interest in American literature, then, was not centered in literary academe. In addition to Menno ter Braak there were other Dutch authors who explored the literary heritage of the United States. Most noteworthy was the novelist, poet, and essayist Simon Vestdijk, who in the thirties and forties published a number of influential essays on Emily Dickinson (1932), Edwin Arlington Robinson (1933), and Edgar Allan Poe (1946).[5] Ter Braak and Vestdijk, though undoubtedly more informed than the majority of the general Dutch cultural public, were not exceptional in their interest in American literature. It is a fact that Dutch culture has been very hospitable toward receiving works from foreign literatures, and there is no reason to think that its attitude toward American literature would be any different. Obviously, as the saying goes, culture follows trade, and also politics. So, we notice an increased Dutch interest in the literature of that country which at any given moment in world history happens to be more or less dominant, whether it be France, England, Germany, or—indeed—the United States.

From the nineteenth century on, then, American literary works found their way into Dutch culture.[6] To be sure, the Dutch were attracted to writers little different from those valued in most other European countries prior to the modern period: Cooper, Hawthorne, Bret Harte, Washington Irving, Longfellow, Whitman, and Harriet Beecher Stowe emerge as the most widely reviewed and translated authors. What characterized Dutch nineteenth-century culture in particular was its receptivity to morally and ethically upright works, a receptivity we have already seen framing Huizinga's discussion of American literature. From this perspective, it will come as no surprise that Harriet Beecher Stowe's *Uncle Tom's Cabin* was by far the most popular American book in Holland. Nor will it surprise that Stowe's other works, and those of her sentimental sister novelists, were particularly welcome in the Netherlands. Consonant with the same pattern, the Dutch Emerson is a very selective one indeed, as some cursory research of my own has revealed: only those of his essays that could stand the test of moral and religious acceptability, or that could be made to stand that test by judicious rewriting, were translated. Similar research by some of my students at Utrecht University has brought to light similar principles governing the selection and translation of American sentimental women novelists.

Although hitherto largely uncharted, the penetration of American literature into the Dutch cultural market has certainly not abated since the early years of this century. On the contrary. It is no exaggeration to say that, especially since World War II, American culture has become so dominant in the Netherlands that it even rivals indigenous Dutch culture. Nor does American literature find its way into Holland only in translation. In most large Dutch bookstores the English-language department is quite as big as the Dutch-language department, and within that department American works clearly dominate. American literary journals like *The New York Review of Books* are widely available, and in the larger bookstores of Amsterdam, The Hague, and Utrecht titles on the best-selling lists of *The New York Times Book Review* are on display, as they are in the United States. American literature is widely translated, too. A new Bellow novel is available in Dutch on the same day the book is brought out in the original; the same thing, by the way, applies to a Gabriel García Márquez. But also books by newcomers, such as David Leavitt's *The Lost Language of Cranes,* are published in Dutch translation within weeks of their appearance in English. The relative contemporaneity of this massive literary penetration, however, can be deduced from the fact that many literary works from before World War II remain untranslated, or are only now being translated. Such is the case with much of Faulkner and Henry James and with all but the most obvious works by Hawthorne, Melville, and their contemporaries.

With all this it should be stressed that reputations, let alone sales figures, of American authors in Holland are not determined by whether or not their works are studied at the university. Some American "classics" are regarded as children's books and are marketed by publishers specializing in such literature: works by Twain, Melville, Cooper, and Stowe. Likewise, Margaret Mitchell's perennial best-seller *Gone with the Wind* is published by a firm that is not otherwise noted for its literary output. Such books achieve relatively high and constant sales, though these are realized entirely outside the literary circuit. For newer authors, financial success is determined by the reviews in the weekly cultural sections of the larger dailies. Most of the reviewers for these newspapers, though they may have had a university education, do not judge by academic standards. If anything, reviewers in Dutch newspapers often actually pride themselves on adopting specifically nonacademic standards. Similarly, what is translated, and sometimes even what is praised in the press, is not always what is sold: even though translated by widely regarded Dutch authors, the few translations of Faulkner and James were quickly remaindered. Similarly, many of the translations of more experimental American fiction, often brought out by small or even ephemeral publishers, fail to sell even when reviewed favorably. In this whole process of cultural interchange, the Dutch academic specializing in American literature can do no more than observe. If he wants to intervene, he has to venture outside academe: he has to write for the newspapers, or he has to act as editor of popular high school magazines such as *Diver,* which introduces high school readers to authors and works absent from standard reading lists. This, then, defines a major area for future research, and indeed there has been a beginning to the synchronic and diachronic study of Dutch-American literary interrelations, and to the policies, the processes of selection, and the economics involved in publishing American titles. Two related areas which, although more academically orthodox, go largely unexplored at present are those of the influence of American authors on their Dutch counterparts, and of wider intertextual relationships.

Given America's enhanced political, economic, and cultural profile after World War II, it was only natural that the study of the United States in the Netherlands would also greatly increase. A first result was the founding of the Amerika Instituut at the University of Amsterdam.[7] This same immediate postwar period also saw the beginnings of official academic interest in American literature. Still, at first this interest was extremely limited, and did not translate into the curricula of the various universities. To a large extent, this had to do with the particular setup of Dutch universities and their faculties of letters. As in most European countries, in Holland the study of languages and literatures, until the 1950s, was concentrated in general departments of Romance and Germanic philology, with a marked emphasis on philology. When these split up into distinct departments or institutes devoted to the study of one particular language and its literature, the creation of English departments or institutes almost naturally favored the purely "English" component, given its established academic credentials in the field of philology. In particular, Dutch universities were dominated by the influence of one school of English literary studies, that associated with F. R. Leavis, *Scrutiny,* and *The Great Tradition.* The influence of Leavis and his followers on the Dutch study of American literature cannot be overemphasized. Leavisites, as we shall see, dominated academic positions devoted to the study of literature written in English. These scholars followed Leavis, who virtually excluded the study of American literature, or only tolerated it insofar as it could be annexed to his particular idea of English literature. In the first instance, then, American literature was at best a side interest of some professor of English literature, most likely one who did not value it much. In the period we are now talking of,

Dutch university departments were extremely small. Most English departments consisted of only a few staff members under one or two
chaired professors. It was only in the midsixties and throughout the seventies that student and staff numbers swelled dramatically. It was this period of expansion, too, that saw the creation of special chairs of American literature and the development of complete curricula of courses in
the subject. In the late eighties, a reversal is occurring as recent cutbacks
in spending on education in general, and on the universities in particular, result in academic retrenchment. I will review most of these issues
separately in detail.

The earliest result of the increased academic interest in American
literature was the publication, in 1946–1947, of the *History of American
Literature* by A. G. van Kranendonk, professor of English literature at
the University of Amsterdam.[8] In many ways, it is a remarkable book. A
hefty two volumes, it shows its author to have had a very good grasp of
American literature and of what was going on in the study of American
literature in the United States itself at the time. Yet, in its independence
of mind and from its European vantage point, Kranendonk's work very
much resembles that of Huizinga's almost thirty years earlier. In fact, it is
not illegitimate to say that Kranendonk's is as much a cultural as a
literary history of the United States, and that as such it is, in spirit and
form, the culmination of the early Dutch interest in America.

With Kranendonk, only a few authors get a chapter all to themselves,
and these of very differing length. From this some interesting observations can be made with regard to Kranendonk's view of the American
canon. First of all, an important omission of Huizinga's is redressed:
Melville is obviously one of Kranendonk's American heroes. Of course,
both Huizinga and Kranendonk only reflect the particular state of
American literary studies in their respective day; still, it is important that
Kranendonk fills his Dutch readers in on the controversial status of
Melville.

Yet Kranendonk's work remains striking for its omissions. A number
of what we would consider major authors are conspicuously absent or
get short shrift in Kranendonk's pantheon. Such is the case with Emily
Dickinson, who gets a mere five pages, and this notwithstanding Vestdijk's earlier extensive and appreciative essay in Dutch. Henry James
also gets less attention than we would now probably be inclined to give
him. In a chapter on the realist novel he is allotted eight pages, and
William Dean Howells, five pages. Indeed, for Kranendonk there exists
little significant difference between the talent and achievement of these

two writers: "From Howells's tremendously prolific oeuvre . . . a lot will be forgotten, but enough will survive to guarantee him a lasting reputation. . . . With even more confidence the same thing can be predicted for Henry James" (318–19). Nor is his final evaluation of James much more consonant with current valuations:

> In a sense Henry James's realist art, particularly achieved and pure, but peculiarly limited, marks the end of a certain development, his work brilliantly signals the end of an era. Shortly after the turn of the century realism will adopt different guises, and the American novel will follow new trails, leading through less narrow territories, opening up wider, larger vistas. (327)

The only poet, next to Poe, to whom an entire chapter is devoted is Walt Whitman. Earlier, Kranendonk had discussed nineteenth-century American poetry in various survey chapters. In these chapters the discrepancy between the treatment of Emerson (five pages) and Thoreau (two pages) as compared to Holmes and Lowell (seven pages each) immediately stands out. Kranendonk explicitly opposes Whitman to these Brahmin poets. He finds much to criticize in Whitman's poetry, but like Huizinga before him concludes by pronouncing him the most American of poets:

> Typically American qualities characterize his work: the defective sense of form and construction; the jovial, somewhat strident, boyish voice that sounds in it; the eager interest in all aspects of life, and not least in its material aspects; the tremendous energy and vitality; the intense joy of living, the unbounded trust in the future; the democratic conviction that all men are equal, and so on. With Whitman's poetry, so original, and so strangely appealing, American literature first found its own and unmistakable national identity. (1:215)

In his chapters on the more contemporary period, too, the amount of attention Kranendonk pays to particular writers may sometimes surprise us, as do his appraisals. He claims that E. A. Robinson's "most beautiful and most important work . . . is the Arthur trilogy: *Merlin*, 1917; *Lancelot*, 1920; and *Tristram*, 1920, and particularly the last volume, a work which gloriously can bear the almost inevitable comparison with Tennyson's recreation of the old legends" (2:145). If our tastes have changed with regard to Robinson's work, it is perhaps well to remember that, likewise, they have with regard to Tennyson's. In other words, given the time of writing, Kranendonk's preferences are not as erratic as they may sound to a contemporary audience. Interesting to note: Kranendonk devotes a few pages to black poetry, music, and writing in general. Another interesting feature is the attention given extraliterary developments: Kranendonk discusses names and works from the most diverse reaches of American intellectual life.

As to his treatment of twentieth-century prose, it is clear from the extended Dreiser chapter that this is where Kranendonk's real sympathies lie. Still, his own preference does not blind him to the merits of other kinds of writers. In this regard his evaluation of Faulkner is particularly revealing. He discusses Faulkner under the chapter heading "Deviations from Strict Realism," yet thinks he is, "in spite of the unevenness of his work, in spite of his many exaggerations and palpable shortcomings . . . the most interesting, the artistically most gifted of present-day American novelists" (2:293). His ranking of Faulkner's work, too, is remarkably perceptive in view of later canonical tastes: *The Sound and the Fury, As I Lay Dying, Light in August, Absalom, Absalom!* and *The Wild Palms* are his favorites. Perhaps the greatest shock to present-day readers is that F. Scott Fitzgerald only gets one page, as does H. L. Mencken, while James Branch Cabell gets two and a half pages—albeit highly ironical and even deprecatingly phrased ones.

Kranendonk's *History* in many ways remains the inevitable yardstick for all subsequent attempts. Kranendonk felicitously combines Huizinga's Dutch home-culture-oriented approach and the American studies perspective then emerging in the United States. As such, his work reflects concerns clearly antedating the impact of *Scrutiny* and Leavis in Holland.

Indeed, the 1950s and 1960s are marked by a coming to academic power of scholars who had either been colleagues or students of F. R. and Q. D. Leavis, or who had contributed to Leavis's *Scrutiny*. The adherents of this school, in their teaching and research, were not so much concerned with exhaustive period study, or even with the entirety of literature, but rather with what they, or their mentor Leavis, saw as the "best" products of English literature. In its most narrow and exclusive form this approach appears in Leavis's own *The Great Tradition* (1948), a book that for decades remained one of the few set course books in Dutch English departments. Leavis's own low opinion of American literature is well known and, in a period when there were as yet no chairs of *American* literature at Dutch universities, it only went to reinforce the prejudices of chaired professors originally appointed to teach and do research on *English* literature. This situation was not helped by the fact that quite a number of new appointees, and not just at the professorial rank, were English and not Dutch. Many of these native English speakers persistently failed to function in Dutch, which effectively excluded them from the decision-making processes in the higher echelons of their universities. Nor did the situation improve dramatically when, in the mid- and late sixties, separate chairs for American literature were created, or separate assignments to teach American literature were made at lesser ranks, for most of these new appointees were Leavisites too.

Despite the fact that some of these appointees made a promising start, their attempts to build a following were all noticeable failures. Yet building a following was precisely what, according to the farewell speech the first and longest tenured among them gave on his retirement, they had set out to do.[9] From the midsixties on through the seventies and into the early eighties, there existed, or there were created, separate chairs of American literature at the Universities of Leyden, Utrecht, Groningen, Nijmegen, and Amsterdam. At the Free University of Amsterdam there was, and still is, a joint chair of English and American literature.

We can understand the state of American studies in the sixties and seventies, and its particular Leavisite slant, by considering the case of T. A. Birrell, a British academic who served as full-time chair in English and American literature at Nijmegen while at the same time serving as part-time professor of American literature at the University of Amsterdam. Nijmegen in particular was receptive to the Leavis influence, a fact underlined by the presence there for decades of the son of F. R. and Q. D. Leavis. Birrell, too, was a confirmed Leavisite, and the literary history he published in 1982, three years before his retirement, is the best illustration of the particular slant his generation gave to the teaching of American literature in the Netherlands during this period.

Birrell's *American Literature* covers American literature from its beginnings to the 1970s.[10] His introduction clearly sets forth Birrell's Leavisite concerns, in that it stresses the personality of the individual writer and the need for evaluation. Notwithstanding a disclaimer, he very much writes *as* an Englishman, a fact underscored by the remarkable circumstance that the book was written in English and translated into Dutch by one of Birrell's Nijmegen staff members.

Birrell is much less far-ranging and comprehensive than his predecessor Kranendonk. He pays no attention whatsoever to anything not strictly literary, and gives only summary attention to social, political, and general cultural conditions. His chapters are subdivided in smaller units, each of which deals with one author. His first chapter, dealing with American poetry up to 1900, is primarily concerned with what American poets borrowed from their English counterparts. The only two poets extensively discussed are Whitman and Dickinson; compared to Kranendonk, a complete transvaluation has taken place, for Whitman gets ten pages and Dickinson eleven.

The same condensation of canon marks Birrell's discussion of the nineteenth-century novel. Although this is by far the longest chapter in the book (one hundred pages), only six authors are deemed worthy of inclusion here: Cooper, Hawthorne, Melville, Twain, James, and Wharton. The inclusion of Wharton and the sixteen pages devoted to her are indicative of Birrell's Leavisite preferences, the more so when we notice that writers of perhaps greater significance get either less or equal coverage: Cooper eleven pages, Hawthorne, thirteen, Melville and Twain, seventeen each. Thus, it comes as no surprise that when Birrell examines Henry James he devotes twenty-six pages to that exemplary Englishman, a central figure in Leavis's *The Great Tradition.*

Birrell's list of twentieth-century poets is also extremely short; it covers a mere five figures in the compass of sixty-five pages. Robert Frost gets twelve pages, as do Pound and Stevens. T. S. Eliot, another good Englishman, is allotted twenty-four pages, in which Birrell significantly devotes more attention to Eliot's relation to England than to America! William Carlos Williams gets very short shrift, all of five pages. Birrell's feelings toward Williams reveal his extreme British provincialism from the start: "He visited Europe various times, but all in all he passed no more than seven days in England" (199). So what!? What is the relevance of this to the "Dutch reader" Birrell so consolingly addresses in his preface? Nor does Birrell grow more tolerant of Williams. *Paterson* he calls "a formless, uncontrolled mash, which strongly reminds one of Pound's *Cantos*" (201). Obviously, Birrell has trouble admitting, or even seeing, that with these works both Pound and Williams had comparable aims, which might even be peculiar to such a thing as an American tradition in poetry. This Birrellian shortsightedness is underscored by his reticence with regard to *The Waste Land* by the otherwise much-admired T. S. Eliot. Birrell devotes barely one page to this poem by Eliot, quite probably because it belongs to the same *American* tradition as the works by Pound and Williams that Birrell so scathingly condemns, cautiously refraining from judging it because he desperately wants to retain Eliot as the epitome of twentieth-century American poets! His highest praise is quite unsurprisingly reserved for Eliot's *Four Quartets*, not by coincidence Eliot's most English and—not irrelevant to Birrell's appraisal—most religious poem. Set beside his most damning rejection of Williams's claim to be writing a particularly American kind of poetry or, in fact, to be writing poetry at all, this praise of the late Eliot clearly reveals Birrell's Leavisite values.

It is clear from Birrell's devaluation of the realist-naturalist movements in fiction, from his cursory treatment of American drama, from his focus only on the modernist novelists Hemingway, Faulkner, and Fitzgerald (he prefers, of course, the latter), and from his grudging recognition of only two contemporary novelists, Bellow and Salinger, that Birrell's is a very insular British literary history of America. The fact that he claims otherwise in his introduction is belied by his bibliography on American literature, composed in its entirety of twenty-four items, nine of which are by either F. R. or Q. D. Leavis! In addition, there are three entries by Marius Bewley, a regular *Scrutiny* contributor. Among the remaining, one is by Eliot, two are by Trilling, and two more are by Yvor Winters, all minds adjacent to Leavis's.

Birrell's book is deserving of such extended examination because it is so representative of what was being taught in Dutch universities in the period since the end of the Second World War. Birrell reveals the narrowness and provincialism of a Leavisite approach to American literature; unfortunately, this approach was the major way of dealing with American literary culture in academe in the fifties, sixties, and seventies. More important yet, the extreme selectiveness, and the application of an English moralism to two cultures, the Dutch and the American, determined what was taught to Dutch students of American literature. Both in scholarly publication and in the classroom American literature was seen almost exclusively through the distorted lens of *Scrutiny* and Leavis.

Thus, the tastes and preferences of the Leavis-oriented approach seem to have dominated the Dutch universities prior to the late seventies. It is extremely difficult to go beyond that "seeming," for reconstituting the shape of the curriculum in this earlier period is next to impossible today. American literature as an official option—an area in which one could write a master's thesis—dates from the early seventies. Prior to that period, not only were official courses of study in American literature nonexistent, but also English departments then were still so small as not to require elaborate procedures of administration such as calling for reproducible course listings. Most American literature courses involved only the teacher and a few students.

My previous remarks were not meant to say that there were not some good things coming out of Dutch universities in the period discussed. Books and articles introduced the Dutch audience to a number of little-known American novelists, or at least then little known in Holland, like John Barth, John Hawkes, James Purdy, Robert Coover, and Thomas Pynchon. There were a small number of scholarly books published.

Things are changing very fast in present-day Dutch academe. The ministry of education and the university authorities are applying pressure both fiscally and managerially: cutting costs and increasing efficiency are the bywords. There is more teaching to be done with less staff. Scholarly output is both demanded and judged more severely than ever before. The generation of chair holders that came to power in the fifties and sixties has all but disappeared. At first, this seemed to create possibilities for growth of American literary studies; for increased scope, too. When Birrell, for instance, retired as part-time professor of American literature from the University of Amsterdam he was succeeded, after a certain interregnum, by Harold Beaver, who became full-time professor of American literature. In his inaugural lecture Beaver spoke "On the American Canon," trying to define his subject for a Dutch audience and a Dutch university.[11] By fastening on a topic increasingly fashionable in American critical interchange at large, Beaver sought to open up and air out the stuffy closet American literature had been consigned to in most Dutch universities. Earlier, Janssens had tried to do the same thing upon the acceptance of his post as professor of American literature at Nijmegen, when in his inaugural speech he spoke on tradition and experiment in contemporary American prose. Both these inaugural addresses, then, tried to maneuver American literary studies in the Netherlands closer to what was going on in the United States itself, and away from the stifling Leavis influence. The same thing was being urged by a number of younger staff members at Utrecht and Leyden.

This concern with opening up Dutch studies of American literature is reflected in yet another *History of American Literature,* published in 1983 by Bertens and D'haen.[12] In their preface, Bertens and D'haen state their explicit intention "to treat American literary history against the background of a more general cultural history" (9). Consequently, they start off each of their ten chapters with a sketch of the historical period under consideration, giving some general indications as to political, economic, social, and cultural developments. Occasionally, they locate the divisions between periods differently than Kranendonk, and they are more prone to trace continuities in theme or technique from the eighteenth or nineteenth centuries to the present day. In general, they show more interest in exploring the reasons why American literature, given its particular social and cultural context, evolved the way it did. In doing this, they follow current developments in American studies in the United States itself. Along similar lines, they are less evaluative than Kranendonk, and certainly less than Birrell, but more concerned with the role, the place, the function, the "slot" a particular author or work occupies in American literature and culture as a whole. Rather than see American literature as a series of exceptional products of singular minds, they view literary culture as a network, a set of interconnected works, themes, and techniques. Unlike the Leavisites—or even the native Dutch moralism of Huizinga—Bertens and D'haen make judgments of worth and significance not on a work's message, not on its moral agenda, not on its aesthetic purity, but on the importance of the work to the tradition, to the developing practice of American literature. They are less interested in choosing the canon than in understanding how it came to be canonical.

In consequence, Bertens and D'haen's book reflects changed patterns of appreciation. Kranendonk only devoted one page to James Fenimore Cooper, and valued him mostly for his non-Leatherstocking books. Bertens and D'haen give him five pages, and single out the Leatherstocking tales for discussion. On the whole, Bertens and D'haen also pay more attention to women writers. They give relatively more space to Emerson and Thoreau, less to James. They rate Dreiser as more important than Birrell did, but less so than Kranendonk. Carl Sandburg, Vachel Lindsay, and Robinson Jeffers occupy little space with them; Frost occupies less than with Kranendonk or Birrell; Pound, Eliot, Williams, and Stevens get an equal amount of space. American drama is treated in a separate chapter, as is black literature. A major difference, especially from Birrell, as both his book and that of Bertens and D'haen were published almost simultaneously, is that the latter devote two entire chapters, almost 90 out of 347 pages of text, to postwar developments in prose and poetry, including sections on postmodernism. In their epilogue Bertens and D'haen remind readers that their book, owing to limitations of space, only deals with those works commonly deemed literary, but that there exists as well an enormous "gray area" of so-called subliterary genres that is of immense interest and importance. In their annotated bibliography they list both classics in the field and more recent works up to 1980. Yet Bertens and D'haen also write in a historical context, and if the new awareness of American research methods and goals is a strength to their study, it is also a weakness, for they rely too readily on the terms and concepts, the underlying "ideology," of American scholars or American literature. The British bias has been corrected in their work, but a wholly or even markedly Dutch approach is not yet in view.

In the early 1980s, then, American literary studies in Holland seemed to be joining the mainstream of American studies abroad, and particularly in the United States. Attention was increasingly being given to the study of postmodernism, ethnic literature, and minority literature. But this widening of the intellectual horizon suddenly faltered as fiscal realities intruded into the university. The new watchwords of the eighties were issued and "to economize" became the most pressing concern. The projected professorship in American literature at Groningen was abolished, or rather appended to the chair of English literature. Upon the retirement of the chair in Leyden that chair was amalgamated with the concurrently vacated chair of English literature. It is an as yet unanswered question whether, with his retirement, Beaver's chair at the University of Amsterdam, of which he was the first full-time occupant, will ever be filled again. The new professor of American literature at Utrecht is caught up in entirely new organizational structures which will merge the administration of the American literature and American studies programs. Next to economizing we now suffer that other terminological catchall of the eighties: "interdisciplinary"!

What the result of all this will be for American literary studies in Holland is hard to say right now. Two lines of defense are open, if American literature is to survive as a discipline in the Netherlands. The first is to further internationalize, especially as far as publications are concerned. Until now most scholars of American literature in Holland have tended to publish much of their work in the local *Dutch Quarterly Review of Anglo-American Letters* (since 1970), and with this periodical's Amsterdam publisher Rodopi; otherwise, they also publish in Dutch, in general trade and literary journals and reviews. This work will have to go on, but in order to prove that they are able to compete internationally, and therefore to merit survival in an environment which is constantly and increasingly questioning the raison d'être not just of American literature but of all the humanities, it will henceforth be necessary to publish in internationally read and refereed journals.

A second line of defense is to stress the Dutchness of what American literature scholars in Holland are doing, and thus to demonstrate the usefulness of their work also to Dutch culture and society at large. This is the kind of research, for better or for worse, that Jan Bakker, from the University of Groningen, has been publishing lately. Such research requires us to look into all aspects of Anglo-Dutch literary interrelations:

influence studies, intertextual relations, translations, the critical and commercial reception of American literature. Hesitant steps in this direction are now being taken in Utrecht, where the American studies brochure, taking notice of the insistent American presence in the Dutch media, claims that Holland, culturally speaking, is the fifty-first state of the Union, and then announces that American studies, by studying this phenomenon, might also "throw some revealing light on the development of Dutch culture." With an almost Derridean *differance*, we have returned here to Huizinga's concerns when talking of America. The best strategy for survival, obviously, will be to combine both lines of defense. We hope the minister of education and our various universities will give us the time to do so.

Notes

1. R. P. J. Tutein Nolthenius, *Nieuwe Wereld: Indrukken en Aanteekeningen tijdens eene reis door de Vereenigde Staaten van Noord-Amerika* (Haarlem: H. D. Tjeenk Willink & Zoon, 1902).
2. Menno ter Braak, "Waarom ik Amerika afwijs," *Verzameld Werk*, Deel 1 (Amsterdam: G. A. van Oorschot, 1980 [1928]).
3. See Rob Kroes, *Amerika in onze ogen: De Amerikanistiek in Nederland* (America in our eyes: American studies in the Netherlands) (Amsterdam: Noord-Hollandsche Uitgeversmaatschappij, 1986), 16–17.
4. Johan Huizinga, *Mensch en menigte in Amerika: Vier Essays over moderne beschavingsgeschiedenis* (Haarlem: H. D. Tjeenk Willink & Zoon, 1918).
5. Simon Vestdijk, *De Poolse ruiter* (Amsterdam: Athenaeum-Polak & Van Gennep, 1976); idem, *Lier en lancet* (Amsterdam: Athenaeum-Polak Van Gennep, 1976).
6. This is most amply documented in J. G. Riewald and Jan Bakker, *The Critical Reception of American Literature in The Netherlands, 1824–1900: A Documentary Conspectus from Contemporary Periodicals* (Amsterdam: Rodopi, 1982).
7. Though primarily concerned with historical and sociological studies, the Amerika Instituut has always also shown interest in the wider cultural aspects of American studies. For instance, its founder, A. N. J. den Hollander, in 1973 published *De verbeeldingswereld van Adgar Allan Poe en enkele tijdgenoten: Bijdrage tot Amerika's ideeengeschiedenis* (The imagination of Edgar Allan Poe and contemporaries: A contribution to an American history of ideas) (Amsterdam: Athenaeum-Polak & Van Gennep).
8. A. G. van Kranendonk, *Geschiedenis van de Amerikaanse literatuur*, in twee delen (Amsterdam: G. A. van Oorschot, 1946–1947).
9. Seymour Betsky, *American Literature in the Market Place: Literature & Cultural Inquiry* (Utrecht: University of Utrecht, 1982).
10. T. A. Birrell, *Amerikaanse Letterkunde* (Utrecht & Antwerpen: Het Spectrum, 1982).
11. Harold Beaver, "On the American Canon" (Amsterdam: University of Amsterdam, 1984).
12. Hans Bertens and Theo D'haen, *Geschiedenis van de Amerikaanse literatuur* (Amsterdam: De Arbeiderspers, 1983).

ಶಿ

Catching Up
The Polish Critical Response to
American Literature

ELŻBIETA FOELLER-PITUCH

The trials and temptations for scholars specializing in a language, literature, and culture not their own were aptly voiced during a 1983 University of Warsaw symposium on the role of foreign philology in Poland. Neophilologists are forever caught between two extremes. One is the urge to embrace a different culture to the exclusion of their own, steep themselves and their students in the alien environment of a foreign language and literature, and concentrate on producing criticism that would match the scholarly response of the "host" country to its literature. The other extreme is that of acting as intermediaries between two cultures, translators and explicators of a foreign literature for the benefit of their countrymen. Between these two extremes most Polish Americanists oscillate, on the one hand translating, commenting, and explaining American literature and culture to fellow Poles, and on the other, producing scholarship in English, based on Anglo-American and European critical methods, often derivative and redundant, yet increasingly written with an eye not merely to the small circle of Polish readers but to the worldwide community of Americanists.

The study of American literature in Poland is of relatively recent date; hence, it is motivated by the necessity of "catching up," of bridging the gap—ideological, temporal, spatial—between the two cultures. Despite the fact that certain nineteenth-century authors such as Cooper, Irving, Longfellow, Stowe, Poe, and Twain were translated quite early, a widespread readership in Poland—not to mention critical and scholarly response—did not appear until our century. Traditionally Poles have displayed great awareness of French, German, and Russian culture. From the partition of Poland in the late eighteenth century to 1918, the languages of the states which occupied Poland were German and Russian. Hence, German and Russian culture played an important role in the concerns of the Polish intelligentsia and in Polish culture in general. Since French was the second language of the elite, French culture also played a significant role in Poland. British literature became better known in the course of the nineteenth century, with the emergence of Great Britain as the dominant economic power of the period and after Polish political emigrés began settling there. The first chair of English philology was established in 1908 at the Jagiellonian University in Cracow with Roman Dyboski as the first professor of English, the emphasis being on British language and British literature. This focus on British rather than American studies continued after the First World War, when Poland regained its independence.

Polish scholars devoted scant attention to American literature in the period between the two world wars, and the reading public as a whole had little access to American literature of any value. Despite such limited exposure, the image of America was powerfully embedded in the Polish imagination. Young readers derived their first impressions of America from western adventure stories by the German Karl May, as well as from the books of Cooper, Twain, and Jack London, whose works are to this day considered children's classics. Since the late nineteenth century the United States had been the primary destination for Polish peasant and Jewish emigrants: America was perceived through its aura of a land of golden opportunity, very much in the style of Emma Lazarus's sonnet on the Statue of Liberty—an aura it has retained to this day. The colloquial Polish expression "an uncle from America" still connotes a life of well-earned wealth. America was more easily associated in the popular mind with high finance, gangsters, and stirring adventure than with literary pursuits of a more serious kind. This sensational image was reinforced by popular prewar films and the cheap thrillers which dominated the market for American books, a fact lamented by Polish critics. Pearl S. Buck became well known after she won the Nobel Prize, and Margaret Mitchell's *Gone with the Wind* has been a constant favorite since its appearance in the late thirties. As for more serious literature, Hawthorne's *The Scarlet Letter,* the poetry of Whitman, the short fiction of Bret Harte and O. Henry, works by Twain, Cooper, Emerson, Dos Passos, Dreiser, Upton Sinclair, and Jack London were translated between the two world wars. During World War II Dyboski wrote an introduction to major

American authors from Benjamin Franklin to Thornton Wilder, but it could only be published much later, in 1958, at which time he added a supplementary chapter on more contemporary writers.

In the difficult years of devastation and reconstruction after World War II critical responses to American literature came to us via France, where the Lost Generation writers and the "literature of violence" (Hemingway, Steinbeck, Faulkner, Caldwell, Richard Wright) were increasingly popular; French enthusiasm made the writers available to Polish critics, who then spread the word in Poland. The critics cited anti-intellectualism, antipsychology, and simplicity as the main traits of American literature, and these traits may explain the appeal of American writers to readers who had just gone through five years of war and Nazi occupation. Also, for the first time large numbers of Poles encountered Americans when they were liberated by American troops from concentration and labor camps in Germany. Moreover, the United States was emerging as an international superpower, with a decisive role to play in the political alignments of a new, postwar Europe. Hence an increasing Polish awareness of things American was hardly surprising.

Articles on Hemingway, for instance, were published a year before his first translated work appeared in 1947. The authors were Stanisław Helsztyński, chairman of the English department at the University of Warsaw, known for his prewar presentations of American writers in journals, and Czesław Miłosz, the poet and future Nobel Prize winner. Miłosz was also the first to point out the analogies between Faulkner's South and prewar Poland, thus doing much to make that author accessible to Polish readers. Steinbeck also was first introduced by the critics and only later translated. This situation is still fairly typical today—first come critical comments or even polemics between the favored few who have read the newest works in English, and only then follow the translations for a wider audience. In the immediate postwar period the interest in American literature was evidently on the rise, as fifty-one books published in 1949 clearly show.

The Stalinist freeze from 1950 to 1955 brought about a fall in the number of American publications. Newer American fiction was translated only after intense ideological scrutiny; hence the popularity of Howard Fast and the publication of a host of virtually unknown proletarian novelists. This situation also explains the exceptionally high esteem accorded John Steinbeck and Jack London, with numerous re-issues of their works. Mark Twain retained his prominent position, joined by James Oliver Curwood, a writer of adventure stories. Although cheap editions of French, Russian, and English classics were made available for mass consumption, American literary classics remained relatively unknown in Poland. New translations of works by Twain, Cooper, London, and Dreiser were issued in this period, but by far the greatest achievement was the publication of a complete translation of *Moby-Dick*. It was, however, largely ignored by the reading public and the critics. The political thaw of 1956 brought with it a revival of interest in American literature and about forty new translations of American prose alone were published each year, mainly of twentieth-century authors. Nevertheless, large areas of earlier prose and poetry still remained untouched and thus much criticism revealed a narrow understanding of the American literary tradition.

The late 1950s and early 1960s were devoted to catching up with American modernists (Sherwood Anderson, Thomas Wolfe, Faulkner, Hemingway, Nathanael West, Thornton Wilder) and some of the writers of classics (Hawthorne, Melville, James). Newer authors also became known—Erskine Caldwell (long overestimated), Carson McCullers, Robert Penn Warren, Truman Capote, Norman Mailer (*The Naked and the Dead*), Philip Roth, J. D. Salinger, John Cheever, John Updike, and William Saroyan (a favorite of the public). Writers of lesser stature, as always, enjoyed quite a vogue; for instance, Herman Wouk and Irwin Shaw have enjoyed great popular esteem. Their popularity has been enhanced over the years by the fact that American films and TV serials based on their novels have been widely shown in Poland.

The gaps in the canon of American literature have been closed during the last three decades, though not in a particularly systematic manner; the complete text of *Walden,* for instance, is scheduled to appear in 1990. This is due not only to publishing policies, availability of paper, complicated negotiations for publishing rights in a situation when our publishing houses have little or no hard currency to offer, and so on, but also depends on what texts individual translators wish to work on. The preference among younger translators is toward more contemporary authors. As an example, we may take the publication lists for 1987 and 1988. Reissues of Hemingway, London, and Faulkner, and volumes of poetry by T. S. Eliot, Ezra Pound, and William Carlos Williams make up for lost time in the category of older American literature. New translations include prose works by Truman Capote, Walker Percy, Thomas Berger, Joan Didion, Susan Sontag, Vladimir Nabokov, William Wharton, Walter Abish, John Barth, Norman Mailer, Robert Coover, John Gardner, John Hawkes, E. L. Doctorow, Raymond Federman, William

Gaddis, and Joseph McElroy, and poetry by Frank O'Hara. The situation is similar into the 1990s. Thus, there is a tendency toward closing the temporal gap between the publication of "serious" American writing and its Polish translation. That gap has already been closed for popular literature and other forms of popular culture. Irwin Shaw, for instance, is so popular that his books are translated without any great delay. It is also worth noting that there is enormous public demand in Poland for detective fiction and thrillers (for example, works of Raymond Chandler and Ross Macdonald) and that there is, as well, a growing popularity of science fiction, which is catered to by a special publisher, Alfa.

American poetry is also, albeit slowly, receiving wider attention. Since 1981 volumes by the following poets have been published: E. L. Masters (*Spoon River Anthology*), E. A. Robinson, Richard Wilbur, E. E. Cummings, Allen Ginsberg (two books, one bilingual), Robert Bly, James Dickey, Robert Lowell, Thomas Merton, and Frank O'Hara. These books are regularly reviewed in literary magazines, such as *Nowe książki* (New books). *Rocznik literacki* (The literary annual) offered a list of translations with a balanced and perceptive summing-up of the year's output; unfortunately, after its temporary closure during the period of martial law in Poland it is grossly behind schedule. The new situation as a result of the semidemocratic elections of 1989 and the dismantling of the communist regime in Poland has liberalized publishing policies, especially by lifting censorship. Hence, for instance, the publication of Jerzy Kosinski's novels, hitherto banned, and the enormous popular success of *The Painted Bird* and Kosinski's public appearances. The underground presses have emerged onto the open market and a number of small publishing firms are springing up, often concentrating on the quick and profitable sale of thrillers, erotic literature, and children's books. The commercialization of all publishers, old and new, large and small, the enormous leap in the price of books, and the lack of funds for subsidizing publishing ventures are causes for concern for translators, publishers, and readers. However, American literature is popular enough in Poland to survive these conditions.

At the universities, post–World War II developments were similar to those in publishing. Despite the supremely difficult postwar conditions, the late forties saw a much greater interest in American literature than before the war. This interest was effectively stifled during the fifties when only the University of Warsaw retained a department of English, under Professor Margaret Schlauch, formerly of New York University, who held the post of chairman from 1954 to 1965. After 1956 the

Ministry of Higher Education gradually reopened departments of English in other university centers (Łódź, Cracow, Poznań, Lublin). "The development of English studies since 1960 has been characterized by an unprecedented dynamism. . . . The number of full-time staff members has increased several times in comparison with the previous period, e.g., in 1982 there were 71 staff members in Poznań, 36 in Cracow and 58 in Warsaw," writes Jacek Fisiak in his informative *English Studies in Poland*. These numbers include lecturers in English, literary scholars, and linguists. The number of students, graduates, and doctoral degree recipients rose accordingly, among them those in American literature. At present there are some twenty American literature specialists with doctorates at Polish universities, including seven associate professors. Apart from the American literature section in the Institute of English Studies, the University of Warsaw also has an active American Studies Center, established in 1976, with a valuable library, a scholarly journal, and a number of university exchanges for students and faculty.

In 1950 a reform was introduced in English studies. Instead of the prewar program of studies, with no limit to the length of study and a minimal course requirement, a competitive entrance examination was introduced, together with a rigid program of course work. This new program culminated in a Master of Arts degree after the presentation of a thesis on language or literature. In 1956 the course of study was lengthened to five years and the number of courses unrelated to English studies was reduced. In 1973 the Ministry overruled strong protests from the universities in order to shorten the course of study to four years and, as Fisiak notes, "again overburdened students with too many subjects unrelated to English studies. Very soon it proved that the quality of graduates went down drastically, and in spring 1980 it was agreed that in 1981 a five-year programme with a new syllabus should be introduced." This syllabus is in effect today.

The period of Solidarity in the early 1980s brought with it a creative ferment and reorganization within the universities, which helped faculty and students to redefine their roles. It was probably in this respect that American studies were most affected by the rise of Solidarity, which a large proportion of the faculty joined. The effect on scholarly research is hard to assess given the gap between writing and publication—there may be a slight decline for that period due initially to the number of time-consuming meetings and strikes, and due later to the organizational difficulties that followed the imposition of martial law in December 1981. As far as teaching is concerned, the trend in the 1980s, at least in the English department at the University of Warsaw, has been toward greater flexibility, with a greater variety of courses offered and freer choice of courses by students. This trend accelerated in 1989; the academic year 1990–91 will bring about a total reorganization of the curriculum in Warsaw, along lines closer to those in American universities.

The number of Master of Arts theses written in postwar Poland on American literature increased from 5 in 1950 to 115 in 1977; the number has been slightly lower in the 1980s, but American literature is still a very popular area of specialization among students, a trend reflecting Polish society's fascination with America in general. On the whole, twentieth-century literature dominates as the subject of most of these theses, with the Lost Generation and contemporary fiction as the most worked, or even overworked, areas. A wide range of critical approaches can be seen, from sociohistorical to structuralist, depending on the individual student's and supervisor's preferences. The students' attraction to contemporary American literature is paralleled by the general Polish fascination with present-day America, a fascination aroused by popular culture in the United States as viewed in movies and on Polish TV, and by American music—jazz, rock, country—which is disseminated by the mass media and widely emulated by Polish singers and musicians. It is an interest stimulated by political events and nourished by the popular conception of America as a land of freedom, democracy, and financial opportunity.

The general interest in newer American literature—fiction, poetry, and drama—is reflected in the changing canon of works taught at the university level. The Institute of English Studies (English department) at the University of Warsaw can be cited as an example. The reading list of the mandatory survey course in American literature, previously top-heavy with realists and naturalists, began to include more experimental writers. Authors such as W. D. Howells and Sinclair Lewis disappeared, while new "classics" like Kate Chopin took their place. In the 1980s the postmodernists were included in the canon: Pynchon, Barth, and also Nabokov. This involved acquiring entire new sets of books for the Institute library. Because of our nonconvertible currency students very rarely can buy American books in Poland and so must use Institute materials for their classes.

After energetic discussions in the American literature section, involving five Polish faculty members and two American professors during the academic year of 1984–85, a number of changes were introduced in the reading list and in the teaching of American literature. Poetry was given much more attention than before, when the course was clearly biased toward fiction. Drama was updated to include Sam Shepard, but that meant that Tennessee Williams and/or Arthur Miller would have to go. This attempt to revise the reading list stressed the unresolved problems of squeezing all American literature into an introductory course of three semesters. The problem was partially solved by the publication in 1985 of *A Handbook of American Literature for Students of English* (edited by Zbigniew Lewicki), prepared by the Warsaw faculty. This provides students with the necessary information and historical background for a better understanding of American literature as a whole, while allowing the lecturer and section instructors (teaching classes in which particular works are discussed in groups of ten to fifteen students) much greater freedom of choice as to what aspects of American literature and critical issues to address, or which of the chosen works to discuss in depth.

Parallel to the continuous adjustments taking place in the reading list, holdings in American and English criticism are continually updated. Books were received at the Institute library—admittedly a privileged one in comparison to other English departments—even during the period of martial law in Poland. The same is true of the American Studies Center library, also in Warsaw and connected with the university. These books are ordered and funded by the American embassy in Warsaw, based on the faculty's teaching and research requirements. And it is mainly this American and British literary criticism that forms the basis for students' Master of Arts theses and faculty members' scholarly works.

A growing number of Polish critical contributions are however, appearing. In 1982–83, for the first time since Dyboski's 1958 introduction to American writers, a history of American literature was published. Written by Andrzej Kopcewicz and Marta Sienicka, it is an outline history of the literature of the United States (*Historia literatury Stanów Zjednoczonych w zarysie*), in two paperback volumes, one dealing with the period from the seventeenth to the nineteenth century, the other with the twentieth century. This new book galvanized Polish Americanists into producing a volley of reviews and criticism. The authors had undertaken the formidable task of writing the first systematic Polish study of the evolution of American literature. In a sense, it tries to be too comprehensive, offering too much for the average reader interested in American literature (the information is at times just a listing of names) and too superficial a view for the serious student of literature. Nevertheless, it gives Polish readers a much-needed explanation of such American phenomena as the American dream, the myth of America, and the concept of the American Adam. On the whole, the authors' viewpoint seems to be based on American criticism. The same is true of their evaluative criteria, never clearly explained; they do not take into account certain discrepancies in Polish and Anglo-American literary terminology (e.g., the term *modernism*) nor do they make any references to parallel Polish or European trends. Despite such lacunae and an obvious imbalance in the treatment of authors (only six lines for Nabokov), the outline history has been a most necessary and welcome reference work.

The Kopcewicz-Sienicka book aptly illustrates the difficulties facing Polish Americanists: the need for informing, explaining, and developing a Polish perspective in uneasy juxtaposition with the necessity of keeping abreast of, but not succumbing to, the criteria and approaches of Anglo-American criticism. This is particularly true of academic critics, who teach in English and whose everyday work depends on the somewhat surrealistic task of re-creating an alien environment and culture in the classroom for an hour and a half at a time.

The task is relatively easier for critics outside academe, who are usually associated with publishing houses or journals and are writing for a nonspecialist audience. The favored medium is the essay, often first published in one of the literary journals, and later collected in a volume. The approaches vary from Aleksander Rogalski's Catholic viewpoint to Wacław Sadkowski's Marxist stance in their essays, collected and published in 1971 and 1972, respectively. Important volumes of essays have also been published by Leszek Elektorowicz (1966), the translator Michał Sprusiński (1984), and Lech Budrecki, the author of two valuable books, one on classic American writers (1976), the other on contemporary fiction (1983). In 1966 Viola Sachs produced a book for the general reader in which she outlined the main themes in American literature, helping Polish readers to understand its historical, religious, and philosophical background, explaining the Puritan origins of America, the influence of the frontier and of black slavery on the American psyche as revealed in literary works. The fact that this book is to be reissued, with a new introduction by the author, testifies to a continued interest in the subject.

Biographies and monographs are also helpful in bringing American authors closer to their Polish readers; for instance, Bronisław Wiśniowski's book on Faulkner, Hemingway, and Steinbeck (1961), Juliusz Żuławski's biography of Walt Whitman (1971), and Aleksander Rogalski's biography of Emily Dickinson, in which she is interestingly paired with the German poet Annete von Droste-Hülshof (1980). Franciszek Lyra's monographs on William Faulkner (1969) and Edgar Allan Poe (1973) appeared in the well-known series of "Literary Profiles" (Profile: Wiedza Powszechna) to which also belongs Halina Filipowicz-Findlay's *Eugene O'Neill* (1975). These books present the life of a given author, give summaries and standard interpretations of the major texts, and also sum up Polish reactions to the writer (translations, reviews, criticism). Another series, entitled "Classics of the 20th Century" (Czytelnik), has published two monographs on American authors, Mira Michałowska's on Gertrude Stein and Sławomir Magala's on John Barth.

The interest of translators, critics, and at least part of the reading public in contemporary formal experimentation in American literature, an interest aptly revealed in the last two studies, is also evident in the prestigious and popular monthly *Literatura na świecie* (Literature in the world), established in 1971 as a journal for the presentation of the latest trends in foreign literature. It publishes the work of young translators and each year several issues are devoted wholly or in part to American fiction and poetry. The usual format is a sample of a writer's work in translation, followed by a critical essay on his or her literary output as a whole or on a given aspect of that work. Articles of a more general nature appear as well. The emphasis is on contemporary literature, and *Literatura na świecie*, under the editorship of Lech Budrecki, Anna Kołyszko, Piotr Sommer, and Leszek Engelking, has done invaluable work in bringing American letters to the Polish reading public, from Pynchon and Barth to John Irving, from Robert Lowell and Ezra Pound to the New York School of Poetry.

Literatura na świecie also prints reviews of more important new works that have not yet been translated, thus keeping its readers more or less abreast of the American scene. The latest news is, however, a somewhat relative concept given the long publishing cycle in Poland (about three years to prepare an issue of *Literatura na świecie*, including a half year for printing). The circulation of this monthly has increased from twelve thousand to fifteen thousand in the 1970s to an average of thirty-five thousand in the 1980s. In the 1990s the circulation is to be decreased and the magazine will appear less frequently, because of budget cuts. The wide range of literature presented by the monthly can be illustrated by the American literature numbers in 1987: selections from Henry Miller's *Sexus* and *Tropic of Cancer,* poems by Robinson Jeffers, W. S. Merwin, Ezra Pound, and Randall Jarrell, an interview with LeRoi Jones, and specimens of Southern literature (Walker Percy and John

Kennedy Toole) with critical sketches (all in no. 5/6 [1987], 40,000 issues). Later numbers contain American feminist writings, Coover's *Spanking the Maid,* Walter Abish's *Alphabetical Africa,* and parts of Joseph McElroy's *Lookout Cartridge.*

Translators from the *Literatura na świecie* circle were involved in producing an anthology of innovative American short stories, entitled *Gabinet luster: krótka proza amerykańska 1961–1977* (The funhouse mirrors: short American fiction 1961–1977 [Warszawa: Czytelnik, 1980]), edited by Zbigniew Lewicki. The choice of writers is representative of the period, including not only postmodernists such as Barth, Coover, and Hawkes, but also Hubert Selby, Jr., Gail Godwin, and Grace Paley. Lewicki has edited a companion volume of contemporary American literary criticism on postmodern literature, *Nowa proza amerykańska: szkice krytyczne* (New American fiction: critical essays [Warszawa: Czytelnik, 1983]). It contains essays by such critics as Gerald Graff, Ihab Hassan, Richard Poirier, and Robert Scholes, and by the writers Barth, Federman, Gass, Hawkes, Anaïs Nin, and Gore Vidal. The two volumes together illustrate a growing interest in postmodern literature on the part of Polish Americanists and a growing awareness of the irreal tendencies in American fiction on the part of the Polish reading public, accustomed to thinking of American fiction as realistic and naturalistic par excellence.

The preference for American postmodernism shown by Polish scholars and translators seems to stem from a twofold interest in America and in formal experimentation. Poland can lay claim to a long native tradition of literary experimentation that dates back to the 1920s, a tradition exemplified by such masters of the surreal and the comic as Witkiewicz, Bruno Schulz, and Gombrowicz. The combination of avant-gardist techniques with the subject of the contemporary United States present in American postmodernism seems to be quite irresistible, particularly as it offers a challenge to translative and critical skills.

The appearance of an anthology of essays by representatives of the American New Criticism (*Nowa Krytyka: Antologia,* edited by Henryk Krzeczkowski and Zdzisław Łapiński [Warszawa: PIW, 1983]), the long overdue publication of Hawthorne's short stories and *The Marble Faun,* as well as the reissue of such symbolic romances as *The Scarlet Letter* and *Moby-Dick,* have perhaps also helped give Poles a more balanced picture of American literature. That a lively interest in it is felt, at least by intellectuals, can be seen by the controversy in the weekly press over the 1983 less-than-successful translation of Nabokov's *Transparent Things,* at the time his first book to be published in Poland, although it has since been followed by *Pnin, The Real Life of Sebastian Knight,* and *Lolita.*

Other ventures aimed at bringing American literature closer to the Polish reader are encyclopedic in character. The entries on American literature in the main *Polish Encyclopedia* (PWN publishers) are being supplemented and revised. *The School Encyclopedia,* important for its potential influence on a young reading public, will contain an introduction to American literature, followed by short entries on twenty-three American authors.

Book-length works in the more rarefied field of academic scholarship, usually published by university presses, are mainly doctoral dissertations or postdoctoral works required for the Polish equivalent of tenure; these are written either in Polish or in English, depending on the preference of the author. They reflect an overwhelming preoccupation with fiction: twelve full-length studies on fiction, six on poetry. Dating from the 1970s and 1980s, when American literature became recognized as a valid field of academic study, these publications are an index to the end of the hegemony of British literature within English departments. The topics in poetry range from a study of early American poetry, to an examination of the Fugitives, to explorations of post–World War II poets. The works on fiction are almost exclusively concerned with the twentieth century, reflecting a general Polish interest in contemporary features of the United States rather than its past. Representative examples include a comparison of the aspect of time in Joyce and Faulkner, a genre study of science fiction, a study of the themes of battle and quest in the "American fable" of the 1960s, a structural study of contemporary American self-conscious fiction, and an examination of American literary nonfiction. Although American plays are well represented on the Polish stage and systematically reviewed in the press, there is an embarrassing lack of scholarly studies of American drama—only two books by Teresa Pyzik, one on the major concepts of tragedy in postwar Anglo-American drama theory, the other on the evolution of character in American drama. Two reasons for this gap are the difficulty of obtaining materials on American stagings of plays and the lack of opportunities actually to attend American theatrical performances. Finally, the reception of American literature in Poland has been treated in two books, which provide useful information about publishing policies and critical responses. When these works are written in Polish they serve as the medium through which Polish Americanists interpret one culture to another, keeping Poles in contact with a different literature. Much scholarly work, however, is written in English; although it can enjoy only a tiny, specialized circle of readers at home, it has a greater chance of reaching an international audience through the medium of the printed word and at conferences.

Conferences are important occasions, for they enable Polish scholars to meet their foreign colleagues and to exchange ideas. In 1977 the English department of Poznań University instituted what was to be a regularly held international conference on American literature, where Polish and European Americanists could meet together with American Fulbright professors in Eastern Europe and with other American specialists, including writers. The *Proceedings of a Symposium on American Literature* (1979), edited by Marta Sienicka, includes only one paper by a Polish scholar, but the proceedings of the second Poznań conference, published in 1981 as *Traditions in 20th-Century American Literature*, includes contributions by eight Polish Americanists. The University of Warsaw Institute of English Studies was host to two international conferences, one in 1978 with Robert Coover as the "guest star" and a second in 1980 with John Ashbery, William Saroyan, Joyce Carol Oates, and Susan Sontag, thus alternating with the Poznań conferences to form a convenient annual series. This development came to an abrupt end with the imposition of martial law in 1981. The resulting gap in conferences on American literature in Poland has been keenly felt. It was not until April 1987 that papers on American literature were presented on the occasion of the triennial Cracow English literature conference. Two of these were Polish and both dealt with contemporary fiction, one on intersubjectivity in Hawthorne and Percy and the other on Maxine Hong Kingston. There followed a Poznań conference on intertextuality in British and American literature in 1989 and a Cracow conference in 1990 on new developments in American and British literary studies.

Papers delivered at conferences and scholarly articles are published in Polish or English by such scholarly journals as *Kwartalnik neofilologiczny* of the Polish Academy of Sciences, *American Studies* (American Studies Center of Warsaw), *Anglica* (University of Warsaw), *Studia Anglica Posnaniensia, Acta Universitatis Lodziensis, Anglica Wratislaviensia*—the more Latin in the title, the smaller the circulation. There are no clear-cut tendencies or "schools," no centralized research plans. The situation allows scholars to pursue their own interests unhampered, except for the difficulty of keeping up with the latest developments in American studies in the world. At the same time, however, apart from a certain concentration on postmodern fiction among scholars and critics of the younger generation, scholarship on American literature proceeds by fits and starts, with unexpected gaps, such as in the study of black American writing.

There are two new developments in the community of Polish Americanists that testify to our "catching up" with the world. In late 1989 the Polish Association for American Studies was established and formally applied for membership in the European Association for American Studies. Joining the latter will strengthen the ties between Polish Americanists and their colleagues throughout Europe. The second development is the publication of works abroad, mainly in the United States, the ultimate accolade for any Americanist. Since 1977 Franciszek Lyra has been summing up East European criticism for *American Literary Scholarship* and so has helped put Polish Americanists on the world map. Jerzy Kutnik's book, *The Novel as Performance: The Fiction of Ronald Sukenick and Raymond Federman* (1986), in the Crosscurrents series, effectively demonstrates the paradox of American experimental fiction being more eagerly seized upon abroad than in its native land. Zbigniew Lewicki's *The Bang and the Whimper* (1984) is concerned with elucidating the development of certain characteristic traits of the American mentality revealed in literary works, traits which are perhaps more clearly visible to an outsider. Lewicki examines the changing concept of the apocalypse present in Puritan writings, Melville's *Moby-Dick,* the last works of Mark Twain, and the fiction of Ralph Ellison and Robert Coover; he then compares it to the more modern notion of an entropic end of the world, as seen in Melville's "Bartleby the Scrivener," the works of Pynchon, Gaddis, Sontag, and Updike. Lewicki argues that "fascination with the vision of universal destruction" is peculiar to American writers.

While Lewicki gives an illuminating overview of important tendencies in American fiction, Teresa Kieniewicz and Agnieszka Salska concentrate on specific aspects of nineteenth-century American literature. Kieniewicz's book *Men, Women, and the Novelist: Fact and Fiction in the American Novel of the 1870s and 1880s* (1982) examines the masculine and feminine success models disseminated by popular American fiction, a field practically untouched by other Polish Americanists. Salska, on the other hand, tackles two major canonical figures in her study, *Walt Whitman and Emily Dickinson: Poetry of the Central Consciousness* (1985). She has undertaken the most comprehensive and in-depth comparison of the two poets published to date. Salska argues that "despite their fundamentally opposing positions as 'public' and 'private' poets, Whitman and Dickinson respond fundamentally to the same philosophical and aesthetic problems. Emerson provides the frame of reference for both when he postulates the ideal of the 'whole soul.' . . ." Salska sees Whitman as a poet of "mediation" who makes "opposition and variety become resolved into unity both on the plane of vision and on the plane of compositional strategies." Dickinson, on the other hand, is a poet of "command," and "whereas Whitman insists on revealing an unbroken continuity, Dickinson shatters it by juxtaposing 'now' with 'always' without offering a discernible route from one to the other. . . . Dickinson's domain is the poem of critical confrontation between the ordering power of consciousness and the tumultuous forces of the unknown." Salska's book is a significant contribution to the large body of criticism that has grown around the two poets.

These books published in the United States represent a new development in the Polish study of American literature and at the same time one of the two extremes within which Polish Americanists function. The books demonstrate that, despite all difficulties, growing scholarly links are being established between Poland and the United States, and that exchanges and scholarships have borne fruit. They illustrate beyond all doubt that Poles have something significant to offer to a wider international audience. We are, indeed, "catching up."

ॐ

Apartheid Defines the Contours of American Literary Studies in Southern Africa

MBULELO VIZIKHUNGO MZAMANE

American literature has no deep tradition in South African schools, whether Bantu, Boer, or British. It is thus possible for a black child in South Africa to go through the school system and obtain a degree without having read a single prescribed American author. There are various reasons, mostly of a political nature, for this state of affairs. Yet African-American literature has been seminal in the growth of South African literature, pointing to a wide discrepancy, as in other areas of black experience in South Africa, between an official and unofficial canon. The situation differs significantly in the other southern African countries of Botswana, Lesotho, and Swaziland (hereafter BLS), where, in order to internationalize the school curriculum, American literature has gained a foothold, along with third world and other national literatures. In determining what American authors are most widely studied, and why they are read, in southern Africa, the BLS countries in the region need to be treated separately from the apartheid enclave in South Africa. In a reformed South Africa it may well be, in fact, that the system adopted in the BLS countries will come to inform the educational structure in South Africa itself. Hence the need to examine the two systems along parallel lines.

The Anglo-Boer Legacy in South Africa

Until South Africa left the British Commonwealth in 1960, and certainly before the apartheid regime came to power in 1948, South Africa belonged to the British sphere of influence: the dominant culture was British. South African English literature was an outpost literature like the early literature of other British dominions, notably Canada and Australia.

Among anglophone South Africans, English literature represented high culture, while American literature sprang from a hybrid culture, rather like the culture of the Australians, Canadians, or Afrikaners, cultures that were regarded as inferior clones to European archetypes. American literature could not be regarded as a subject for lofty discourse any more than popular or cockney culture. American literature might be possessed of a more civilized point of view but it was no less upstart and marginal than Afrikaner literature and culture. Such Anglo-centric attitudes are deeply lodged in the psyche of anglophone South Africa and continue to inform literary discourse in English-language institutions, so that at the University of the Witwatersrand, South Africa's premier institution, even African literature in English is offered, not in the Department of English but in a separate unit still to be elevated to the status of a fully fledged department.

As English-speaking South Africans had previously controlled education in schools set up for Africans by missionaries of British extraction, English values and parochial concerns became dominant in most African schools. The Bantu Education Act, implemented in 1956 despite widespread African opposition, removed African schools from missionary control and placed them under state control, through the creation of a separate department of African education. However, the removal of African education from English control did not open the floodgates in African schools, or Afrikaner schools for that matter, to American literature or any other national literature. "The African will be taught from infancy that there is no place for him in the European community above the level of certain forms of labour." These words had been uttered in introducing the Bantu Education bill by H. F. Verwoerd, chief architect of apartheid from 1948 until his death by an assassin's knife in 1966. Verwoerd intended to educate succeeding generations of Africans for a life of meager privileges and low horizons of expectation in the African reserves. A system of education had been designed accordingly to save the Bantu (an African word meaning *people*) from the frustration that came with exposure to, as Joseph Lelyveld says in *Move Your Shadow*, "the green pastures of European society in which he was not allowed to graze." Bantu education was designed to program Africans and such programming required that Africans be inoculated against possible intellectual contamination, especially by those external influences which would impart to them liberal or revolutionary ideals. Contemporary American literature, especially from the civil rights movement then moving into gear in America, had the potential to radicalize African readers in South Africa. Such tendentious literature from America was deemed particularly undesirable and suffered censorship, along with South African protest literature and Soviet literature.

In the 1960s students from South Africa who went to school in the former British High Commission territories of Botswana, Lesotho, and Swaziland used to complain about how South African border patrols confiscated titles such as *Black Beauty*, because it was feared they might be linked to the black power movement in America, with the same indiscriminate zest with which they pounced upon works by Lenin and Dostoevsky and Solzhenitsyn. The situation in the BLS countries, however, contrasts starkly with the situation in South Africa, where a list of banned books, publications, and objects is issued weekly in the government *Gazette*.

American Literary Studies in the BLS Countries

The British system of education continued to flourish outside South Africa's borders in the British protectorates of Botswana, Lesotho, and Swaziland. As Africans continued to identify more with British traditions than with Afrikaner culture, African parents in South Africa who wished to protect their children from "mental retardation" under Bantu education sent them to schools in the British protectorates. Many of these schools were still run by missionaries, as schools in South Africa had been before Bantu education.

In the 1960s, during the period of decolonization, as the educational systems of the BLS countries came increasingly under African control, diversification of the school curriculum began to take root. American and other national literatures were introduced. However, this encounter with American literature was, at first, of a very conservative kind, consisting of American classics supplied, one suspects, by the United States Information Service, which in the Kennedy era began to export American literature and culture more aggressively than ever before. The library at St. Christopher's High School in Swaziland in the 1960s, one of the best libraries in any African school in southern Africa at the time, kept a complete set of F. W. Dixon's Hardy Boys series and several copies of *The Adventures of Tom Sawyer* and *The Adventures of Huckleberry Finn* as prime examples of universal childhood and adolescent themes. These books complemented British children's series such as Enid Blyton's Secret Seven series and British classics by Charles Dickens, presumably gifts from the British Council like most of the other novels by British authors in the library at St. Christopher's.

The establishment in 1964 of the University of Botswana, Lesotho, and Swaziland (UBLS), which conferred its first autonomous degrees and diplomas in 1967, and the independence in 1966 of Botswana and Lesotho, followed in 1967 by Swaziland, ushered in far-reaching changes in the literature syllabi at the university and in schools in all three countries. The Department of English at UBLS began to teach African literature, which gradually came to form the core of the syllabus. At the same time, the syllabus was expanded to encompass American, Russian, Commonwealth, and other European literatures. A recent development in the BLS countries and in Zimbabwe, independent since 1980—a development matched elsewhere on the continent—has been the addition of Caribbean, Asian, Latin American, and other third world literature.

At UBLS in the 1960s and 1970s the favored American authors and texts were Hemingway's *For Whom the Bell Tolls* and *A Farewell to Arms;* Steinbeck's *The Grapes of Wrath, Of Mice and Men,* and *Cannery Row;* Arthur Miller's *Death of a Salesman* and *The Crucible;* Mark Twain's *The Adventures of Huckleberry Finn;* Harper Lee's *To Kill a Mockingbird;* Tennessee Williams's *A Streetcar Named Desire* and *Sweet Bird of Youth;* and Henry James's *Washington Square.* The same range of American authors offered at the university was represented in the secondary schools' curriculum by selections from their work deemed more suitable for younger readers, such texts as Ernest Hemingway's *The Old Man and the Sea* and John Steinbeck's *The Pearl.* Although this became the official canon, student reception of such authors and their texts followed an intricate but decipherable pattern conditioned by cultural affinity, historical and political circumstances, and their economic situation. A few examples will explain attitudes which influenced reader reception of such prescribed texts.

The "other" Hemingway, the Spanish Civil War Hemingway, continues to have the greatest significance for readers in southern Africa, accustomed to social and political turmoil, whereas for most of the rest of the world the alienated "lost generation" Hemingway is important.

Their efforts to overcome tyranny, to avoid destabilization by the apartheid regime, and to attain authentic freedom are similar to the concerns
that ignited the Spanish Civil War or the American War of Independence. People in southern Africa live on a footing of constant war. Along
similar political lines, southern African readers are attracted to the
depression-era Steinbeck, who subscribed to socialist values and wrote
as the voice of the dispossessed, the American underclasses, and the
Mexican-American "wetbacks."

Mark Twain's *Huckleberry Finn,* with its abolitionist theme, and Harper
Lee's *To Kill a Mockingbird,* with its civil rights message, elicited positive
responses among students at UBLS. From the late 1960s, however, as
black consciousness spread to the university campus, a reassessment of
such white liberal authors as Mark Twain and Harper Lee followed. A
certain amount of disquiet set in over white liberal spokesmanship, with
its implicit paternalism, wherein the black voice in what is, after all, a
black problem is stifled. In *Huckleberry Finn,* for instance, we see Jim, an
elderly man of African origin, guided like a helpless pup by a "European" boy young enough to be his son. Jim's dependence on Huck, who
hatches all the brilliant schemes, projects an unflattering image of slaves.
Jim's thought processes have yet to mature beyond Huck's. White liberal
patronage characterizes Mark Twain's depiction of Jim in a way that
recalls the condescension we find in the region among white liberals like
Alan Paton, author of *Cry, the Beloved Country,* a novel in which, as in
Mark Twain, no political role model acceptable to politicized blacks
emerges. *Huckleberry Finn* was still prescribed in 1988–89 at the National
University of Lesotho (NUL), formerly a constituent campus of UBLS
but autonomous since 1975, but only in a course on World Literature:
Images of Childhood, where it was taught along with works by James
Joyce, William Fielding, Maxim Gorky, Camara Laye, and R. K. Na-
rayan. The adoption of such a comparative approach does not mean,
however, that American literature has been marginalized over the years.

The training in American universities (rather than in Britain where
the cost of university training for overseas students has become prohibi-
tive) of an increasing number of young academics and civil servants
responsible for education in the BLS countries may well mark a significant shift from the periphery to the mainstream of American literary
studies in these countries. In 1987–1988 two doctoral students and one
master's student graduated from American universities, all of them
members of staff in the Department of English at the University of

Botswana; in the same period, two lecturers in the Department of English at the university of Swaziland were completing their doctorates in American universities.

As in the rest of Africa, American studies in the BLS countries have had a twofold thrust that is likely to persist into the future. First, one sees a dominance of African-American literature that is likely to remain unchallenged. NUL exemplifies this trend: the only full course on American literature at the university in 1988–89 was a course on African-American literature. The full course description reads:

> A study of Black American literary culture in its historical contexts, from slavery into the 20th century.
> Prescribed Texts:
>   R. Wright, *Native Son*
>   M. Berman (ed.), *A Chronological History of the Negro in America*
>   F. Douglass, *Narrative of the Life of Frederick Douglass*
>   D. Randall, *Black Poets*
>   L. Hansberry, *A Raisin in the Sun*
>   J. Baldwin, *Go Tell It on the Mountain*
>   J. H. Clark (ed.), *American Negro Short Stories*.

Next, one encounters a smattering of American classics chosen largely for their emphases on civil rights and abolitionist themes. There are also a few texts chosen, as far as one can see, on the whims of American academics appointed since independence through the Peace Corps, academics who occasionally still find their way to these institutions. *Death of a Salesman* was one such text that seemed to make little sense to students in the region, many of whom came from communities where the village shopkeeper, the closest figure to a salesman, is definitely on a sounder economic footing than the rest of the village community. By contrast, one found that among favored American classics, texts with a Southern setting were preferred over others set elsewhere in North America.

Southern literature strikes a responsive chord in many southern African readers for reasons which are not too difficult to decipher. The South, down to its vegetation and climate, elicits recognition in southern African readers. The literature abounds with stories of the racism, sexism, and poverty which one recognizes are indigenous not only to the American South, but also to South Africa.

The situation of the American South bred writers in much the same fashion as did that of nineteenth-century Russia, or present-day South Africa. In such situations of social and political repression and upheaval the writer must bleed, on paper, to flush out the poisons of corrosive bitterness, human degradation, social injustice, and racial antipathy. Rather than encourage self-indulgence and metaphysical escape, the literature of the American South exhibits an immediacy and engagement with life that aim at both recognition and exorcism. It is a literature of deep social and personal crisis, one that calls for a wide range of human resources and responses from writers and readers alike.

Coming from South Africa to the American South, one soon realizes that it is no accident that the South has produced such marvelous writers, ones read more avidly than northern writers by South Africans: William Faulkner, Eudora Welty, Robert Penn Warren, Tennessee Williams, and Margaret Mitchell. In addition, the South African reader comes to associate African-American writers with the South, since the Southern experience is their sounding board. Part of the Southern literary tradition, like the South African literary tradition, has to do with the fact that Southerners, black and white, are story-tellers: theirs is a more elegantly verbal culture than that of the North.

Also, as many whites in South Africa know, guilt and tragedy seem essential for good literature. The South is a place redolent with these qualities. As reflected in the work of Faulkner and others, most native white Southerners are subconsciously trying to deal with the guilt of slavery and its racist aftermath. White Southerners somehow have to come to grips with the fact that if their families were wealthy before the Civil War, that wealth was based upon the ownership of human beings. If they were poor, the only thing that gave them any status was their superiority to the black slave. This is a difficult burden: Southerners somehow have to explain how their ancestors could be "good people" and still engage not only in the abomination of a trade in human beings, but also base their society, their wealth, and their status upon it. This compensatory reaction takes many forms: some try to set things right; others deny that slavery was all that bad; and still others become aggressively racist as if to assert that slavery was all right because blacks are/were inferior anyway. This concern for the moral integrity of predecessors might not be important in a culture which is not quite so concerned about people's origins, but Southerners dwell with ghosts. They are ancestor worshipers. In the South, wealth is not the marker of class; it is family. So Southerners cling to putative, and quite often fictive, past family glory as a source of status and pride.

Southern society is still trying to recover from the impact of the Civil War and Reconstruction, which decimated the economy after 1864. In

addition, Southerners are the only Americans ever to have lost a war
(with the exception of the war in Vietnam), in much the same way as the
Afrikaners lost the Anglo-Boer War of 1899–1902. These factors, plus
the guilt of slavery and segregation, have created a fairly serious in-
feriority complex for Southern whites. They peddled flesh, they lost a
war, they lost their wealth, and the rest of the nation has been calling
them ignorant racists for over 120 years. This explains in part some of
the bravado of Southerners: why they take sports, especially contact
sports, seriously; why they are embarrassingly patriotic; and why they
insist upon doing provocative things like flying the Confederate flag although they know it is an insult to blacks. Southerners feel that they must
prove themselves worthy, and this often results in overreaction and exaggerated behavior which can be matched on all counts, from the rugby
field to the houses of Parliament, by *platteland* Boers in South Africa.

There is no doubt that many Southerners were racist, but one soon
learns from reading African-American writers who relocated to the
North that racism is not that much more prevalent in the South than in
the rest of the country. Moreover, as James Baldwin, Imamu Baraka, and
others show, the racism which one encounters in the South is somewhat
different from the racism of the North. First, Southerners are (with the
exception of the subhuman goons one reads about of the Klu Klux Klan
and Forsythe, Georgia, variety) almost unfailingly polite. Also, like
speakers of Afrikaans (as opposed to English-speaking South Africans),
Southerners have always known black people on an intimate level, and
they often feel a great deal of personal affection for individual blacks, as
plantation stories demonstrate. It is the black race in general that is the
target of their racism. The reverse is true with Northerners. They pro-
fess great affection for the black race, but are afraid of individual blacks
because, as James Baldwin's *Nobody Knows My Name* or Ralph Ellison's
Invisible Man reveal, they have never known any.

These various attitudes toward race and class that characterize Southern literature and society are matched by the attitudes of whites in South
Africa. In Athol Fugard's play, *Master Harold and the Boys*, which pre-
miered in 1982 at the Yale Repertory Theatre, Harold, Fugard's alter
ego in the play, exhibits a range of attitudes and emotions toward blacks
that are familiar to readers of William Faulkner, Harper Lee, and other
white liberal American writers—from dependence, condescension, rejection, guilt, and atonement, to outright animosity culminating in
crushing shame. Southern literature addresses all these problems and
thus seems, like African-American literature, to speak to South Africans,

too. Southern literature and culture are complicated; and if the South is sometimes maddening and ugly, it keeps one's interest and elicits partisan responses among South Africans who read the literature.

Pan-Africanism and Cultural Affirmation

In the Republic of South Africa readers seek out American literature relevant to their experience: they seek more than a mere classroom acquaintance with the literature. Their response to American literature is conditioned by their South African experience. This response is best demonstrated by an examination of the impact of American literature and culture on South African writing, an impact we can more systematically trace by reaching back in time to the founding of the Pan-African movement, which set the stage as much for African-American as for Caribbean and African literature and politics in the twentieth century.

The year 1900 was important in the history of black political thought in Africa, America, and the Caribbean. The year saw the first Pan-African Congress convened under the leadership of such prominent blacks as the Trinidadian lawyer, H. Sylvester Williams, and the African-American leaders, W. E. B. Du Bois and Booker T. Washington. The feeling of solidarity engendered by Pan-Africanism led to political interaction on an unprecedented scale between Africans in the diaspora, in America and the Caribbean, and on the continent.

In the 1910s Solomon Tshekiso Plaatje, founding secretary-general of the African National Congress when it was formed in 1912 and the first African in South Africa to write a novel (*Mhudi*) in English, embarked on travels to carry out research "through several farms and cities of nineteen different states in America and compare conditions under which blacks lived in America with conditions in South Africa." Plaatje met and held discussions with many founding members of the Pan-African movement. In addition, he wrote a fifteen-page pamphlet against the prohibition of mixed marriages in South Africa. The pamphlet sold eighteen thousand copies in New York in 1921 and influenced the views of many African-Americans who read it.

Such interaction as Plaatje and others had initiated in the first quarter of the twentieth century with Africans in the diaspora continued under the umbrella of Pan-Africanism. At the fifth Pan-African Congress in 1945, held in Manchester and attended by such figures as Kwame Nkrumah and Jomo Kenyatta, who were to lead their respective countries to independence, the South African novelist Peter Abrahams was co-secretary with George Padmore, widely regarded as the father of African emancipation from British colonialism.

Pan-Africanism stirred black nationalism and set the tone for black writing from the Americas, the Caribbean, and Africa. The examples in the 1920s of African Americans, and in the 1930s of people of African origin in the West Indies and Africans living under French colonialism, illustrate the cultural and political affirmation brought about by Pan-Africanism. The Harlem Renaissance in the 1920s and the rise of negritude in the 1930s were literary expressions of a political and cultural reawakening among people of African origin. The literature was part of the cultural nationalism that accompanied Pan-Africanism.

In the 1920s writers of the Harlem Renaissance, such as Langston Hughes, Countee Cullen, and Claude McKay, began to assert their identity as black people, in some ways by trying to reach back to their African roots. Although Pan-Africanism remained an important aspect of their political program and despite Marcus Garvey's "Back to Africa Call" (which largely went unheeded), the Harlem Renaissance never became a roots movement the way negritude, Rastafarianism, and some of the American black power organizations of the 1960s were to become. Writers of the Harlem Renaissance, who have had a profound influence on Peter Abrahams and other African writers even up to the present day, were more concerned with the problem of being black in America than with the liberation of the African continent as such and people of African descent universally. That task was left to writers and political activists of the civil rights and black power movements: they had a more direct influence on black consciousness writers and activists in the 1960s in South Africa. Steve Biko, on whom the movie *Cry Freedom* by Richard Attenborough and Donald Woods is based, was one such black consciousness activist.

In the 1930s and 1940s the scene shifted from New York to Paris with the rise of negritude, which spilled over into Africa and America. The shift from a concern with purely political matters to a preoccupation with cultural affirmation among writers of African descent began with writers of the negritude movement. They saw the assertion of their cultural identity as people of African origin, and their psychological and cultural emancipation from European domination, as prerequisites to the liberation of the black race universally. In the 1930s, negritude was propounded by Aimé Césaire and Léopold Senghor, who later became the first president of Senegal; in their writing they attacked European civilization and celebrated an African orientation and influence. In the first period of black writing in French there was a deliberate attempt by writers such as René Maran, Birago Diop, Bernard Dadie, and Max-millien Quénem to dislodge their European disorientation and return to their African cultural heritage, to preserve and to introduce this African heritage into their writings by transcribing and translating into French the legends, myths, and folklore of their own people. This formed the basis of a valid literature in the French language, written by Africans from the continent and in the diaspora, and associated with the maga-zine *Présence Africaine* founded in 1947 by Alioune Diop to serve as an important voice for people of African origin everywhere.

The 1950s and 1960s were a time of turbulence and violence, when Southern blacks protested, demonstrated, and even died in order to achieve integration into the American system. In "Cultural Nationalism in the 1960's: Politics and Poetry," Jennifer Jordan describes the forces that shaped African-American literature and politics in the following terms:

> The stench of death and terror . . . the sight of police dogs biting defenseless children, Bull Connor's red face scowling on the living room television set, and King's, and even Kennedy's, bloody finales, frozen on front pages and incessantly re-enacted and rerun in black and white or even living color, made Elijah Muhammad seem promising, turned Malcolm into a saint and a prophet, and sent Black folks into the streets. The nationalism that resulted was a protean force that sheltered a number of divergent movements, the most prominent of which, according to James Turner, were the religious nationalism of the Nation of Islam, the Marxist revolutionary, Black capital-ism, the political nationalism of the Republic of New Africa, Pan-African nationalism, and cultural nationalism.

The civil rights movement in the 1950s and black power in the 1960s precipitated some of the most profound struggles of the postwar era by oppressed groups in America: many found their inspiration in the great struggle for decolonization in Asia and Africa. Out of the civil rights campaigns in Montgomery, Alabama, in the mid-1950s and the up-heavals of the 1960s in Watts, Cleveland, Detroit, Los Angeles, New York, and other places, emerged important leaders from black commu-nities in America: Martin Luther King, Elijah Muhammad, Malcolm X, Stokely Carmichael, LeRoi Jones (Imamu Amiri Baraka), and many others. Many had no university education. Malcolm X, George Jackson, Eldridge Cleaver, and H. Rap Brown were "more closely associated with the jails of the United States and not with the universities." Yet they had risen to become important spokespersons for the black cause; their autobiographies had made a significant impact on the American political and literary scene.

Their example struck a responsive chord in the souls of the emerging writers of the black consciousness era in South Africa. Many of my contemporaries in South Africa had the doors of the universities in their country slammed in their own faces; a few of them were not strangers to prison either, usually having been sentenced for petty offenses under apartheid legislation or for suspected political offenses which were never proved. The black struggle in America provided precedents. Black writers in South Africa could emulate their African-American counterparts by stirring people's hearts and reactivating the fighting spirit among blacks. The new writers and activists in South Africa, like their counterparts in America, maintained the Pan-African concept, which was essentially an exercise in self-definition by black people "aimed at establishing a broader definition of themselves than that which had so far been permitted by those in power."

The legacy of Pan-Africanism lies in its contribution to the decolonization of the black mind. The founding fathers used Africa as a point of reference, as much in literature as in music, art, sculpture, religion, and politics: they used Africa to develop an unvarnished style, and depended on images, metaphors, and subject matter drawn from the black world to produce culture designed primarily for blacks. Pan-African literature and culture, as an affirmation of the sum total of black values and their emancipationist ideals, strove with increasing vigor for a hearing side by side with Pan-Africanism in the political arena, for the total liberation of black people universally. South African writers have been contributors to, as well as beneficiaries of, the unfolding Pan-African ethos that has informed twentieth-century politics and culture among people of African origin the world over.

Impact of African-American Literature on South African Writing

After Sol Plaatje, Peter Abrahams was the next significant African novelist in English to emerge from South Africa. In *Tell Freedom* Abrahams conveys his sense of exultation at discovering African-American literature in the 1930s. Abrahams made connections between the African-American predicament and the conditions of Africans in South Africa. Recalling his first encounter with *The Souls of Black Folk* by W. E. B. Du

Bois, he discovered an American giving him words that could voice what was within him, "words that had the impact of revelation. . . . The mood and feeling he described were native to me." Alain Locke's anthology, *The New Negro*, led to a feeling of great pride: "These poems and stories were written by Negroes! Something burst deep inside me. The world could never again belong to white people only! Never again!" He recounts similar responses to Countee Cullen, to Langston Hughes, to Sterling Brown, to Claude McKay, to Georgia Douglas Johnson, to Jean Toomer. "I became a nationalist, a colour nationalist, through the writings of men and women who lived a world away from me. To them I owe a great debt for crystallizing my vague yearnings to write and for showing me the long dream was attainable."

Nor is Abrahams a solitary voice in this regard: the example of an America which had served as a seedbed in which Pan-African ideas had flourished so that they could return, invigorated, to their home continent recurs again and again in South African writing. For Sipho Sepamla it was not so much the literature as the other aspects of African-American culture—film, music, and advertisements—that left lasting impressions on his world. He describes the era of his teens in the 1940s in the following terms:

> This was the era of the Juke-box, Louis Jordan being the hit-maker. The music of the time was boiling hot with a heavy rhythm. The jitterbug, illustrated in such movies as *Cabin in the Sky* and *Stormy Weather* was very popular. . . . It seemed like an act of God to identify with all things by black Americans. The very fact that these brothers came from Africa and were baptised as slaves was equated to the massive oppression experienced by local Africans.

In his poems Sepamla sometimes uses Americanisms and jazz rhythms. "The Blues is You in Me" employs the jazz idiom to explore various aspects of life under apartheid. In a foreword to Paul Oliver's *Blues This Morning*, Richard Wright observes that "the most astonishing aspect of the blues is that, though replete with a sense of defeat and down-heartedness, they are not intrinsically pessimistic; their burden of woe and melancholy is dialectically redeemed through sheer force of sensuality, into an almost exultant affirmation of life, of love, of sex, of movement, of hope." The blues idiom is eminently suited for Sepamla's purpose in the poem, in which he unburdens himself of the melancholy that assails him and demonstrates how he never loses faith in life. The poem explores typical problems in the lives of blacks and whites, in the manner of a blues song. He complains about underpayment, censorship, residential segregation, discrimination in education, and other apartheid measures. He argues that these same measures designed to keep blacks in subjugation also serve to constrain white happiness and curtail progress. While whites are inclined to wallow in their complacency and to accept the stagnation, blacks are striving to change the status quo and to counteract their oppression:

> We are the blues people all
> the whiteman bemoaning his burden
> the blackman offloading the yoke.

Whites are victims, too, of an apartheid that ironically has become burdensome to them as well to maintain. The title signifies the inseparable destiny of blacks and whites in South Africa. The black person is the soul of the white person in South Africa; any white person who refutes the complementary nature of the relationship consigns his soul to perdition.

Don Mattera, three years younger than Sepamla, completed high school at a Catholic institution, then formed a gang called the Vultures, named after the American movie *Where No Vultures Fly*, before he became a poet and a political activist. Influences on his writing, as on his life, have been truly eclectic, ranging from the 1950s writers of the Sophiatown renaissance, and the writers who are associated with *Drum* magazine, to writers of the Harlem Renaissance and the Pan-African school. He elaborates in an 1987 interview with Hein Willemse:

> I was influenced by people like Can Themba, Bloke Modisane, people like Zeke Mphahlele, and many other journalists. Lewis Nkosi, he was my agent, but he didn't really influence me. More for me was the influence of the Harlem renaissance, W. E. B. Du Bois and Langston Hughes, the black American life style, the novels of James Baldwin, the novels of Richard Wright. These were direct influences. Also the writings of Kwame Nkrumah, the writings of Pan-Africanism.

Among South Africa's new generation of poets, Mafika Gwala emerged in the late 1960s as the leading exponent of black consciousness, the movement founded by Steve Biko that was heavily indebted to the ideas of Charles Hamilton, Stokely Carmichael, and others. Certain features of African-American cross-cultural influences manifest themselves in the following lines from Gwala's "Gumba, Gumba, Gumba":

> Witness a dachshund bitch shitting
> A beautiful Black woman's figure too close by,
> Her hand holding the strap;

In a white lonely suburb.
Tramp the city
Even if you're sleepweary
'cos your Black arse
Cant's rest on a 'Whites Only' seat.

Gwala admits as much, while appearing to dispute the fact, when he writes in *Staffrider*:

> I grew up in a mixed environment. I have Coloured and Indian cousins, nephews, and nieces, uncles and aunties. Some who even pass for whites. English, especially in the youth stage, is spoken with lots of American and Afrikaans slang. So where I had sounded American in my poems it is not because of the influence of Black American literature as Nadine Gordimer so readily concluded in her book, *The Black Interpreters*. It's just that American movies, American comics, and paperbacks, American advertisements came down on us in typical imperialist fashion. (July/August 1979)

Gwala makes heavy weather of the issue. Admittedly there are elements of decadence which undiscriminating nonwhites ape from American culture; nonetheless, it is essentially healthy for the growth of any culture to be able to co-opt all those aspects from other cultures which enrich one's own. That should be the advantage (which whites deny themselves to their own detriment) of living in a multicultural environment. The strong language in Gwala's poem is typical of the uncompromising stance adopted by black consciousness poets. The linguistic features of the new poetry are closer to African-American than to British or Anglo-American poetry. The recurring image of the "black beauty" in the new poetry derives in part from negritude and in part from black power in America, and perhaps in equal measure from common sense and the cultural background of African poets. A strong South Africanness, however, clings to Gwala's "Gumba, Gumba, Gumba." The title, which has acquired wide usage in America through South African musicians, is of South African coinage and refers to the township style of all-night entertainment with plenty of food, drink, music, dancing, and lovemaking in African Shebeens. Gwala does not need to feel defensive about such cultural fusion, which can be a sign of great vitality.

Reverse Influences

Despite my focus on the seminal role American black writing has played in South African literature, a brief recognition must be made of the fact that the relationship has been two-sided, that American black writing of the 1960s owes much to the influence and ideas of exiled South Africans.

There is wide recognition of the contribution to the American musical scene of the 1960s and 1970s of South African musicians such as Miriam Makeba, Hugh Masekela, and Dollar Brand (Abdullah Ibrahim), and most recently Jonathan Butler. Paul Simon's "Graceland" album brought, along with political controversy, the indigenous South African sound of the Ladysmith Black Mambazo to the drawing rooms of middle-class America. In theater, Athol Fugard's Yale plays have elicited rave reviews, and they have found no lack of emulators at the Yale Repertory Theatre. *Sarafina,* another South African production, with music by Hugh Masekela and playwright Mbongeni Ngema, received five nominations for the 1988 Tony Awards. There has yet to develop, however, an appreciation of the contribution of South African poets to the unfolding, especially, of African-American literature. Kgositsile is a case of the lack of recognition that reverse influences of South African writing on American black writing could be found as much in Plaatje's time as in African-American writing of the 1960s and 1970s.

Keorapetse Kgositsile, aspirant to the poet laureateship of the black power movement in America through his association with Malcolm X and other radical African-American voices, typifies the poets of the second wave of the African diaspora in a number of ways. His poems straddle Africa and America. "For Afro-America," in *Seven South African Poets,* cements the relationship between Africans on the continent and in the diaspora. His references range widely. "Exile," from *The Present Is a Dangerous Place to Live In,* contains quotations from Gwendolyn Brooks and Aimé Césaire, together with an invocation of the anti-imperial spirit of Patrice Lumumba, the Congo's first prime minister, who was assassinated. Kgositsile's poems deal with the cultural and political regeneration of black people worldwide. His black perspective embraces a third world rather than an ethnic outlook. He conceives of himself as a poet of the liberation struggle and describes his symbiotic relationship to the liberation struggle as follows: "The revolutionary poet concretizes the dreams of a people for a better life; the liberation movement fights to make these dreams a reality." His social vision brings him closer to Cabral than to Nkrumah. He is as assertive as he is optimistic about the triumphant outcome of the black people's liberation struggle universally. He supports the armed struggle; fire, a recurring image in his poems, endorses the Fanonesque concept of purgation by violence. Many poets of the black consciousness era, notably Mafika Gwala and

Mongane Serote, have gravitated toward Kgositsile's internationalist outlook. With Kgositsile the resources of African poetry were exported to America and exported back, mediated by his American experience. He remains an important figure as much in the South African liberation movement, where he is assistant director of the African National Congress's Department of Arts and Culture, as in African-American poetry.

Conclusion

Political considerations play the most decisive role in determining what American authors and literary movements are most widely studied or read in southern Africa. In the BLS countries, as in the Republic of South Africa, domestic political concerns—which include not only an apartheid that spreads its tentacles to every country on the subcontinent but also a widespread opposition to it—play a role in what is read and what is studied, and in how these works are approached. Further, in the Republic of South Africa the reading canon and the academic canon differ, while by contrast in the BLS countries the two are integrated in a manner that suggests the direction educational structures in postapartheid Africa may eventually take. African-American writers are the most widely read in the region; literature of the American South, which springs from the same impulse as South African literature, is better appreciated than literature from the rest of the United States. The seminal role African-American literature has played in the development of protest literature in South Africa is reciprocated by the radicalization of African-American literature, culture, and politics through the input of exiled South Africans. In the final analysis, apartheid defines the contours of American literary studies in southern Africa.

The Dual Canon
A Swedish Example

ROLF LUNDÉN

In March 1902, a famous Swedish historian, Harald Hjärne, wrote an article entitled "Americanization," in which he deplored the European servility toward the United States. He likened America to a rattlesnake which had the power to hypnotize its victims with its charm before it sank its poisonous fangs into their trembling bodies. Professor Hjärne felt, to his dismay, that not only European politicians and businessmen but also representatives of the church and the universities had been bewitched by the American rattlesnake.

Ever since the nineteenth century Sweden has been the victim of the kind of ambivalent feelings toward the United States that are expressed in Professor Hjärne's article. In that respect Sweden is no different from many other European countries which have experienced a similar love-hate relationship.

American literature was initially looked upon by Scandinavian critics as being crude and superficial. Knut Hamsun, the well-known Norwegian author, wrote a book in 1889 which had a tremendous impact in Scandinavia called *The Cultural Life of Modern America,* in which he castigated American literature as being hopelessly unreal and devoid of talent. Whitman's "Song of Myself," he wrote, was "no more a song than is a multiplication table." In Sweden, American literature fared little better. Up to the 1920s, the American books that were accepted on the Swedish market were books of adventure and humor; writers like Twain, Cooper, and London were in demand. During the 1920s the understanding and appreciation of American literature improved, but it is interesting to note that the first American to receive the Nobel Prize for literature was Sinclair Lewis, whose depiction of American culture gave sanction to the Swedish derogatory view of the United States. A majority of the selection committee within the Swedish Academy had on several occasions expressed negative views of America and its culture.

Since then, the Swedish opinion of American culture and literature has steadily improved, with setbacks in the 1960s and 1970s, but this unwillingness to fully acknowledge the United States as a producer of quality literature comparable to the best European literature is still noticeable in Sweden. As we will see, American literature has been accepted by the critics, the publishing houses, and the readers, but the academic bastions have not yet fallen.

This will suffice as a background, underlining the tradition of ambivalence that has characterized Sweden's attitude toward American literature. This study will focus on what has taken place during the last fifteen years and try to answer such questions as whether any radical changes have occurred in the appreciation of American literature; which American writers and books are being read and studied; which writers have been excluded from the cultural debate in Sweden; and whether Swedish scholars have approached American literature from a particular theoretical standpoint.

But before I enter into such a presentation, let me make a few sweeping statements about literary theory in Sweden and about the literary canon. By tradition, Swedes in general have not been a theory-oriented people. Sweden has never produced a de Saussure, a Jakobson, a Derrida, a Foucault, a Lévi-Strauss, or a Kristeva. Nor have we given birth to literary theorists like Bakhtin, de Man, Iser, Benjamin, or Barthes. There are several reasons for this, including the size of the population and the fact that Swedish is not an international language. But maybe the basic factor is that Swedes have always been slow to accept new, esoteric theories, which they have regarded as newfangled trendiness. Sweden has been characterized by a weak theoretical tradition, and until recently there has been little theoretical debate. With certain exceptions, Swedish university students are not trained in theoretical analysis. To generalize even further, one may say that the Swedish mind is traditionalist, eclectic, and pragmatic. I do not mean this as a derogatory remark, but merely as a crude distinction from the cultural climate of other countries, such as France, a distinction which may explain some of the attitudes in Sweden toward American literature. Sweden has not been open to foreign cultures like Holland; it lacks Poland's avant-garde tradition; it is not experiencing the anarchic or hysterical freedom that Greece seems to be enjoying right now. Sweden is, by and large, a stable, traditional, dependable, predictable society.

This study will try to establish the canon of American literature in Sweden. This is obviously no easy task, since the whole concept of a canon has been under attack, and scholars trying to write literary histories have felt themselves to be in a quagmire. One could discuss the Swedish literary canon in general—the total interest in literature in Sweden—and try to find out how large a portion of that interest is directed toward American literature and whether the interest has been growing. I will devote only a little space to this. One may also concentrate on establishing the canon of American literature in Sweden, that is, which American authors and works have been translated, reviewed, performed on stage, included in literary histories and reading lists at the universities, and accorded serious scholarly concern in articles, books, and dissertations. This will be the primary interest of this investigation. There is one further issue concerning the canon that one needs to notice and that has been made the basis for the structure of this study.

There seem to be two canons in Sweden: one more popular canon consisting of works accepted by the well-educated reading public and discussed in the press and in cultural journals; and one canon comprising the works studied and written about at the universities. As a result of its small size, its homogeneity, and its limited book production, Sweden may highlight a pattern of a dual canon, one readerly and one academic, that is common but less noticeable in other countries as well. As a consequence of this division, this essay will first deal with the well-educated general reader's response to American literature and then discuss the presence and status of this literature at the university.

During the last fifteen years there has been a remarkable growth in the interest in American literature in Swedish society in general. When I speak of American literature read by well-educated readers, I exclude popular literature like detective stories, thrillers, and romances, and discuss only "quality" literature. There has been a tremendous inflow of American novels, short story collections, plays, and collections of poetry, primarily during the last ten years. Compared to other foreign literature, American literature is capturing an increasingly larger portion of the Swedish market. American writers and their works are consequently more highly visible today than they were fifteen years ago.

More books by American writers are being translated. The selection of

American literature in the original is wider and more easily accessible. American writers, such as Vonnegut, Cheever, Gardner, Updike, Oates, Marilyn French, and Jayne Anne Phillips are interviewed with regularity on Swedish radio and TV. The Swedish radio has run serials of novels by Anne Tyler, Hemingway, Steinbeck, McCullers, and Philip Roth. American writers are constantly visiting Sweden to attend book fairs and to create publicity for their books when they appear in translation. During the fall of 1987 Sweden received visits from Updike, Oates, Auel, Mary Hood, and Marilyn French.

Many factors have contributed to this increasing interest in American literature. In the first place, the cultural climate of Sweden has changed. Sweden is no longer as anti-American as it was during the 1960s and early 1970s. During those years Prime Minister Palme demonstrated against the Vietnam war side by side with the North Vietnamese ambassador, he likened the bombing of Hanoi to Treblinka, and Swedish demonstrators threw eggs at the American ambassador. Now Prime Minister Carlsson has paid an official visit—the first in twenty-five years by a Swedish prime minister—to the United States. Those of us who twenty years ago worked in the field of American literature kept a low profile. When I received in 1970 an ACLS fellowship to do research at the University of Pennsylvania, friends and acquaintances had difficulties understanding why I would want to go to such a country. Today thousands of students go every year to study in the United States.

Another reason for the increasing interest in American literature is the fact that there has been a shift in the publishing world from London and Paris to New York. American publishing houses are pushing their products in a much more aggressive way than their British, German, French, or Italian counterparts. Swedish editors feel that it is much easier to do business with American publishing houses than European ones. This is partly a language problem when it comes to Germany and France and Italy, but not only that. Americans are undoubtedly more skillful in "hyping" their books. Publishing houses in the United States also make use of the competition that exists in Sweden between several fairly large publishing firms by playing one firm against another. If I am correctly informed, it is much more difficult for American publishing houses to place their products in Denmark, where the market is dominated by the large publishing house Gyldendal, or in Norway.

In Sweden during the last fifteen years, some five hundred American literary works have been translated or performed on stage. The overwhelming majority of translations have been works of prose, primarily novels. There have been about ten times as many prose works as there have been collections of poetry. There have been five times as many novels and short story collections as there have been theater productions. Compared to the novels that have appeared, there have been few collections of short stories. During the last three or four years more short stories have been published by writers like Grace Paley, Peter Taylor, and Mary Hood.

Almost without exception, the American novels that have been translated are of a realistic/naturalistic mode of expression; often they have been novels of manners. Almost the entire body of work of a core group of writers has been translated into Swedish, with most works appearing very soon after they first appeared in the United States. This core group is comprised of such highly appreciated fiction writers as Mailer, Roth, Updike, Vonnegut, Bellow, Doctorow, Anne Tyler, John Gardner, Gail Godwin, Malamud, John Irving, and Joyce Carol Oates. Joseph Heller's books have often been best-sellers, selling more than one hundred thousand copies, a very high figure in Sweden, which would correspond to an edition of some three million copies in the United States. Maybe the most successful of them all has been Isaac Bashevis Singer: more than fifteen of his works have been translated since he received the Nobel Prize for literature in 1978. In 1984 his books had sold more than a million copies, which rarely happens to a writer in Sweden. What may have contributed to Singer's success is that he has returned to Sweden several times since 1978, that he has regularly been interviewed in the media, and that two books on his art have been published in Swedish.

American feminist writing has been extremely well received in Sweden. Innumerable books on feminist issues have been translated, such as the theoretical works of Kate Millett, Betty Friedan, and Marilyn French. A long list of feminist novels has been published, works by such influential writers as Sylvia Plath, Mary McCarthy, Marilyn French, Gail Godwin, Marge Piercy, Alix Kates Shulman, Judith Rossner, Tillie Olsen, Mary Gordon, Lisa Alther, and Erica Jong. But also a number of lesser-known feminist novelists have been introduced to the Swedish reading public: Rita Mae Brown, Laurie Colwin, Nora Ephron, Margaret Mitchell Dukore, Nancy Hayfield, Shirley Hazzard, Isabel Miller, Gloria Naylor, and Emily Prager. The reason for this interest in American women writers is in part because the feminist movement has been very vital in Sweden for several decades, so that these novels have had a ready audience waiting for them.

What has also characterized the output of American novels in Sweden is the large number of first novels that have flooded the market. Due to the stiff competition between publishing houses referred to earlier, editors are constantly in search of new talent and thus first novels often appear in Sweden a very short time after they have seen light in the United States. One editor recently stated that ten years ago it was still possible to wait for a promising writer to prove himself, but now, because of the severe competition, "the publishing houses dare not risk being left out in the cold, but feel forced to buy immature and mediocre books and hope that at least one of these unsafe bets will pay off in the future." There is consequently a large element of risk-taking in this venture, and many of the American novelists whose first books are translated are never heard of again. A few of the authors whose first novels have recently been offered to Swedish readers are: Joan Chase, Peter Collier, Joe Cottonwood, Jacob Epstein, Laurel Goldman, Jim Harrison, Joyce Reiser Kornblatt, Bret Easton Ellis, Bobbie Ann Mason, Lorrie Moore, Hank Searls, Brett Singer, Marian Thurm, Douglas Unger, and Meg Wolitzer.

The number of first novels translated has grown so much that reviewers have become skeptical of new American fiction. One critic wrote, for instance, of Gloria Naylor's *The Women of Brewster Place*—a critique I do not share—that it would have been sensible to postpone the introduction of this author to the Swedish public "until the future shows whether this first book is the beginning of an authorship." Another reviewer said of Brett Singer's first book: "One deplores the Anglo-American dominance over Swedish culture in general and over translation literature in particular. If this book had been written in Italian, would it have been translated? I doubt it." A third critic stated: "Mediocre novels are published by authors in all countries, also by Swedes. But why do we have to publish so many of that kind from the United States in particular? What is it that makes that country so magnetic that evidently even its run-of-the-mill authors are quite irresistible?"

A large group of American novelists, however, have not been translated into Swedish and thus are not included in either the popular or scholarly canons of American literature in Sweden. These are the experimental writers. Few of the postmodernist novelists have been introduced to Swedish readers, and the works that have been translated have been their most conventional. Two short pieces by Brautigan have been published; the early work by Pynchon, *The Crying of Lot 49* and *Slow Learner*, but not *V* or *Gravity's Rainbow;* William Gaddis's *Carpenter's Gothic*, comparatively short and more easily accessible, was recently translated, but *The Recognitions* and *JR* are still waiting to be published. Barthelme's *City Life* has appeared in a Swedish translation. But John Barth, Robert Coover, Ronald Sukenick, John Hawkes, and Raymond Federman have not been translated at all. This apparent lack of American experimental writing in translation creates among Swedish readers a false picture of American literature in general. One may try to explain this preference for traditional, realistic fiction and the indifference to postmodernist forms of writing by pointing in part to the fact that the Swedish reading public, with a total Swedish population of only eight million, is too small for such an elitist form of writing; and in part to the fact that Swedes are not particularly interested in a theory-conscious, post-Saussurean discourse. During the last few years, however, a change seems to be taking place. During 1987 and 1988, William Gaddis and William H. Gass were published for the first time; a critical debate on postmodernism took place in leading journals and newspapers; an exhibition of postmodernist art, and a conference on postmodernism and poststructuralist theory were arranged.

In the field of poetry, Swedish editions of American collections are much more scarce. Only some thirty collections of American poetry have appeared during the last fifteen years. Poets whose work has appeared in magazines and who have also had whole collections translated are Gary Snyder, W. S. Merwin, Denise Levertov, John Ashbery, Kenneth Rexroth, and Mark Strand. In 1985 a landmark publication appeared, which may have an impact for a long time: a nine-hundred-page anthology of American poetry translated into Swedish and covering the period from 1910 to 1983.

In drama, some seventy-five different productions of American plays have been staged at theaters and on TV. Plays by Jack Gelber, David Mamet, Arthur Miller, Marsha Norman, and Tennessee Williams have been presented in various parts of the country. Three playwrights, however, have dominated the scene: Edward Albee, Sam Shepard, and Eugene O'Neill. There have been at least five different productions of *Who's Afraid of Virginia Wolf*, and Albee's *The Zoo Story* has also been staged. Seven of Shepard's plays have appeared on Swedish stages. O'Neill still has a special relationship to Sweden. As is well known, his last plays had their world premiere at the Royal Dramatic Theater in Stockholm. His last wish was that the same theater produce the first performance of *Long Day's Journey into Night*. This play has since then been staged several times, and of late such plays as *Hughie, The Hairy Ape*, and *A Moon for the Misbegotten* have been produced anew. The Swedish interest in O'Neill has not only been expressed in a long list of productions but also in several books devoted to him. Moreover, one of the more influential Swedish playwrights today, Lars Norén, has in a very obvious way been influenced by O'Neill's art.

In conclusion, most of the translated literary works—fiction, poetry, drama—reflect the contemporary scene in America. Sweden is getting a comparatively representative picture of what is happening at the moment in American literature, with the glaring exception of the postmodernists. But we do not get expressions of the literature of earlier periods. There are extremely few editions of the works of Hawthorne, Melville, James, Fitzgerald, and Faulkner available. A few attempts have recently been made to renew the interest in older American literature. Translations have appeared of Dos Passos's *U.S.A.*, Chopin's *The Awakening*, Charlotte Perkins Gilman's *Herland*, Cabell's *Jurgen*, James's *Washington Square*, Stein's *Tender Buttons*, and Thoreau's *Civil Disobedience*. Ayn Rand's *Atlas Shrugged* was recently translated for the first time, twenty-nine years after it appeared in the United States, and so was Hubert Selby's *Last Exit to Brooklyn*, twenty-three years after its original publication. In 1983, Whitman's "Song of Myself" was presented in a new translation; the most recent collection of Dickinson's poetry appeared in 1986.

As stated above, Sweden is characterized by a dual canon in American literature. There is a striking difference between, on the one hand, the keen interest in American literature that is expressed by the readers, the publishers, and the media, and, on the other, the lack of interest that characterizes the universities. To give a few examples of the latter, the first chair in American literature was established in 1968, and it still remains the only one in Sweden. Apart from this post, there are only two more positions in American literature in Sweden, an associate and an assistant professorship; both of these are affiliated with Uppsala University, which is the only Swedish university that has a doctoral program in American literature. Compared to other European countries, two positions in American literature is a ludicrously low figure. Norway, for instance, which in population is about half the size of Sweden, has at least five times as many positions in American literature and American studies as Sweden. Italy has twenty full professors in American literature, and West Germany has well over a hundred academic teachers in this field. This imbalance may to some extent explain why the scholarly output in Sweden is comparatively small.

I have stated that Swedes traditionally have not been particularly interested in viewing literature from a theoretical point of view and that this may be a partial explanation for the Swedish indifference to American postmodernism. This is presumably also the cause of the universities' unwillingness to apply new critical approaches to the study of American literature. Yet I feel the need to qualify and perhaps hedge on my view that Swedish scholars are indifferent to theory. Of course there are individuals and groups that are theory-conscious. Courses on literary theory are given at the universities, at least for the graduate students. There has long existed a Marxist group of critics. A number of scholars in Stockholm are now applying poststructuralist theories to the study of literature. A recently published study on Pär Lagerkvist's art was based on Lacanian theories. Hardly any scholars, however, have devoted themselves to structuralism. But in many instances these theoretical approaches are met with skepticism by the majority of Swedish scholars. Right now there seems to be a generation shift taking place. The theory-conscious scholars are by and large younger, whereas the skeptics belong to an older generation.

Furthermore, Swedish critics in general have become much more conscious of the shape of, and questions concerning, the literary canon. It is the writing of new literary histories that has caused this awareness. As the writing of the Columbia and Cambridge literary histories has created a similar consciousness in the United States, Swedish scholars have become engaged in a debate on what criteria should decide the selection of and approach to specific genres, periods, writers, and their works. A new Nordic history of world literature has just been published, edited by a Dane, and a new Swedish literary history is being produced right now. Looking into this history of world literature it is interesting to see the significance, or rather lack thereof, that this Nordic perspective accords American literature. In the third volume, dealing with world literature from 1600 to 1720, only three pages are devoted to American literature, and in the fourth volume, covering the period 1720 to 1830, merely two out of four hundred pages discuss the literary achievement in America. The rest of the volumes have not yet appeared.

The scholarly research that has been done in the field of American literature has been done, with few exceptions, in the English departments. In the departments of literature, which in Sweden are prestigious institutions, American literature is being neglected. In the latter departments few American works have been included on the reading lists for undergraduate studies. In Sweden, a student studies one subject at a time. If one tries to make up a composite list of which American literary works a student in the departments of literature at one of the four largest universities would be exposed to during four terms of full-time study, it would look something like this: one short story by Poe, ten poems by Whitman, ten poems by Dickinson, a selection from Eliot's *Waste Land,* two poems by Pound, one play by O'Neill, and one novel by Hemingway, Faulkner, Bellow, or Mailer. During the third and fourth terms, a system of elective courses is often used: the student chooses two courses per term and writes a longer essay. At Uppsala the student can choose, from a selection of twenty-nine courses, one course on the American twentieth-century novel; and in Lund a similar course from a choice of fifty-eight courses. As can easily be noticed such writers as Hawthorne, Melville, and James are not represented at all. One can easily see that the student who graduates with a major in literature has a very limited knowledge of American literature. Many of these students become teachers in the Swedish secondary schools and hand down to their students the literary canon they have received at the university, a canon from which American literature is virtually absent.

If a student in a department of literature decides to enter the doctoral program, he or she will not be exposed to a significantly increased number of American literary works. At Lund, for instance, the graduate program is based on a system of elective courses. Students can choose ten courses from the fifty courses offered. There are courses on English, German, French, and Russian literature, but none on American literature. When it is time for graduate students to write their dissertations, they will choose a topic in areas where they have done extensive reading and in which their teachers are competent. It is consequently very unlikely that a graduate student in literature will write a dissertation on American literature. It is equally unlikely that established scholars in the field, who are then responsible for establishing the existing literary canon, will devote themselves to the study of American literature. As a consequence, as far as I have been able to find out, no dissertation in a department of literature has been written on the art of an American author since 1968, when Egil Törnqvist wrote his book on O'Neill. The closest one can come is a sociological study on the reception of Jack London in Sweden (1974) and a theater study on the relationship between O'Neill and the Royal Dramatic Theater in Stockholm.

The reasons for excluding American literature from the canon are several. The emphasis of study in the comparative literature departments is to a large extent on periods when American literature had not yet come of age. Another reason is that of tradition: the emphasis is first on Swedish literature, second on European literature. Swedish scholars in comparative literature have done important work on French and German literature, but hardly any on American literature.

Most of the research on American literature done in Sweden has, as I stated above, been done in the English departments. Dissertations, books, and articles have been written at all five major universities. Nevertheless, most English departments are long since oriented toward Great Britain. There are six times as many jobs in British and Commonwealth literature as in American literature. Only Uppsala University has a fully developed doctoral program in American literature. Consequently most Swedish graduate students—aside from those in linguistics—take their degrees in British literature. Out of the seventy-nine literary dissertations produced in the English departments since 1973, only twenty-four have been devoted to American literature. But at all universities, in the English departments, students can take some courses on American literature both at the undergraduate and graduate levels.

One reason why the English departments are so very much oriented toward British literature is that the Swedish school system has the same orientation. School anthologies have for many years contained more material on England than on America. Although this is now slowly changing, the preferred way of pronunciation is still British English; American English is tolerated but few teachers use it. There is consequently a built-in prejudice in the Swedish school system, a prejudice the teachers vehemently deny. Swedish students are unconsciously taught to believe that British English is the norm and that American English is, if not substandard, at least a less acceptable form of the language. When students get to university they carry this preference for British English with them, and when they leave university as teachers of English they perpetuate these values. Again, a change toward greater tolerance of American English is now noticeable. But this preference for things British certainly still has an impact on the study of literature, making university students of English subconsciously choose courses in English literature rather than American literature.

Most of the research that has been done in the English departments during the last fifteen years has been of a traditionalist, historicist nature. With few exceptions these articles, dissertations, and books have been devoted to thematic, biographical, or ideological/philosophical investigations. One should maybe point out that all dissertations in Sweden are published and reach a rather wide, international distribution. Few scholars during this period have applied new literary theories to American literature. There are no structuralist or poststructuralist studies. The closest one comes is a book on Gertrude Stein's *Lucy Church Amiably* which is inspired by feminist poststructuralist critics like Kristeva.

If one compares the literary canon of the educated reading public to the canon that emerges at the universities, it is not surprising that the latter is more conservative than the former. Scholars deal with writers of the past more than with contemporary ones. They study the well-established, mainstream writers who wrote before World War II. But there are exceptions to this tendency: studies have been devoted to best-sellers and to postmodernist fiction. Most of the scholarly work analyzes American prose, but surprisingly many articles and books have focused on poetry, a striking difference from the taste of the well-educated reader. Few scholars have devoted their energies to the study of American drama.

If we first look at the scholarly work that has been done on prose writers, the forty plus articles and books that have appeared during this time can be subdivided into four areas.

First, an unusually large number of studies have been devoted to major nineteenth-century writers, with a specific emphasis on the American Renaissance. Books have been written on Emerson, Melville, Hawthorne, and Thoreau, and articles have also been devoted to these writers. The book on Hawthorne deals with isolation and interdependence in his fictional characters, and the work on Henry David Thoreau traces his intellectual development with a special emphasis on the influence of Hinduism on Thoreau's thought. The Melville study argues that *The Piazza Tales* should be seen more as a unified whole, in which one of the unifying elements is Melville's hatred of oppression. An interesting book on best-sellers between 1895 and 1920 investigates the popular values of the time not only by analyzing the central concerns of these books but also by delving deeper into the issues that were avoided in these books.

The second group of prose writers that Swedish scholars have found worthy of analysis can be associated with the golden age of the 1920s. Dissertations have been published on Cather, Faulkner, Glasgow, Dreiser, and Gertrude Stein. I myself have done work on Dreiser in which I took a closer look at a dialectical pattern that characterizes much of Dreiser's thought and art, a belief that, for instance, good and evil, or poverty and wealth, strike a necessary balance, an "inevitable equation," to use Dreiser's term. The Faulkner study is concerned with the theme of war in his novels, dividing the Faulkner chronology up into three phases dealing with the Civil War, World War I, and World War II. Even though several studies have dealt with the fiction between the wars, it is remarkable that some of the influential writers of this period have been neglected. Very little has been written on Hemingway, Sherwood Anderson, Fitzgerald, and John Dos Passos. To take Hemingway as an example, it is strange that so little scholarly work has been done on his fiction in view of the tremendous influence he has had in Sweden. His books have been extremely popular, in the original and in translation; they have been included on many reading lists at the universities; numerous newspaper and magazine articles have discussed his life and art; and several Swedish writers have testified that he has been a great influence on their writing. In spite of all this, no longer study on Hemingway has appeared during the last two decades, if ever.

A third category of novelists studied by Swedish critics is the realists after World War II, primarily Baldwin, McCullers, Isaac Bashevis Singer, and Joyce Carol Oates. Here one may hold forth the study of McCullers which sets out to investigate the nature of McCullers's style in *The Member of the Wedding* by comparing the novel's text to the Brown corpus. The result of the study is a negative one, in the sense that McCullers's text does not deviate noticeably from the Brown corpus. Consequently, one cannot state that McCullers's style is particularly lyrical or "literary," which many scholars have felt it to be.

I have stated above that Swedes have had little interest in American experimental postmodernist fiction. However, at the universities this interest is growing, and this is the fourth group of novelists and short story writers that has received some attention. A few books and articles have studied the art of Nabokov, Vonnegut, Barth, Coover, Barthelme, and Pynchon. These studies concern themselves primarily with structure, stylistic devices, foregrounding, and aesthetics. One recent dissertation focuses on what the scholar terms "duplex fiction," by which is meant that certain postmodernist texts function on two levels at the same time, one "naive" level and one "self-reflexive" level.

About forty academic articles and books have been written on American prose in the past fifteen years. About half as many were devoted to American poetry. This is an astonishingly high figure, if one keeps in mind proportions between prose and poetry being translated into Swedish. Ten times as many American novels have been translated as collections of poetry. In academic research only twice as many studies deal with prose as with poetry. I see no explanation for this unusual interest in poetry except perhaps that modern poetry is by nature more academic than popular.

The Swedish interest in poetry has been limited to the poets after World War I. Again one may see two subcategories. Several studies have analyzed modernist poets like Eliot, Pound, and Stevens. Two books by the same scholar have studied Eliot's poetry, one on *The Waste Land* and another on Eliot's use of animals in his art. Another book compares Pound's China cantos to the old French histories of China on which they were based, trying to answer the question of how Pound transformed historical sources into poetry.

The rest of the studies on poetry are concerned with more contemporary poets like Berryman, Stafford, Bly, and Adrienne Rich. The book on Berryman analyzes the poetics of *The Dream Songs* by means of his essays and interviews with him. In particular, this critic is interested in the influence of Whitman's "Song of Myself" on Berryman's attempt to "record fully the soul under stress." But there are hardly any studies on poetry prior to World War I. There are no studies on Whitman, Dickinson, or Stephen Crane, which is remarkable if one keeps in mind that academics often have a predilection for the literature of the past, as has been seen in the case of prose.

In drama little work has been done. There have been five times as many studies on poetry as on drama. Here, however, the popular canon and the academic one coincide in one particular instance. As Eugene O'Neill is the playwright whose plays were most often performed during these past fifteen years, so O'Neill has been shown far more interest by the scholars than any other dramatist. One O'Neill study records the history of his works in relation to the Royal Dramatic Theater in Stockholm; another is a close reading of *A Touch of the Poet*. The only other playwright to get serious academic attention is Lillian Hellman. Nothing during this period was written on Albee or Shepard, whose plays are regularly performed on Swedish stages.

To sum up, American literature in Sweden during the last fifteen years has been very popular among readers and newspaper critics, but has received very limited interest in the academic world. American prose has received much more attention than poetry or drama. Swedes have shown little urge to read theory-conscious literature or to approach American literature by means of post-Saussurean theory, even though a change is now in the making. And finally, the readerly canon has comprised primarily contemporary literature, whereas the academic canon has encompassed literature of the past and literature of a less popular nature like poetry and postmodernist fiction.

One may, finally, speculate on what may happen in the future to the dual literary canon that I have tried to outline above. Will the two canons, which now, at least superficially, seem rather disparate, coalesce into a more unified whole? There are signs pointing in that direction. An increasing number of scholarly works have been written recently on contemporary American writers. Dissertations are now in the process of being written on Adrienne Rich, Gail Godwin, John Gardner, William Styron, Walker Percy, Theodore Roethke, William Stafford, Gary Snyder, and on contemporary native American fiction. The readerly canon simultaneously seems to be starting to include more experimental fiction. Newspapers and journals are expressing an ever-deepening concern with American postmodernism, and publishing houses seem to express a growing interest in avant-garde forms of writing. It is too early to say however, whether the steady flow of American literature into Sweden, and the increasing interest it evokes among well-educated readers, will also affect the comparative indifference to it that now characterizes the academic world. As a representative of that world, I naturally hope it will not take too long before American literature will gain, at the universities as well, a respect that is long overdue.

ﻬ

Contributors

Huck Gutman is the author of *Mankind in Barbary: The Individual and Society in the Novels of Norman Mailer* (New England). He is a coeditor of and contributor to *Technologies of the Self: A Seminar with Michel Foucault* (Massachusetts). He is completing a history of American literature and has published essays on Whitman, Dos Passos, and Mailer. A former Fulbright senior lecturer at the University of Lisbon and the New University of Lisbon, he is a professor of American literature at the University of Vermont.

Keiko Beppu is the author of *The Educated Sensibility of Henry James and Walter Pater* (Shohakusha, in English). She is also an accomplished editor, having co-edited *A Literary History of the United States* and edited both *Women and Language in Literature and Society* and *After a Hundred Years: Essays on Emily Dickinson* (Appollon-sha, in English). She has contributed chapters on Toni Morrison, Joyce Carol Oates, Charles Brockden Brown, Susannah Rowson, Hannah Forster, Marianne Moore, and "Women and Literature" to various Japanese collections of essays. She has published articles on Hawthorne, Melville, Twain, James, and Dickinson. A councillor of the American Literature Society of Japan, she is on the editorial board of two Japanese journals, *Studies in English Literature* and *Kansai American Literature*. Since 1974 she has been the major Japanese contributor to *American Literary Scholarship*. She has taught at Michigan State University, and is a professor at Kobe College.

Michele Bottalico has published essays on British and American literature and has contributed articles and entries to *Novecento Americano, Grande dizionario enciclopedico UTET, Dizionario Bompiani degli autori*, and *Chicano Literature: A Reference Guide*. He has translated George Eliot's *Middlemarch* and is currently working on a book on early nineteenth-century American literature. A former Fulbright research scholar, he teaches at the University of Bari.

Marc Chénetier is the author of *Richard Brautigan* (Methuen) and of the recently published *Au-delà du Soupçon: la fiction américaine de 1960 à 1987*. He has edited *Critical Angles: European Views of Contemporary American Literature* (Southern Illinois) and the *Letters of Vachel Lindsay* (B. Franklin). He has written *By Signs Obsessed: The Aesthetics of Vachel Lindsay* and numerous essays on American postmodern fiction. He was French contributor to *American Literary Scholarship* from 1981 to 1988. The editor of the *Revue Française d'Etudes Américaines*, he is Professor of American Literature at the University of Orléans.

Theo D'haen is the coauthor of the recent *History of American Literature* (De Arbeiderspers, in Dutch), *Literary Post-Modernism* (De Arbeiderspers, in Dutch), and *Text to Reader: A Communicative Approach to Fowles, Barth, Cortzar and Boon* (Benjamins, in English). He is the editor of *Convention and Innovation* (Benjamins), *Yearbook Postmodernism 1: Fiction International* (Rodopi), and *Linguistics and the Study of Literature* (Rodopi), and he has published articles in English and Dutch, in Holland and the United States, on Cheever, Hawkes, Fowles, Gardner, and John Clellon Holmes, and others on postmodern fiction, the apocalyptic imagination, Defoe, Kafka, Orwell, and Burgess. He holds the chair in English and American literature at the University of Leyden.

Elżbieta Foeller-Pituch has published ten articles on the fiction of John Barth and John Gardner. She has published other articles on Thornton Wilder, William Faulkner, Henry David Thoreau, and Hawthorne. She has a deep interest in literary uses of mythology, particularly in the domain of postmodern writing. She wrote the essays "Innovative Fiction between the Two World Wars" and "Recent Innovations in American Fiction" for the recently published *A Handbook of American Literature for Students of English.* She has been a visiting scholar at Harvard University and is currently an assistant professor in the Institute of English at the University of Warsaw.

Jan Nordby Gretlund has published widely; the bulk of his essays has been on Southern writing and culture, which are his consuming interest. He is a member of the editorial board of *American Studies in Scandinavia,* is the Danish board member of the Nordic Association for American Studies, and is the current bibliographer for the section on Scandinavian scholarship for *American Literary Studies.* A member of PEN, he is the head of the English department at Odense University.

Natalia Klissourska has published extensively on American literature. She is the author of essays on black and native American writing, on Arthur Miller and Lorraine Hansberry, on Melville, Faulkner, and Robert Lowell. She is coeditor of two anthologies of translations into Bulgarian: *An Anthology of American Short Stories* and *An Anthology of American Drama.* She teaches American literature in the Department of English Philology at Sofia University.

Robert Lawson-Peebles is the author of *Landscape and Written Expression in Revolutionary America: The World Turned Upside Down* (Cambridge). He is as well the coeditor of a forthcoming book on American landscape. He has published essays on Henry George, Meriwether Lewis, Edgar Allan Poe, and William Carlos Williams. Formerly a visiting fellow at Princeton University, a fellow of the Philadelphia Center for Early American Studies, a research lecturer at Christ Church, Oxford, and a lecturer in English at the University of Aberdeen, he is currently a lecturer at the University of Exeter.

Rolf Lundén is the author of two books on Theodore Dreiser and of articles on James Baldwin, Sherwood Anderson, and John Updike. His most recent book, published in 1988, is *Business and Religion in the American 1920s* (Greenwood

Press). He was the Scandinavian contributor to *American Literary Scholarship* between 1973 and 1980 and is now coeditor of *Studia Neophilologica*. He holds the chair of American literature at Uppsala University, where he is also the chairman of the English department and deputy director of the Swedish Institute for American Studies (SINAS).

Mbulelo Vizikhungo Mzamane is the author of *Mzala: The Short Stories of Mbulelo Mzamane*, which has been reissued as *My Cousin Comes to Joburg* (Longman), and *The Children of Soweto: A Trilogy* (Longman). He has edited *Hungry Flames and Other Black South African Short Stories* (Longman), *Selected Poems: Mongane Wally Serote* (Ad Donker), and *Selected Poems: Sipho Sydney Sepamla* (Ad Donker). His essays have been widely published in journals and books, and he is on the editorial board of seven African journals. He teaches at the University of Georgia.

Federico Patán is a fiction writer, critic, poet, and translator. His most recent work is *Nena me llamo Walter* (Baby, call me Walter, short stories); *Imagenes* (Images, poetry); *Ultimo exilio* (Last exile, novel), which was the winner of the Xavier Villaurrutia Award; *En esta casa* (In this house, short stories); and *Dos veces el mismo rio* (Twice the same river, anthology). As readers of his essay will become aware, he has translated a wide variety of important American literature into Spanish. He is a professor at the University of Mexico.

Savas Patsalidis is the author of two books of poems, *Paroles* (Greek-Canadian Tribune) and *Diaphragm* (Wire/Athens). His book *The Death of the Author and the Dissemination of Meaning: De-Constructing Modern Theatre* (Hyacinth) is forthcoming. He has written extensively on modern and contemporary theater, with a particular emphasis on the implications for performance of contemporary literary theory. He is a professor of drama at Aristotle University of Thessaloniki.

Hans-Peter Wagner is the author of *Eros Revived: Erotica of the Enlightenment in England and America* (Secker & Warburg). He has written, also in English, *A Short History of English and American Literature* (Klett), a monograph on American Puritanism (Lang), and a bilingual study of eighteenth-century licentious prints: *Lust and Love in the Rococo* (Greno). He is the editor of the critical editions of John Cleland's *Fanny Hill* (Penguin), of Smollett's *Launcelot Greaves* (Penguin), and of Anstey's *The New Bath Guide*. He has published essays on early American literature, eighteenth-century English literature, and postmodern American writers. He teaches at the University of Eichstätt.

Hana Wirth-Nesher has published essays on Saul Bellow, Henry James, Philip Roth, V. S. Naipaul, Virginia Woolf, D. M. Thomas, I. B. Singer, Twain, Dickens, Kafka, and Joyce, among other authors. She is at work on *Legible Cities: A Study of Urban Poetics* and *What is Jewish Literature?* (a collection of essays). She is associate editor of *Prooftexts: A Journal of Jewish Literary History* (Hopkins). She is a senior lecturer in English at Tel Aviv University, where she serves as department head.

Xiao-huang Yin has edited several books and published more than a dozen articles and essays on American literature and history. He has also translated stories by Malamud, Cheever, Crane, and others into Chinese, as well as novels by such popular writers as Ken Follet, Leon Uris, and Frederick Forsyth. An assistant professor at Nanjing University, he is currently doing research on Asian-American studies and Sino-American relations at Harvard University.